D1105940

*Irish Voices from the Great War*

# Irish Voices
# from the Great War

Myles Dungan

IRISH ACADEMIC PRESS
DUBLIN · PORTLAND, OR

*First published in 1995 by*
IRISH ACADEMIC PRESS
44 Northumberland Road, Dublin 4, Ireland

*and in the United States of America by*
IRISH ACADEMIC PRESS
c/o ISBS, 5804 NE Hassalo Street, Portland, OR 97213 3644.

*Website:* http://www.iap.ie


© Myles Dungan 1995
Reprinted 1998

British Library Cataloguing in Publication Data
A catalogue record for this title is available from the British Library.


ISBN 0-7165-2573-9

Library of Congress Cataloging in Publication Data
A catalog record is available from the Library of Congress

Set in 10.5 on 12.5 point Ehrhardt

Printed in Ireland
by Colour Books Ltd, Dublin

*To Iseult, partner and icon*

I call
and shorten your way with speed to me
I am love and hate and the terrible mind
Of vicious gods

Fragment from *War*, an uncompleted poem
by Francis Ledwidge.

# Contents

# Abbreviations

| | |
|---|---|
| ASC | Army Service Corps |
| Bn. | Battalion |
| BEF | British Expeditionary Force |
| Connaughts | Connaught Rangers |
| DCM | Distinguished Conduct Medal |
| DSO | Distinguished Service Order |
| Inniskillings | Royal Inniskilling Fusiliers |
| IWM | Imperial War Museum |
| Leinsters | Leinster Regiment |
| MC | Military Cross (officers only) |
| MM | Military Medal (NCOs and other ranks) |
| RA | Royal Artillery |
| RAMC | Royal Army Medical Corps |
| RAP | Regimental Aid Post |
| R.D.F. | Royal Dublin Fusiliers |
| R.I.F. | Royal Irish Fusiliers |
| R.I.R. | Royal Irish Rifles |
| R.I. Reg. | Royal Irish Regiment |
| R.M.F. | Royal Munster Fusiliers |
| VC | Victoria Cross |

# Preface

It is a shame and a serious injustice (though not altogether surprising) that the stories of the thousands of Irishmen who participated in the Great War should have been left largely untold until the era of 'revisionist' history. Why did we have to wait until one mode of recording and narrating the history of our nation and nationhood became 'unfashionable' before writers began to look at this neglected corner. With a few honourable (and one or two execrable) exceptions, the Irishmen who, for many different reasons, opted to join the British, American, Australian and Canadian armies and fight in the 1914–18 conflict, have been ignored by historians until the 1990s. Over the last five years three excellent volumes, Terence Denman's *Ireland's Unknown Soldiers*, Tom Johnstone's *Orange, Green and Khaki* and Phillip Orr's *The Road to the Somme* have, thankfully, redressed the balance

This volume is to be the first of two which, I hope, will slightly extend the scope of the examination which has already taken place of this subject. The emphasis in these two volumes will be on the words and feelings of the ordinary Irish soldiers who participated in this brutal, savage and cynical conflict. This first volume will deal, specifically and in detail, with a selection of the most important battles and campaigns in which the three Irish Divisions (and other Irish regiments of the old Regular Army) participated. The second volume will deal with some of the issues which arose during and out of the war itself (trench warfare, command structures, nationalism, unionism, etc.)

The content of both volumes will be based on near-contemporary archive material from a variety of sources, notably the Imperial War Museum, the National Army Museum and the Somme Association Archive as well as on the published diaries and reminiscences of soldiers in Irish regiments. In addition there is a wealth of audio archive material compiled many years after the events recorded, most of which which has not been used in a publication.

Here the author must (as authors do) enter a number of caveats. Neither volume should be seen as an academic treatise. My aim is to allow the men who lived in the mud and blood of Flanders and Gallipoli to speak for themselves, not to theorise at length about the significance of their experiences. I hope it may prove to be a useful sourcebook for those involved in further work on the subject, but I tread warily in the footsteps of the likes of

Orr, Denman and Johnstone. In addition, although this is a work devoted to Irish soldiers and regiments, its pages will be full of the recollections of many non-Irish officers who served with those Irish regiments. I believe this to be a perfectly legitimate means of conveying something of the experiences of the ordinary soldiers, few of whom wrote diaries or memoirs preserved in archives, or even letters deemed worthy of being kept by family members. (Though, tragically, a rich store of such material as did exist has been lost to historians over the years as veterans died off and their effects were disposed of.) It must also be said of the RTE radio archive material that while most of it is highly atmospheric and descriptive some of it is factually inaccurate and unreliable (most of it was recorded at least sixty years after the events described). Insofar as possible I have attemped to eliminate the more egregious lapses of memory or descents into special pleading.

I have approached this material as a journalist attempting to tell a series of personal stories trying not to lose sight of those stories as they flit in and out of the small number of selected battles covered in the book. Though I have attempted, as succinctly as possible, to convey some idea of the bigger picture in the case of each battle, with limited space available to me and without a background in military history the concentration is, of necessity, on the individual stories. It may well be, therefore, that the initiated will find details of battles oversimplified and the uninitiated will find them over-complicated and confusing. I hope not. My own personal fascination with this topic is derived, not from any fixation with the trivia and details of Great War campaigns but from a deep regard for the humanity of the men who survived horrors, depredations and traumas which should have quenched the flame of even the most resolute human spirit.

My thanks are due to a number of people for their help in assembling and compiling the material on which this book is based. To Kevin Healy, Director of Radio Programmes, RTE for permission to use material from the Sound Archive, to Kieran Sheedy (from whose work in 1973 the bulk of the taped recollections comes), Joe Little and Jim Fahy for allowing me to use material from programmes they have compiled over the years and to Ian Lee for patiently winkling out what was there and copying it for me. To Pat Ryan for some tricky tape transfers.

To Billy Ervine of the Somme Association for his advice and help over the last year and for his selection of material from the Somme Association archive which has, I hope, enhanced the material in this volume on the 36th (Ulster) Division. Billy's scholarship and enthusiasm goes far beyond the involvement of the Ulstermen in the war. Richard Doherty, war historian *extraordinaire*, has been equally generous in letting me have access to the tapes on which one of his excellent 'Sons of Ulster' programmes on World War I, was based. I would also like to thank the administration of Leopardstown Park Hospital for access to Joseph Cahill and Jack Campbell, two Great War veterans whom I interviewed there.

A wealth of material was made available to me in the Imperial War Museum in London and I would like to acknowledge the help of Nigel Steel of the Department of Documents in tracking down the copyright holders for the many memoirs and diaries from which I have quoted. C.M.F. Coleman granted permission to reproduce extracts from the diaries of Guy Nightingale, Cdr. V.M. Lake from the papers of his father W.V.C. Lake, D.E. McElwaine from the papers of his father, Mrs J.P. Brennan from the memoirs of her husband, Rose Hunt from the memoirs of her father, Charles Cecil Miller, and Peter Kirkpatrick from the Ivone Kirkpatrick papers. Dr Peter B. Boyden, Head of the Department of Archives, Photographs, Film and Sound at the National Army Museum, allowed the inclusion of material from that source, most notably the diaries of Capt. Noel Drury. Some additional documents relating to Guy Nightingale and others were researched at the British Public Record Office in Kew. Permission to quote from Frank Hitchcock's *Stand To* was granted by Gliddon Books, who recently re-published the volume, and Lavinia Greacen allowed me to quote from *Chink*, her work on the life of General Dorman O'Gowan. Despite every effort having been made it has not been possible to obtain permission from the copyright holders of all the collections used.

Finally, I would like to thank Michael Adams of Irish Academic Press for his interest in Irish military history. Frank McGuinness, who, without knowing it, sparked my interest in this whole area through his wonderful *Observe the Sons of Ulster Marching Towards the Somme*. He, like me, had 'never been told'. And Kevin Myers, whose enthusiasm for the subject, in the conversations we have had, has been highly infectious.

## BACKGROUND NOTE

The use of military terminology and jargon is unavoidable in an enterprise such as this. The following note provides background information which may be of assistance in the reading of this book. Some, but not all, is repeated elsewhere in the text.

Before 1914 the small British Regular Army was composed of regiments which, in the main, consisted of a 1st and 2nd Battalion of about 1000 men each. A third battalion was often attached to the Regimental HQ and was used for training purposes. From 1914 to the beginning of 1918 with the creation by the Secretary of State for War, Lord Kitchener, of a huge volunteer Army (compulsory conscription in England, Scotland and Wales came later), the Regular Army battalions were augmented by Service battalions of fresh, inexperienced troops. Thus, for example, the Royal Irish Fusiliers was composed of its two original battalions, a third and fourth battalion based at home and responsible for training and recruiting, and seven service battalions (5th to 11th) at different times during the course of the war.

Battalions, as a rule, were divided into four companies; these in turn were further subdivided into platoons. Before the officer corps became badly depleted a battalion would normally have been commanded by a lieutenant-colonel, a company by a major or captain and platoons by a full lieutenant. A second lieutenant (also known as a subaltern) might have commanded a 'section' within a platoon, though, depending on numbers command of sections would often fall to a non-commissioned officer (sergeant-major, sergeant etc.).

Battalions were banded, in groups of four, into brigades under the command of a brigadier-general. In early 1918, because of the extent of casualties brigades were reduced to three battalions each. Above brigade level was the division, consisting of three brigades. The 10th (Irish) Division, for example, the first Irish division to be recruited, was made up of the 29th, 30th and 31st Brigades. A division was usually commanded by a major-general. Above that again was the corps, there were three or four divisions within this unit, which was under the command of a lieutenant-general. Four combined corps made up an army, under the command of a general. At the outset of the war, in 1914, the British Expeditionary Force which went to France, had two armies, This number had grown to five by 1917.

The first commander of the British Expeditionary Force was Field Marshal Sir John French. He was succeeded in December 1915 by General Sir Douglas Haig, who was elevated to the rank of Field Marshal in 1917. He held his position until the end of hostilities in November 1918. When it became clear that the war was not going to be swift and decisive, a general proclamation was issued by the British government calling for 100,000 men to volunteer for three years service. This force, raised by Lord Kitchener, became known as K1 and included the first Irish division, the 10th. Further proclamations followed, and the Second New Army (K2) included the other nationalist division, the 16th. In the Fifth New Army was the loyalist 36th (Ulster) Division.

The battles and campaigns covered in this book have been selected as the most significant involving Irish troops. Others may argue that important engagements (such as the Battle of Loos) have been left out. Given the space available, however, it was not possible to include everything and I felt it better to devote more time and space to a smaller number of key battles. The period from the arrival of the British Expeditionary Force (the bulk of the Regular Army at the time) until just before the First Battle of Ypres saw the beginning of the destruction of the famous Irish units of the old Regular Army. This process continued with the destruction of the 1st Dublins and 1st Munsters at Gallipoli in 1915 at the V Beach landing.

The numbers of Irishmen involved in the war then grew exponentially with the introduction of the first volunteer unit, the 10th Division, at the Suvla Bay landing in Gallipoli in August 1915. Later that year the 36th (Ulster) Division and the 16th (Irish) Division were introduced to the Western Front. These two divisions were unionist and nationalist mirror images, based on the politically oriented militias of the Ulster Volunteer Force and the National Volunteers. Both would suffer appalling casualties at the dismal Battle of the Somme in 1916, the 36th on 1 July, the opening day of the offensive, and the 16th in the September attacks on the tiny French villages of Guillemont and Ginchy.

The 10th Division, unlike the two other Irish divisions, became engaged in hostilities against two of Germany's allies, the far-flung Ottoman Empire of Turkey, and the Bulgarians. After being withdrawn from Turkish territory in Gallipoli, the 10th found itself assisting the Serbians against an opportunistic attack by their traditional Bulgarian enemies towards the end of 1915. The division was based in Salonika in neutral Greece. By 1917 it had been moved to Palestine to assist General Allenby remove the Turks from the Holy Land.

Meanwhile the two other Irish divisions found themselves side by side in the Second Army of General Plumer (who ranks alongside Allenby as one of the few capable British commanders of the war) and took part in the successful offensive at Messines-Wytschaete in Belgium, a prelude to the long, wearisome and bloody Third Battle of Ypres (often referred to as Passchendaele). Here the 16th and the 36th came under the wing of the Fifth Army, led by an Irishman, General Gough (one of the least competent British commanders). The result was a disastrous erosion of morale and manpower and the continuation of the loss of the 'Irish' character of the two divisions as events at home (in the aftermath of the Easter 1916 Rising) reduced recruitment to a trickle.

Things got worse in 1918 when the war was almost lost to a massive German advance in March of that year. The Fifth Army, with its numbers greatly depleted, bore the brunt of that assault and the 16th (Irish) Division ceased to exist. Many of the Service battalions which had been recruited during Kitchener's 1914 initiative were merged or disbanded. What was left of the 36th Division stayed together, but the battalions which made up the nationalist divisions (10th and 16th) were spread throughout the Army, giving rise to accusations of lack of trust in their committment to the cause for which they had signed up to fight.

When the curtain came down on the Great War, in November 1918, few of the men whose stories are carried through this book and concluded in the final chapter were still with the same units with which they had started out.

# 1　The Old Contemptibles

In the world of paranoid alliances which existed in Europe in 1914 it was not at all illogical that the shot fired by a Serbian nationalist which killed an Austro-Hungarian potentate in modern-day Bosnia should have forestalled a possible Irish civil war. That shot reverberated in Ireland like a loud bang which distracts two men involved in a squabble of their own. It was as if a neighbour's house was on fire. Both ran to join the chain gang. Neither did so entirely from the purest of motives. They wanted to be seen with buckets in their hands dousing the flames. Both expected the neighbour would reward them once the fire was extinguished.

The Great War had loomed as the country hurried towards a war of its own between the supporters of the Union and the advocates of Home Rule. But instead of fighting each other, thousands of Irishmen, of unionist and nationalist persuasions, had joined the British forces and, for very many different and often conflicting reasons, fought the Germans, Turks and Bulgarians in World War I.

It was to take nine months for the uninitiated (and often naive) volunteers of August and September 1914 to begin to be ground through the human 'sausage machine' which the Great War quickly became. But there was no shortage of Irish soliders, already in uniform, to feed the frenzy of the generals and the politicians when the Germans marched into Belgium in early August 1914. These were the men who had chosen (frequently by default) the Army to provide them with a livelihood. Men who did not need to be drip-fed stories of German atrocities, the rape of nuns, the ravaging of 'Little Catholic Belgium'. These were the Irish soldiers of the Regular Army, often in Irish regiments, which constituted the British Expeditionary Force, despatched to France and thence to Belgium, in August 1914.

The men of nine Irish infantry regiments were represented in that force. The cavalry regiments, because of the static nature of the fighting, were of little consequence other than in the opening and final days of the war. As casualties mounted, many cavalry officers and men were simply drafted into infantry units. Even in the early, mobile stage of the war cavalry was used sparingly enough. John Breen, a regular with three years experience in the 2nd Battalion, Royal Irish Regiment, didn't see many German cavalry charges after he arrived in France: 'The Germans had cavalry all right but they didn't like the shell fire or the rapid fire. They didn't put many of them up. They'd put them up now and again.'[1]

Eight units, the Royal Irish Regiment, the Royal Inniskilling Fusiliers, the Royal Irish Rifles, the Royal Irish Fusiliers, the Connaught Rangers, the Leinster Regiment, the Royal Munster Fusiliers and the Royal Dublin Fusiliers, each had two battalions in the Regular Army, some on overseas, colonial duty; the Irish Guards had a single battalion. Each regiment had its own natural recruiting hinterland, some (Dublins, Munsters, Leinsters, Connaughts) are self explanatory but, broadly-speaking, in the case of the Royal Irish Regiment it was mostly the South East; the Inniskillings drew their men from Donegal, Derry and parts of mid-Ulster; the Rifles from Belfast, Antrim and Down; and the Royal Irish Fusiliers from Armagh, Monaghan and Cavan.

Nine battalions of these famous regiments became members of an elite group. They called themselves 'The Old Contemptibles', the pejorative nickname being an ironic comment on the order conveyed to the German First Army by the Kaiser as it cut a swathe through neutral Belgium. Incensed by the intervention of Britain he commanded his invading army to 'exterminate the treacherous English. Walk over General French's contemptible little Army'.[2] The 'Tommy' in the BEF was not impressed with this rhetoric, tending anyway to a comic opera view of the German soldier. 'The field grey, rather baggy uniforms, comic boots, and helmets amused us. Anything strange or foreign was inferior, to the mind of the common soldier.'[3] They adopted the 'Contemptible' tag as their own and turned it against the Germans.

Field Marshal Sir John French, who had been forced to resign for his pusillanimous approach to the recalcitrant officers in the 1914 Curragh Mutiny, was given charge of the British Expeditionary Force of 70,000 men who were mustered from the home based units (French lasted just over a year before being replaced by the ambitious First Corps Commander, General Sir Douglas Haig). The BEF was quickly despatched to France by the Secretary of State for War, Lord Kitchener. Thanks to some stubborn and unexpected Belgian resistance it got there before the Germans did. The men were pitched straight into action as the hammer blows of the Schlieffen Plan descended on the towns and cities of Flanders and Picardy. Within three months 40,000 Irish soldiers,[4] regulars and reservists hauled in to fill the gaps left by the earliest casualties, would be involved in the fighting on the Western Front. This figure does not include the thousands of Irishmen in English, Scottish and Welsh regular Army units.

Before their departure for France each soldier received a personal message from the Secretary of State for War admonishing him to be on his best behaviour and to treat the natives (these particular natives were, of course, white) with due respect and deference. 'Be invariably courteous, considerate and kind. Never do anything likely to injure or destroy property, and always look upon looting as a disgraceful act.' On the other hand, the French being the French, renowned the world over for moral laxity and 'fast' women the innocent 'Tommy' was warned to be on guard against 'temptations both in wine and women. You must entirely resist both temptations, and, while treating all women with perfect courtesy, you must avoid any intimacy.'[5] Such avuncular counsel was to be kept by every soldier in his Army Service Pay Book. This also contained a form which was to be filled out should a soldier wish to make a will. More importantly it told the Tommy that he would get higher pay while in the field risking life and limb.

John Lucy, a 20-year-old corporal, from Cork, had joined the 2nd Royal Irish Rifles, along with his brother, who was a year younger, in January 1912, shortly after the death of his mother. Studying the men (mostly from Belfast) who formed this battalion, Lucy concluded that, on the basis of this representative sample, most of those in the regular army had been driven to the colours by 'unemployment and the need of food'. There were some exceptions:

> There was a taciturn Sergeant from Waterford who was conversant with the intricacies of higher mathematics, and who was very smart and dignified and shunned company. There was an ex-divinity student with literary tastes, who drank much beer and affected an obvious pretence to gentle birth; a national school teacher; a man who had absconded from a colonial bank; a few decent sons of farmers. The remainder of us in our Irish regiment were either scallawags or very minor adventurers.[6]

Jack Campbell was one of a family of five brothers all of whom served in the forces during the war. Like Lucy, Campbell was an 'Old Contemptible' but he had been attached to a Scottish regiment on enlistment. He arrived in France, a raw private, with the 1st Royal Highlanders (the Black Watch) and served with them until 1918. Campbell and Lucy were fortunate in one respect: both were young and fit. Many of the men who made up the BEF were reservists who had been out of khaki for up to seven years. They were to find the going particularly rugged. Often, because of their return to 'Civvy Street', they were under the command of much younger men and tended to grouse more about the absence of home comforts.

The troops of the Irish Regular Army battalions left the country without much fuss or ceremony, the dour Kitchener being more inclined to secrecy than to show. There were a few good send-offs in some garrison towns but, by and large, they slipped out of Irish or British barracks, sailed for the Continent and were soon traversing the paved roads of Northern France (some singing a popular marching song 'Tipperary' as they did so). Edward Byrne,

a Waterford man, who had been assigned to the 72nd Battery Royal Field
Artillery in 1912, was 23 years old when Gavrilo Princip fired the shots in
Sarajevo which precipitated the global confict. He handed in his dress uniform, like all the others in his unit, got on the train from Waterford to
Queenstown and sailed to France—on a ship called the *Kingstonian*. Bad
weather forced the ship to return to Southampton, but not before having to
jettison some terrified horses somewhere in mid Channel.

It was a member of one of those Irish regiments who acquired a dubious
distinction. At 7 a.m on 22 August, outside Mons, men of the Royal Irish
Dragoon Guards spotted a group of German soldiers. Cpl. E. Thomas, an
enthusiastic Irishman, fired. The Germans withdrew. They were the first
shots fired in battle by a soldier of the British Army on the continent of
Europe for almost a hundred years. (An anonymous Irishman was also the
inspiration for one of the first famous recruiting posters. This depicts a
British soldier lighting his pipe nonchalantly, while a German cavalry regiment hurtles towards him. The caption reads 'Half a mo', Kaiser'. The sketch
emanates from a report of an Irish Guardsman who coolly cadged a cigarette
from a fellow soldier and lit up with the cavalry approaching.)

Had Kitchener been given his way, the BEF would have been nowhere
near Mons; it would have deployed much further to the south. The old
warlord feared that the small force, by advancing so far north to meet the
Germans, would open its account in full retreat. The Prime Minister, Asquith,
on the advice of French, overruled him. Kitchener was proven right. Within
a matter of days the BEF was retracing its steps at much greater speed. But
on their pleasant late summer march in mellow August sunlight to Mons the
BEF was feted by grateful French villagers giving a hearty welcome to their
new saviours and encouraging them, by means of a universal gesture, to cut
the throats of the 'sale Boche': 'Their promiscuous kissing, the cut throat
gesticulations, useless presents, mad hatred of the "dirty Germans", and their
petty pilfering of our cap-badges, buttons, and numerals, "browned" a good
many of us off.'[7] Astonishingly requests for mementoes continued with the
BEF going in the opposite direction, in full retreat, a few days later. It was
too much for one Dublin Fusilier in the 10th Infantry Brigade, 'who was
wearily dragging himself along in the ranks of his company. Hearing the too
familiar cry of "souvenir" he turned an angry glance over his shoulder and
growled "Here, you can have my blooming pack for a souvenir!" '[8] Naturally,
the cheers were for 'Les Anglais', a misapprehension corrected by John Lucy
in the case of the 2nd Royal Irish Rifles, ' "Nous ne sommes pas Anglais,
nous sommes Irlandais." They liked that and laughed with pleasure, and then
shouted: "Vivent les Irlandais", and we cheered back at them: "Vive la France".'[9]

Jack Campbell, who survived the war and died in 1993 at the age of 96,
landed at Rouen with the Black Watch and entrained for Mons the following

day. 'It was Sunday evening when we arrived in Mons and as we marched through the town the church bells were ringing, calling the just to prayer, but we weren't interested in prayer or anything like that because in a matter of hours we'd be engaged with war that'd kill thousands and bring hardship and misery to millions all over the world.'[10] A few miles outside of the town the battalion left the road and formed 'a kind of front' in a wheat field. The stalks had already been cut and lay around the field in sheaves; Campbell and his Scottish comrades made comfortable bedding for themselves and settled in to wait and see what would happen. The calm was shattered at 5 a.m. the following morning when three batteries of field artillery opened up on a small wood a few hundred yards away from the Black Watch. Campbell quickly found out why:

> A horde of cavalry came out of there. I didn't think there was so much cavalry in the world to tell you the truth. They came heading straight for us. We could see they were losing heavily because there were other troops in front of us ... They got to about 100 yards from where we were; then they seemed to falter and those that were left galloped back in the direction they came. A short while after that we got the order to fall in. We fell in and that started the retreat from Mons.[11]

Campbell had watched a German cavalry unit being torn to shreds. He wondered why, after that morale-boosting achievement, the BEF was pulled back. He was not alone in querying the move. John Lucy had been similarly blooded with the 2nd Rifles against an equally unsuccessful German infantry battalion. 'Why did we retire?' he asked. 'We had beaten off an enemy calculated on the spot as being from five to seven times our number. We alone had wiped out at least one whole enemy battalion with the loss of a few men. We had beaten our enemy and were full of fight. Now we looked as if we were in full flight.'[12] They were, and at breakneck speed.

In fact Lucy's impression was erroneous, as might be expected from an individual infantryman blinkered by a lack of information or awareness of what was going on outside of the reach of his own temporary entrenchments. The BEF had not defeated the enemy; it had barely managed to hold the enemy at bay. As French was well aware, the Germans could quite easily outflank the overextended British force to the west (the French Army was positioned to the east) and cut off the BEF, 'so we turned our backs on Mons, and it was a long time before our soldiers sang their songs again thereabouts.'[13] John King, from Waterford, a seven-year veteran of the Royal Irish Regiment, knew when he was beaten and why:

We were badly up against it. We had nothing to defend ourselves with. They outnumbered us by about six or seven to one and they had plenty of armaments and other things which we hadn't. We were only learning as we went. We thought we were the best equipped army in the world but we found we were up against it when we went there.[14]

The withdrawal to a more defensible front, despite the presence of thousands of French and Belgian refugees going in the same direction and on the same narrow country roads, was well executed and saved the tiny force from embarrassment at best and annihilation at worst. Among the wild rumours which circulated through the ranks of the gullible or superstitious was that the saviour of the British regular army was the 'Angel of Mons'. It was said that clothed in white and on horseback she had turned back the German tide. From 23 August until the rot was finally stopped at the Marne in the first week of September it was helter-skelter back towards Paris for both the British and French Armies. Units which looked for guidance and leadership often found themselves left to their own devices in the pandemonium which frequently attended the withdrawal. Isolated individual and collective acts of courage and futile sacrifice were common as the BEF 'ad libbed' its withdrawal. Some units adopted the Falstaffian approach and put discretion before valour, retreating in a dangerous, uncoordinated, 'every-man-for-himself' manner. Others put the welfare of the Army before their own personal safety. At a canal bridge in Nimy, near Mons a 25-year-old Sandhurst graduate, Lt. Maurice James Dease, 4th Batt. Royal Fusiliers (City of London Regiment) from Drumree, Co. Meath became the first officer to win the Victoria Cross in the Great War. He manned a machine-gun and was killed preventing the advancing Germans from crossing the bridge.

At Cambrai, later to be the scene of fierce fighting, some of the Dublin Fusiliers were preparing for a rearguard action. As they waited for the Germans they sang rebel songs. One of the songs to which they gave full voice was 'Dear Old Ireland', better known by its chorus, 'Ireland, Boys Hurrah'. It was a strange echo of half a century before when soldiers of Thomas Francis Meagher's Irish Brigade of the Union Army in the American Civil War had sung the same song on the banks of the Rappahannock River before the carnage of Fredericksburg. As they sang they were joined in the chorus by Irish units of the Confederate Army camped on the other side of the river. There is no record of the Germans having joined in the rousing Dublins' chorus at Cambrai!

Where units beat a hasty retreat they ensured the Germans didn't benefit directly from the withdrawal by spiking whatever guns they couldn't take with them on a rapid march. But the 2nd Munsters probably took to extremes the injunction to leave nothing behind the Germans could use. After beating off one attack by a German Uhlans cavalry battalion, the Munsters realised that the horses which were supposed to pull their field guns had been killed in the fighting. They rounded up some of the riderless German steeds and yoked those highly strung beasts to the guns instead. But they would still have been forced to leave guns behind. Rather than do that, some of the Munsters yoked themselves to the guns and dragged them for about five miles until they came across some more horses. 'As we had not enough horses we made mules of ourselves, for we were not such asses as to leave the guns to the enemy', a wounded Munster is supposed to have commented later in hospital in Tralee.[15]'That retreat from Mons was one test of endurance,' for Jack Campbell.

> We got ten minutes rest every hour and what rest you got during the night depended on the proximity of the German Army that was advancing after us. Some times you got three or four hours, maybe you might get five hours. After a few days with the lack of proper rations we began to have hallucinations. You'd see evacuees going along, or a line of transportation and then you'd pull yourself together and there was nothing on the road at all.[16]

Rudyard Kipling, in his book on the Irish Guards (his son lost his life serving with the Regiment, hence his interest), described a similar phenomenon four days into the retreat, four days of footsore exhaustion and sleepless nights,

> By this time, the retreat, as one who took part in it says, had become 'curiously normal'—the effect, doubtless, of that continued over exertion which reduces men to the state of sleep-walkers ... At night, some of them began to see lights, like those of comfortable billets by the roadside which, for some curious reason or other, could never be reached. Others found themselves asleep, on their feet, and even when they lay down to snatch sleep, the march moved on, and wearied them in their dreams.[17]

'Our minds and bodies shrieked for sleep,' wrote John Lucy of the trudge southwards undertaken by the Royal Irish Rifles. 'In a short time our singing army was stricken dumb. Every cell in our bodies craved rest, and that one thought was the most persistent in the vague minds of the marching men.' Men who could go no further dropped out. They seemed to Lucy to be the bigger, stronger looking specimens. 'The smaller men were hardier.' Officers rode up and down the ranks on horseback encouraging and cajoling (which must have rankled with some) knowing that the best the stragglers could hope for was a POW camp. 'The pained look in the troubled eyes of those who fell by the way will not be easily forgotten by those who saw it.'[18] Food was scarce and living off the land could have unwelcome side effects. 'There was a lot of orchards in that part of France and we'd dip into the orchards and fill our pockets as full of fruit as we could then we'd eat that stuff and the bowel movements weren't that comfortable.'[19]

Some units almost allowed themselves to be outstripped by the advancing Germans. A private in Lucy's 2nd Royal Irish Rifles remembers his battalion getting too close for comfort and escaping one night into the sanctuary of a small forest. 'We got on like the Babes in the Wood, holding each others hands ... so as not to lose touch with each other. We dare not light a match or make a sound that would betray our presence ...'. The ploy worked, but only just.

> Once when they were looking for us their searchlight played in the open just where we were, only we were in the shade, and if we had moved another inch our shadows would have been seen. We heard them talking and shouting to each other, but they gave no chase, think-ing we had got away in another direction.[20]

One man who got very little opportunity on that hectic retreat to display either the leadership qualities which would vault him to prominence in World War II or the edginess and arrogance which were to bring about his downfall was 2nd Lt. Eric Dorman-Smith of the 1st Battalion, the Northumberland Fusiliers, garlanded after the first Battle of Alamein, subsequently bypassed and humiliated, largely through unpopularity due to his prickly and overbear-ing manner. He would return to his Cavan home in the 1950s and become an active supporter of the IRA's border camapaign, changing his name to Dorman-O'Gowan.

But all that was in the future in 1914, and a very uncertain future it looked indeed, on 22 August, as 'Chink' (so called because of his resemblance to the regimental mascot—a Chinkara antelope) waited for the advancing Germans with his platoon at a bridge over the Mons canal near the town of Mariette. His orders were to hold the bridge for as long as possible and then withdraw. Many of the men in his platoon were, surprisingly enough, Irishmen also. Like a lot of other regular army regiments the Northumberlands (also known as the Fifth Fusiliers) found the working classes of Dublin and Belfast easier to recruit than those in their own natural hinterland (in the tense moments preceding the arrival of the Germans two Dubliners in his platoon exasper-ated a nervous Dorman-Smith by asking him if they could keep their rifles after the war—we don't know for what purpose).

German infantry arrived in force and allegedly used local children as cover to get close to the far side of the canal from Dorman-Smith's B Company. By mid-afternoon a field gun had been brought up to the canal bank to shell the Northumberland's positions. Unknown to the men of B Company they were on their own; the rest of their battalion had withdrawn an hour before. Their signaller had been one of the first to die in the initial German rush. They held out, waiting for the order to blow the bridge. Finally, after taking heavy casualties for an hour they withdrew. As they fell back towards the town of Frameries, instructions arrived to destroy the bridge which was now in German hands. The experience of the Northumberlands in Frameries was similar to that of B Company in Mariette. As the Germans attacked orders came to different battalions to pull back. The 1st Northumberlands were the last to get such an order. By the time they joined the general retreat the town had been almost completely overrun, and the Germans were snapping at their heels.

Initial setbacks had been turned into defeat which had, by 24 August, become a rout. Dorman-Smith became a part of the tired and exhausted column of soldiers which, outnumbered and outgunned, now wound its way southwards. But their retreat was not fast enough to elude the German advance. The first phase of Chink's war ended near Inchy on 26 August when a German shell overshot the hastily prepared defences of Gen. Smith-Dorrien's retreating Corps and burst near Dorman-Smith in a reserve position. He suffered a shrapnel wound to his left arm and severe surface cuts. He was evacuated to the base hospital at Rouen and from there to England.[21]

The most spectacular rearguard action by an Irish battalion was also the most costly and led to the virtual annihilation of the 2nd Royal Munster Fusiliers at Etreux on 27 August. The battalion had been ordered to hold a position east of the Sambre-Oise canal (roughly fifty miles south of Mons) until ordered to withdraw. The move was designed to keep the Germans as far off as possible while General Haig's I Corps beat an orderly retreat. The Munsters, led by Major Paul Charrier, an excellent commander, described as a 'hearty, genial Kerryman',[22] fulfilled their role superbly, fighting to hold off 7 battalions of German infantry, 3 artillery batteries, as well as cavalry. This was done with considerable panache and not a little black humour. A couple of hours after contact was first made with the advancing Germans, at about midday, the battalion cooks rapidly had to abandon operations and their base. Showing something of the same spirit which had prompted their colleagues to yoke themselves to artillery pieces and drag them for five miles, the cooks were determined to bring their food with them. As they scampered across a lane, under heavy German fire, hefting large unwieldy dixies they were greeted by raucous and unsympathetic shouts of 'Don't be emptying all the tay down your trousers', 'Come out of that, Micky; what are you stopping in the middle of the road for.'[23]

An hour later and the 2nd R.M.F was still holding out. Gradually, however, the battalion's position was chipped away until finally it became untenable. Charrier waited for the order to pull back, but none came. Finally,

> To the meadow near the bridge where the Munsters were collected an orderly carrying a despatch came up at about three o'clock in the afternoon. The time of the dispatch was not marked upon the message, which was to order the Munsters to retire 'at once'. The orderly who carried the message had, he said, been chased by the enemy, and after lying hidden for a time under the nearest cover, believed that it was not possible for him to bring the message through to Major Charrier. Upon this incident the tragedy of the whole day turned. Time had been lost, time too precious ever to regain ...[24]

As they withdrew the odds were against any of the Munsters getting back to rejoin I Corps. By evening their retreat, along the road to Guise, which lay a few miles to the south, had been cut off, their ammunition was running out and their guns were silent. 'The last unwounded gunner met his fate struggling to carry an 18-pounder shell to the gun, standing on the road, surrounded by a small heap of huddled-up bodies.'[25] 'The enemy had entirely surrounded the Battalion, but, encouraged by the few remaining officers, the men fought on until 9.00 p.m. Sounds of approaching help were listened for in vain.'[26] While attempting to force a way through, Charrier, having cheated death many times like a dishonest poker player on a roll, was finally killed.

Accounts differ as to his exact fate. Capt. H.S. Jervis in a letter to Charrier's wife written on 29 August 1914, while a prisoner of the Germans, told her that her husband had already been hit twice: 'Still leading and setting an example to all, he was shot a third time and mortally. He fell in the road.'[27] But Jervis might have been sparing her the gory truth. Another officer, Lt. Thomas, in a letter to his mother wrote that ' ... he was blown to pieces in the end by a shell'.[28]

Thomas himself was too badly wounded to be taken to a POW camp with the other officers. A bullet had penetrated his windpipe and a shell had ripped the biceps from his left arm. To allow him to breathe a tube had to be inserted in his throat. He was able to eat and drink as a result but was unable to speak. Conditions in the field hospital where he lay with three other Munsters, more seriously wounded than he, were grim. 'This town is about the size of Bandon, and is just one big hospital; every house is full of wounded, and flies and the smells are awful.'[29] The low opinion Thomas formed of German medical care was partially corroborated by a man with far greater expertise in the area, Col.

H.N. Thompson of the Royal Army Medical Corps (RAMC), also a prisoner, who held that 'The pure surgery was good, but the administration, sanitation, and feeding arrangements were very poor.'[30]

By dusk the position of the Munsters was untenable. Totally surrounded and having lost nearly 130 dead and with most of the rest wounded, the 250 or so Munsters who remained were forced to surrender. Only 155 members of the battalion escaped death or capture, one of those, a gunner, Pte. Donovan, hid for months in France before making his way through Belgium to neutral Holland and home to England.[31] The Germans gathered and buried the dead of both sides in two huge trenches in an orchard. A cross carved with the motto 'Freund und Freind in Tod vereint' (*Friend and Foe united in Death*) was placed over the graves. As the only medal which could be awarded posthumously was the Victoria Cross and, as it had to be granted for an act of courage seen by a superior officer, Major Charrier was given no gallantry award. But in 1919, after their release from their German POW camps, fifteen medals were presented to members of the battalion whose action had held up the equivalent of two German brigades for twelve hours. Almost 60 years after the event one of the last of the 'Old Contemptibles', Frank Hyland (joined up in 1902) of the Dublin Fusiliers, at the age of 88, would still get highly emotional at the memory of the Munsters at Etreux: 'They were there and they were getting terrible cut up and when I think of it now it makes me cry. They were good men and all their lives were worth nothing.'[32]

The 2nd Battalion of the Royal Dublin Fusiliers had only marginally more luck than the Munsters. Two companies of that unit, under a Major Shewan, found themselves in much the same position, isolated, devoid of information and holding high ground east of Haucourt, directly in the line of the German advance. When the Germans occupied Haucourt in strength, though lacking any orders to withdraw, and unaware that the rest of the 10th Brigade had already done so, Shewan decided to retire to the south, towards the village of Montigny. An advance party, under Capt. Trigona, moved ahead of the main force and was fired on outside the village. Reluctant to believe that the Germans had already penetrated this far south they chose to believe that they were the victims of what has since become known as 'friendly fire'.

Checking the assumption, in the dim light just before dawn on the morning of 27 August, they communicated to the men firing at them that they were the Dublin Fusiliers. Some of the soldiers opposite responded by waving their headgear and shouting 'Dublin Fusiliers, right, come on!' Trigona was suspicious and decided to investigate further. By the time Major Shewan and the main body of the two companies, plus various strays they had picked up along the route, had arrived, he had identified the defenders of Montigny as Germans! Growing impatient, and concluding that their ruse had failed, the Germans began firing again. Shewan and his men retraced their steps and sought refuge in a nearby farmhouse but it quickly became clear that they couldn't remain there for long. Shewan himself, and a number of others, had been wounded in the withdrawal so Capt. N.P. Clarke took command of the two companies and ordered a further retreat before the isolated farmhouse became completely surrounded.

As they pulled out of their temporary lair the Dublins took more casualties. They moved back towards Haucourt, bypassed the town and began a hazardous march across German lines through Vitry and Lens to Abbeville and thence to Boulogne, where they managed to get transport back to England. Like some sort of Pied Piper, Clarke had picked up so many stragglers that by the time his group reached the coast it included two officers and 73 men from ten different units. The remainder of the members of those two unfortunate companies of the 2nd Dublins were either killed or imprisoned, the battalion losing a total of 450 men, including Maj. Shewan, who spent the war as a POW.

The ultimate German objective as they pushed southwards, was Paris, and they got perilously close. When the Irish Guards engaged them in a standing fight on 1 September it was at the densely wooded Villers Cotterets, near the Marne, almost within sight of the lights of Paris. Kipling describes the engagement as 'that heathen battle in half darkness'.[33] On 31 August the Guards had covered an extraordinary 35 miles, in extreme heat, with the loss of only five dropouts. But still it wasn't enough. The Germans were inexorable, and the Guards CO Lt.-Col. Morris decided it was better to choose a favourable location and a good moment to face them. The skirmish took place in the middle of a vast wood, ten miles long by three across. Pte. O'Shaughnessy from Tuam, Co. Galway remembers being told the Germans were coming through the wood and that the Guards would go in and meet them. By Kipling's account, 'The action resolved itself into blind fighting in the gloom of the woods, with occasional glimpses of men crossing the rides, or firing from behind tree boles ... when a man dropped in the bracken and bramble, he disappeared.'[34] Pte. Patrick Joseph Bennet of Thurles later wrote to his siser, however, claiming that the Guards were unruffled by the onslaught of the Germans: 'The Irish boys were cool when the shots were flying around us. They were calmly picking berries.'[35]

Lt.-Col. Morris chose to stay on horseback rather than seek the safety of the thick vegetation. He rode up and down the line encouraging his men. As the Germans launched shellfire into where they suspected the Guards positions were, according to Kipling's account he hollered, ' "D'you hear that? They're doing that to frighten you." To which someone replied with simple truth: "If that's what they're after, they might as well stop. They succeeded with me hours ago". '[36] Pte. O'Shaughnessy saw the CO, at one point, calmly sitting astride his horse smoking a cigarette. He never saw him again. Morris was shot dead, along with Maj. H.F. Crichton and the commander of No. 4 Company, Capt. C.A. Tisdall. (Tisdall's name is commemorated on one of the windows of the tiny Church of Ireland church in Julianstown, Co. Meath.) Among the wounded was the Battalion adjutant Capt. Lord Desmond Fitzgerald. Lt.-Col. Morris left behind in Ireland a son who was barely a month old at the time. He had been born ten days before Morris had sailed for France with the BEF. The child, Michael, in time, would see service in World War II, and play a small but significant role in the planning of D-Day before his post-war involvement in the Olympic movement led to him becoming, as Lord Killanin, President of the International Olympic Committee.

One of the junior Guards officers who survived the Villers-Cotteret engagement was a young lieutenant, Neville Woodroffe. One 3 September, two days afterwards, he wrote to his mother. The letter conveys some sense of the losses suffered by the Guards. 'The wood was very thick and the enemy was no less than 100 yards off. We lost considerably including nine officers three of whom only can be accounted for.'[37] In a subsequent letter he enlarges on what happened. 'The Coldstreams and us were together but the wood was so thick that I fear many shot one's own men [*sic*] ... The Germans are very fond of wood fighting and detail snipers to get up trees where they are not seen and pick off the officers, others lie on the ground and if caught pretend they are dead.'[38] Despite heavy losses Woodroffe reported that the Guards entrenched in the woods and held their positions for six days. During that time the British and French rout was dramatically turned around and it was time to move forward again.

What happened was that the Germans had refined (i.e. abandoned) the Schlieffen Plan which for years had dominated their strategic thinking for a renewed war with France. Instead of pounding Paris to dust with their guns or encircling and rounding up the remnants of the BEF, the Germans turned their attention to the French Armies east of Paris. In doing so they weakened their right, left a gaping hole in the process and allowed the British and French to counter-attack. What followed, from 6 to 10 September, was the Battle of the Marne. 'That was the time the Germans started moving back', recalled John Breen of the 2nd Royal Irish. 'We knew we were attacking and that gave you great heart, to know you weren't being hunted all the time.'[39] Suddenly the Germans were falling back, over the Marne to the Aisne thirty miles beyond. They had clearly been caught unawares, overstretched and overconfident.

> Across the Marne there were many encouraging sights of an army in rapid retreat. Discarded uniforms, equipment, and carts lay about along roads and hedges. We saw ammunition in large quantities ... The aban-

doned German transport was the most heartening sight. The British Army was certainly getting its own back.[40]

Like a ball kicked firmly against a wall the BEF bounced back at their erstwhile pursuers.

By the time the Battle of the Aisne began on 13 September (the Germans having been pushed a further 30 miles back towards Mons) the pace was beginning to tell on the 'Contemptibles', who had trudged south for twelve consecutive days without respite and who were now footsore and feeling sorry for themselves. The Connaught Rangers was the Irish regiment which took most punishment from the Germans at the Aisne. Losing 222 officers and men. They were employed at Soupir, on the northern side of the river, near the town of Soissons on 14 September. In the same battle Major W.S. Sarsfield, acting CO of the Rangers, died of wounds. He was a direct descendant of Patrick Sarsfield, earl of Lucan, the great Irish soldier of the eighteenth century. The Rangers' losses had helped secure the position of the Irish Guards, who had heavy casualties of their own. Woodroffe wrote to his mother on 30 September. In retrospect the tone was naive. 'This is a terrible war and I don't suspect there is an idle British soldier in France. I wonder when it will end; one hears so much. There has been more fighting and more loss of life crowded into seven weeks than there was in the whole of South Africa.'[41] At that stage of the conflict the 'sausage machine' had not even begun to crank into action. Losses in the first seven weeks were, in military terms, within acceptable bounds. When compared with what was to follow Woodroffe's letter sounds like a man falling off a cliff complaining of toothache.

Woodroffe didn't live long enough to experience the 'total wafare' of the trenches. What he did bear witness to was the first sign of strain among some of the men around him. Nervous exhaustion so debilitating that it led to the first incidents of self maiming in the war. 'It seems a favourite and old trick to shoot one's finger off when one is cleaning one's rifle. Two men were admitted to hospital having blown their fingers off ...'.[42] The practice was widespread. John Lucy was almost hit by a bullet which had already achieved the purpose for which it was intended: 'One evening in billets a man who had already said he was fed up, deliberately shot himself through the left hand. He was in the room below that in which I was billeted, and the bullet came through the floor near my feet, narrowly missing me. The man said that the wound was an accident and that it occurred while he was cleaning his rifle, but others later confessed unofficially to have known his purpose.'[43]

Despite this the fighting of 1914 was, qualitatively, a different conflict altogether to the type of warfare we associate with the Great War. The historian of the Leinster Regiment, writing about the preparation of the 2nd Leinsters for the battle of the Somme in 1916, contrasted the comprehensive bombardment which preceded that offensive with the earlier, almost gentle-manly, phase of the fighting:

> There were a few veterans of 1914 who related to us how on the Aisne nearly two years ago a message would be sent round to say that our howitzers 'would fire ten rounds at 4 a.m'. This was to prevent the infantry becoming perturbed by the sound of such devastating bom-bardment and imagining that a great battle had begun. Veterans of course are never believed, but apparently ammunition was not fired away for fun in those far off days.[44]

The speed of the German onslaught (similar in nature to the 'Blitzkrieg' of World War II) had forced them to bypass Antwerp rather than risk putting their schedule of conquest out by even a day. In mid September, with the first signs of the war becoming bogged down on the Aisne, the city was still (just barely) held by the Belgians. The BEF had espoused a policy of breaking for the sea in order to circumvent the German armies. The Germans followed suit. What could be more prejudicial to this plan than the collapse of one of Europe's premier sea ports. Accordingly a Naval Division was landed there to stiffen Belgian resistance. Phillip Doyle was one of about 100 Wexfordmen who had joined the pre-war British Navy. He did so along with a friend, Jack Conway, who was to be killed at the Dardanelles the following year. But not even enlistment in the Navy meant that he could avoid trench warfare. Shortly afer the outbreak of the war this man of the sea was transferred from the Navy proper to the Naval Division and early in September found himself, with virtually no infantry-type training, in a trench helping King Albert's Belgian Army defend Antwerp. The First Lord of the Admiralty, Winston Churchill, crossed the Channel to see for himself. 'Mr Churchill got up on a box in a big shed in Antwerp and told us we were going to meet the enemy but they were all old men. Well, we found out our mistake, they weren't all old men.' Sixty years after the event Doyle could afford a wry chuckle at the recollection. Given the way they were armed he would have needed a sense of humour at the time. 'We had nothing ... only Japanese rifles and Japanese bullets ... We were only on a bluff, bluffing the Germans.' The Naval Divi-sion was able to do little to prevent the fall of Antwerp on 9 October and when it changed hands Doyle and his colleagues were safely back in England after a stay of about six weeks: 'We never seen a German ... We were in the trenches for about a fortnight and then they withdrew us ... we got out in the dark, back into Antwerp and from there we docked in Dover.'[45]

The stasis along the Aisne and the British race to the sea secured a front which hardly varied for the next three and a half years. The opposing war machines were like stricken dinosaurs, unable, through their own sheer weight and lack of formidable brainpower to push each other far beyond the country-side where the fighting started. One of Neville Woodroffe's last letters reflected the reality of what life held in store for the Irish Guards for the next fifty-two months of attrition.

> Things look very much the same, and it is comparatively monotonous after our previous adventure. We had a small patrol out in front of our trenches yesterday and it was awful to see the massacre and refuse which a wood to our left disclosed. Dead Germans and a few of the Wiltshire regiment which had been there fully a fortnight ago and in terrible conditions. Legs stuck in boots lay out in the open and corpses shattered from shell fire lay at short intervals. Kits and rifles, ammunition, helmets, tools etc. all lay in heaps. The stink was awful. We buried what we could, but the most one could not touch. However, enough![46]

Less than a month after sending that letter Woodroffe himself was dead; he had failed to survive the first 100 days of the war. In a photograph taken of him in his Irish Guards' uniform he looks more like a pre-pubescent drummer boy than a soldier, but the conflict was to claim younger lives than his. He had barely been a year out of school, and had experienced little of what life had to offer, when he died.

An indication of the haemorrhage which was taking place even at this relatively early stage in proceedings was that the 2nd Royal Irish Regiment, to maintain its complement, was sent seven drafts of new recruits or fresh soldiers between the flight from Mons and the 'Race to the Sea'. A draft of six officers and 353 men arrived on 15 October, in time for an attack on Le Pilly, a small town on the spine of a ridge near the Ypres sector, a low-lying area of fields, dykes and muddy streams. The town was taken in the afternoon of 19 October. The failure of a French attack, however, left the 2nd Royal Irish, under its acting CO Maj. Daniell, exposed and vulnerable. Early on the morning of the 20th the Germans, who had only retired about 400 yards from the town, countered and surrounded the isolated Irish battalion. According to John Breen, Maj. Daniell offered them the choice of capitulation, so hopeless was their situation, ' ... he gave us the option. Would we fight through or would we surrender. We said we'd fight through and we'd get through some way or another.' Some did, including Breen, but most died or were taken prisoner. Daniell himself was shot and killed along with six other officers and 170 other ranks. The Germans took more than 300 Royal Irish prisoners, most were wounded.

On that day the Germans attacked along a line between Arras and the sea and the 2nd Leinsters were back on the defensive, baulked in their attempt to reach Lille, the great industrial city of the French north west. In defence of a town called Premesques, near Armentieres, one of the most bizarre incidents of the entire war occured. It involved the historian of the Leinsters, F.E. Whitton, then a captain, and Capt. R.A. Orpen-Palmer. The latter was the son of a Kerry-based Church of Ireland rector, Revd Abraham Orpen-Palmer. His younger brother later commanded a battalion of the Royal Irish Fusiliers. R.A. Orpen-Palmer was known, simply as 'O-P 1' while his brother was 'O-P 2'.[47] Both Whitton and Orpen-Palmer were wounded and captured. Whitton was unable to walk, and Orpen-Palmer, who had lost an eye in the fighting, was temporarily blind. Somehow both managed to escape from their captors, members of a Saxon regiment. But their hopes of reaching the British lines were slim, given their disabilities. Nonetheless they managed to overcome them. Writing two years later Frank Hitchcock, whose diary of the trenches *Stand To* became a classic of the war, recalled that, 'Some years afterwards I met a Sergeant in the 1st Royal Fusiliers who recalled the fact of seeing Leinster officers stumbling into their entrenchments. The blinded one, he said, was being directed by the one he was carrying.'[48] Under cover of darkness and with a single pair eyes and legs the two men had managed to stumble onto the British lines.

The war now settled into a slough of entrenched immobility from which unimaginative generals, 'widow makers', were unable to tug it loose. All along the line from Alsace-Lorraine to the sea a narrow strip of land was given over to the belligerents; civilians (who are rarely mentioned in World War I diaries) simply left the armies to it. In retrospect many were to see the first three months of hostilities as the heady halcyon days of innocence. Then the war was fought, largely, between professional soldiers who were disposed to take a broadminded approach to the prospect of unalloyed discomfort and violent death. These were men who cared little who their enemy was nor who their allies were. As their ranks thinned they were replaced by a far less jaundiced breed, men to whose youthful idealism a cynical government had appealed. That moral stand would be suborned, twisted and corrupted by shells, machine-guns, generals and politicians over the next four years. From the trauma of the Great War a new moral order would emerge. One in which the bloom of aristocratic hierarchy would begin to fade and wither. But that was in a future not yet pre-determined. Let us leave the last word to the men digging trenches across Northern France and Southern Belgium and coming to grips with narrowing horizons and the shock of the new quotidien. 'No sooner is a trench dug than it fills with water ... the soil is clay, and so keeps the water from draining away even if that were possible ... pumping has been tried, but not with much success. The weather continues wet, and there does not seem to be any likelihood of a change. Consequently, we may expect some fresh discomforts daily.'[49]

# 2    Gallipoli: The V Beach Landings

'Murphy's Law' ('Everything that can go wrong, will') in all its military applications is wasteful and profligate of human life. When such misfortune is allied to human error and incompetence on a vast scale the result is pure tragedy. Such was the confluence of physical and metaphysical forces which resulted in the carnage of Gallipoli, a campaign which could have changed the trend of the war (even of history itself) but which is remembered only with bitterness and recrimination where it is commemorated at all.

The underlying idea was as flawless as the planning and execution were flawed. Force the Dardanelles, draw thousands of German troops from the Western Front to reinforce a tottering Turkish army, take Turkey out of the war and open up a short, warm-weather supply route to your Russian ally. It was worth the committment of the resources of the Navy and the overstretched army. But like so many of the grand designs of the Great War it was bungled by men inadequate to the tasks allocated to them. The plan was conceived by Winston Churchill, First Lord of the Admiralty. Kitchener was unenthusiastic, already overcommitted to the Western Front, and preparing for a Spring offensive in 1915; he had only one division (the 29th) to spare and his new volunteer troops were not yet adequately trained.

The Gallipoli campaign began as a naval operation. Royal Navy vessels bombarded Turkish forts along the Gallipoli peninsula, and Royal Marines even effected a landing. But the element of surprise seemed to apply to both sides. The Marines withdrew for lack of follow-up support, and the Turks, with the aid of German officers, led by Field Marshall Liman von Sanders, began to prepare for the invasion they now knew would come sooner or later. Kitchener, finally succumbing to the notion that the landings were necessary, appointed Gen. Sir Ian Hamilton as Commander of what would be known as the Mediterranean Expeditionary Force. The forces he had at his disposal included the 29th Division (a regular Army unit based in India) a Royal Navy division, a French division and the troops of the Australian and New Zealand Army under Gen. Birdwood who had expected to be serving in France. The main landings were to take place near the southern tip of the Gallipoli peninsula at Cape Helles on beaches designated by the initials  S, V, W, X, Y and Z. Having established a beachhead, the troops would then take the heights of Achi Baba (six miles to the north east of V Beach) and the town of Krithia.

Two famous Irish battalions of the 29th Division, the 1st Royal Dublin Fusiliers and the 1st Royal Munster Fusiliers (86th Brigade, accompanied by the 2nd Hampshires of the 88th) were assigned V Beach for their landing. It was overlooked by the quiet coastal village of Sedd el Bahr. (The Australian landings, which took place at night, near Ari Burnu, were stalled when the local Turkish commander, an obscure officer named Mustapha Kemal, pushed them back to the beach which became known as Anzac Cove. Kemal later became the far less obscure Kemal Ataturk, the 'Father of Modern Turkey'.)

Hamilton's intention was to disorientate the Turks with a series of simultaneous landings on 25 April 1915. Some, as it transpired, were virtually unopposed. But the Commander-in-Chief was less than adequately aware of the state of the Turkish defences on individual beaches. Also, by allowing so many separate landings to take place, communications became snarled up. As with the future landings at Suvla Hamilton was effectively incommunicado. He was on board ship, out of radio contact with his divisional commanders and, 'out of the loop'

The plan for landing the Dublins and Munsters was quite well thought out. It just didn't work. It had two essential elements. An old collier *River Clyde*, with openings cut into her port and starboard bows, was to be run ashore and beached. Troops were then to descend via gangways to barges and walk across these to the shore without getting their feet wet. In addition, lighters with the 1st Dublins on board (40 men per boat) would be towed offshore and would row up to the beach before discharging their troops. From offshore guns of two naval battleships would pound the Turkish defences around the fortress of Sedd-el-Bahr, which dominated the beach. 'It was surmised that by 8.00 a.m. the ground above the beaches would have been won; by noon we should be in the vicinity of the village of Krithia, and have taken the hill of Achi Baba that night,'[1] wrote the CO of the Munsters, Lt.-Col. Tizard. The supposition was outrageously optimistic; in fact by nightfall the Dublins and Munsters had not even secured the beachhead.

V Beach itself was narrow, crescent-shaped and raked, with, as the Dublins and Munsters would have seen it coming ashore, a sheer ridge to the left, about fifty feet in height, and the old fortress to the right. Beyond the fortress was the village of Sedd-el-Bahr, the beach itself provided little cover against machine-gun or rifle fire for invading troops. The operation was in the hands of a Royal Navy officer, Commander Unwin, who had conceived the idea of using the *Clyde* for the landings. Over two thousand troops were squashed aboard the boat as it approached V Beach. 'That night I don't think anyone slept' wrote Tizard. ' ... When it became light enough the ships began the bombardment of the fort and the village of Sedd el Bahr and the ground adjoining the beach and we slowly steamed in.'[2] Each man was well supplied (too well, as it transpired) carrying 200 rounds of ammunition and three days

iron rations as well as a greatcoat and a waterproof sheet. Packs weighed
about 60 pounds.

Disaster struck the Dublin Fusiliers first. Initially their boats were towed
and then set adrift with sailors manning the oars which would take them to
the shore. At first it appeared that the landing would be virtually unopposed.
One unidentified officer of the Dublins wrote,

> The ships' shells were simply ripping up the ground, and with my field
> glasses I could see many of the Turks running for their lives. I thought
> then that we would have no difficulty in landing. Then machine-guns
> galore were played on us from a trench unseen at the bottom of the
> cliff, not ten yards from us. Shrapnel burst above our heads at the
> same time and before I knew where I was I was covered with dead
> men. Not knowing they were dead, I was roaring at them to help me
> up, for I was drowning ... We got the dead and wounded off on to the
> mine-sweeper, and gathered another three boatloads of men to take
> ashore and face the same thing again.[3]

Capt. A.W. Molony, writing home, told of a 'perfect tornado of fire, many
men were killed and wounded in the boats, and wounded men were knocked
over into the water and drowned, but they kept on, and the survivors jumped
into the water in some cases up to their necks and got ashore; but the slaughter was terrific. Most of the officers were killed or wounded.'[4] The CO of the
Dublins, Col. Rooth, made it to the shore but was shot dead at the edge of
the water. Major Fetherstonhaugh, his second-in-command, was mortally
wounded in his boat. The litany of death continued with five more officers
killed, most before they got as far as the beach. The men fared just as badly.
The 1st R.D.F. was, largely, recruited from among the working classes of an
impoverished Dublin. The diet of the average Dubliner in the early years of
the twentieth century was nutritionally deficient. As a consequence working
class Dubliners were small in stature, averaging around 5' 4" in height. The
water, even quite close to the beach, was more than a fathom deep.

Lt.-Col. Tizard watched the carnage from on board the *River Clyde* waiting to send his own men into the same shambles:

> I saw many cases just then where men who had jumped out of the
> boats having to wade ashore got hit and fell face downwards in the
> water; a chum, who had got ashore, seeing this, would come back and
> pull him out of the water so that he should not be drowned. In nearly
> every case the men who did this were killed. Men in the boats who
> were hit tried to get away from the hail of lead by getting out of the
> boats on the far side in order to keep out of sight, thus getting the boat

between them and the shore. There were four or five boats along the shore at intervals broadside on to it, and behind each of them were four or five men who had been hit. Some were holding on to the gunwales and others were hanging on with their arms through the ropes which are looped round the boats so as to prevent themselves sinking in the water which was up to their waists. After a time I noticed these men sank from exhaustion and loss of blood and were drowned. The water by this time all along the shore and especially around the boats was red with blood.[5]

This could even be seen from the skies: a Royal Navy flier, Lt.-Com. Sampson, monitoring the invasion beaches flew over V Beach and noticed that the water was a peculiar colour. On closer examination he realised that it was red with blood to a distance of about fifty yards from the shore.

Some did manage to make it to the beach. Lt. Maffet of X Company found himself in a boat where most of the sailors fell victim to Turkish shrapnel and small arms: 'The men had to take over their oars, and as they did not know much about rowing the result was that we often got broadside on to the shore and presented a better target to the enemy.' Then the boat was hit by incendiary shells. 'Several of the men who had been wounded fell to the bottom of the boat, and were either drowned there or suffocated by other men falling on top of them; many, to add to their death agonies, were burnt as well.' Maffet himself was hit in the head by a machine-gun bullet; others tore into his pack. In this instance its bulk certainly saved his life but he was knocked out of the boat: 'I went under water and came up again and tried to encourage the men to get to the shore and under cover as fast as they could as it was their only chance. I then went under again. Someone caught hold of me and began pulling me ashore.' Sheltering behind a bank he looked out to sea and saw 'the remnants of my platoon trying to get to the shore, but they were shot down one after another, and their bodies drifted out to sea or lay immersed a few feet from the shore.'[6]

Sgt. J. McColgan was in a boat with 32 men; only six of whom got out alive. He himself was hit in the leg as he dived overboard. 'One fellow's brains were shot into my mouth as I was shouting to them to jump for it. I dived into the sea. Then came the job to swim with my pack, and one leg useless. I managed to pull out the knife and cut the straps and swim ashore. All the time bullets were ripping around me.'[7]

Lt. Henry Desmond O'Hara, the only son of W.J. O'Hara, R.M. of Ballincollig, Co. Cork, and a nephew of the bishop of Cashel, was more fortunate than most of his fellow officers. He would play a leading role in the drama that followed the landings, but as he watched his battalion being torn to pieces he was aboard the *Clyde* with W Company: 'Meanwhile, our ship, instead of grounding as had been arranged, struck about 15 yards from the shore, and it was that that saved our lives, as we had to stay where we were.'[8] When he came ashore about midnight he would be forced to assume command of what was left of the battalion. His level-headedness and quiet heroism would help him survive and earn him a DSO, the second-most prestigious gallantry award. He was youngest officer at that time to have received the honour. But in the early hours of the morning of 25 April he could only watch with horror as the remnants of the 1st R.D.F. dragged themselves up the shore and took some shelter under cover of a bank.

Then it was the turn of the 1st Royal Munster Fusiliers who had been witnessing the slaughter with rising apprehension from on board the *River Clyde*. Unlike the Dublins who had, at least, been caught by surprise, the Munsters now knew what to expect. While they waited, bodies of dead and drowned Dublin Fusiliers floated by. As with many of the regular Irish battalions the Munsters, though overwhelmingly Irish among the NCOs and other ranks, were, in the main, led by English officers. A number of these have left accounts behind, most notably the CO, Lt.-Col. Tizard, Capt. Geddes, who commanded X Company, and Lt. Guy Nightingale, who, like Henry Desmond O'Hara, found himself, briefly, in effective charge of his battalion on the beach. Their narratives, relatively free of military humbug and bombast, provide a blood-curdling account of the slaughter of the Irishmen under their command.

The plan for the Munster's landing went wrong from the start. The *River Clyde* beached too far from the shore, as we have already heard from O'Hara, and the barges, which were to have formed the gangway from the vessel to the beach, instead of going straight ahead went wide of the collier and had to be pulled back, under a hail of murderous fire, by crew members and Fusiliers. (Unwin and one of his midshipmen won VCs for this action, awards which, though well-deserved, were in marked contrast to the treatment of the unsung heroes of the two Irish regiments who actually landed.)

With the barges in position Tizard gave the order to disembark. Capt. Henderson was in position with Z Company on the starboard side, and Capt. Geddes was to lead X Company down the gangway on the port side. The gangway on the port side jammed and briefly delayed X Company. Once again the barges let the Munsters down. Strong currents caused the barge on the port side closest to the beach to break adrift into deep water.

> Capt. Geddes leading his men jumped over the side and had to swim about 20 yards before he could wade ashore. A good many who followed him sank owing to the weight of their equipment and were drowned. The crew again went out to try and get the barges straight. These barges were filled with dead and wounded, very few of the men

from the two companies had got ashore. Those who had were taking cover behind a bank about eight feet high that ran along the beach ten yards from the water's edge. In front of this bank was a line of barbed wire entanglements about 25 yards distant.[9]

Geddes made it to the shore by swimming, but many of the men of his company, unable to swim or weighed down by their huge packs, drowned in the treacherous currents. 'We got it like anything', Geddes later wrote; 'man after man behind me was shot down but they never wavered. Lt. Watts who was wounded in five places and lying on the gangway cheered the men on with cries of "Follow the Captain". Capt. French of the Dublins told me afterwards that he counted the first 48 men to follow me and they all fell ...'.[10] The first of the Munsters to actually make the beach was Sgt. Patrick Ryan, who swam ashore in his full kit. He subsequently received the DC for some risky reconaissance work.

Henderson's company, on the starboard side of the *River Clyde*, was faring no better. One of his platoon commanders, Capt. Lane, survived to write an account of the nightmarish assault on the beach.

> All the way down the side of the ship bullets crashed against the sides but beyond a few splinters I was not hit. On reaching the first barge I found some of the men had collected and were firing. I mistrusted the second barge and the track to the shore so I led them over the side, the water nearly up to our shoulders. However, none of us were hit and we gained the bank. There I found Henderson badly hit and heaps of wounded. Any man who put his head up for an instant was shot dead, and we were rather mixed up with the Dublins. Nearly all the NCOs were hit.[11]

Out of the first 200 men down the gangway 149 were killed outright and 30 were wounded. Pte. Timothy Buckley, of the Munsters, a native of Macroom, Co. Cork, counted 26 men down the gangway before him: 'I stood counting them as they were going through. It was then I thought of peaceful Macroom, and wondered if I should ever see it again.' Instead of running down the gangway he jumped over the rope and straight onto the pontoon. Two more followed suit and lay flat on the pontoon bridge. ' ... the shrapnel was bursting all around. I was talking to the chap on my left, and saw a lump of lead enter his temple. I turned to the chap on my right. His name was Fitzgerald. He was from Cork, but soon he was over the border.'[12]

A safe distance (or so he thought) from the massacre on V Beach on board a Royal Navy monitor was 17-year-old Thomas Leavy from Dublin. He was well acquainted with a number of the 1st Dublins; some were boys close to his own age; and he watched with sickening dismay as they went to their deaths. His vessel was maintaining a constant fire in support of the landing. 'After things settled down we were out in a boat pulling the dead bodies onto an island there called Rabbit Island ... it was terrible to see it, we couldn't do anything, all we could do was fire over their heads with our two 14" guns.' Almost sixty years after the landings he still believed that, 'The undertaking was all wrong ... it was a blunder. There wasn't a hope in hell of taking the place.'[13] Also watching from naval vesels offshore were a number of newspaper war correspondents. One of the more naïve members of the group, watching through field glasses, noticed the the men lying on the beach and was heard to ask, 'Why are our men resting?' It was pointed out to him by the veteran correspondent H.W. Nevinson that they were not resting but dead.

By the time he got to the shore Geddes felt badly in need of a rest. He

> was completely exhausted and lay on the beach until I was able to crawl up to the slender cover the Dublins were holding—ten yards from the water's edge ... It was the most ghastly hell you can imagine and you might just as well have walked the plank. You can form no idea of the horror of the undertaking—two splendid regiments practically wiped out.[14]

Movement on the beach was practically impossible. As Capt. Lane discovered, any man who worked himself into an exposed position was inviting instant death. Lane was hit running for cover: 'The bullet went through my right ankle and carried on sideways smashing my left leg to bits. One of my platoon then came out very pluckily and pulled me into safety. I had only been on the beach five minutes and never saw a Turk.'[15]

Tizard, watching from the *River Clyde*, realised that it was impossible to carry out the original plan of attack which had been arranged by Brig.-Gen. Hare, Commander of the 86th Brigade:

> ... nothing could live on the ground about the beach. Men who left the cover of the bank for an instant were killed and five men of the R.M. Fusiliers who had been sent forward to cut the wire had all been killed within ten yards after leaving cover. The concentrated fire from the beach on to the one point of landing from the vessel, and also on to the gangways and exits was so heavy and accurate our losses had already been very severe. More than half of those who had left the vessel were either killed or wounded.[16]

There were also fatalities on board the ship. The Munster's second-in-command, Maj. Monck-Mason, was wounded there, as was the adjutant, while the CO of the Hampshires was killed on the ship's bridge.

Various efforts were made to reinforce the survivors ashore. Some of the Dublins who were fortunate enough not to have been allocated seats in the lighters which had turned into death traps were despatched down the makeshift pontoon bridge to the beach. Men from W Company of the 1st R.D.F, among them Sgt. C. McCann (later promoted to lieutenant), were met with the same Turkish fusillade which greeted everything that moved off the *River Clyde*.

> [We] reached the two barges that formed the landing stage when we came under heavy rifle and machine-gun fire again. We threw ourselves flat on the barges and lay still for some time; I was between two men of the Munster Fusiliers who were dead, but I did not realise this until I asked one of them to make more room, and as he did not move I pushed him with my hand, and then found that his head was blown away.[17]

On shore Geddes, who estimated that he had lost about 70 per cent of his Company, was trying to extricate what was left of the Munsters and the leaderless Dublins from their exposed position. Breaking for shelter near the old fort, along with half a dozen others, he was wounded. 'However we got across and later picked up 14 stragglers from the [Dublins]. This little party attempted to get a lodgement inside the Fort but we couldn't do it so we dug in as well as we could with our entrenching tools'.[18] Geddes continued in command until he was evacuated from the beach after dark. Gradually he had worked the vestiges of the two Irish regiments into a more defensible position and into place for a possible counter-attack against the well-protected Turks.

The *River Clyde* was now a distinctly uncomfortable place to be, well within range of the Turkish artillery and machine-guns, filling up with wounded who had been evacuated from the beach or from among the heaps of bodies in the barges. At about 9.00 a.m. the Turkish firing abated and Tizard decided to try and get some more men ashore. Major Jarret and some of Y Company were despatched.

> A ship's cutter had been put into position and with the two barges and a gang plank formed a way from the vessel towards a spit of rock that jutted out from the beach on the right of where the *Clyde* was beached. This spit of rock was thickly covered with dead, and the enemy had got the range of this spot to a nicety making it a veritable death trap.[19]

Elsewhere, in accordance with the lottery of war, the landings had been more successful (in some cases virtually unopposed). At W Beach, where the 29th's Divisional commander had concentrated his own attentions to the exclusion of all other landings, there had been stiff opposition but it had been over-come. A flanking movement from that beach could have caught the Turks at V Beach in the rear. During the afternoon Tizard spotted, from the *Clyde*, a party of men on the cliffs to the left of the bay, but a message he sent to the 29th Division HQ asking that they be used to outflank the Turks was ig-nored. Also at W Beach the 86th Brigade's CO Brig.-Gen. Hare had been wounded, so Tizard took command of the brigade. The CO of the 88th Brigade, Gen. Napier then came aboard the *River Clyde* along with a platoon from the Worcester Regiment. Instructions came from 29th Division HQ that the landings must continue, so, reluctantly, Tizard sent out another company of the Hampshires. Once again the barge closest to the shore had broken away and, unable to move forward, the Hampshires began to crowd back into the boat. Seeing this Gen. Napier and his brigade major went to investigate. Both were killed by Turkish shellfire. Lt. Guy Nightingale watched Napier die:

> He was hit in the stomach on the barge between our ship and the beach. He lay for half an hour on the barge and then tried to get some water to drink but the moment he moved the Turks began firing at him again and whether he was hit again or not I do not know, but he died very soon afterwards, and when I went ashore for the second time, I turned him over and he was quite dead ...[20]

Nightingale, who had served with the Munsters in India, was sent to join the remains of Maj. Jarret's company trapped behind a bank on the beach. 'We jumped into the sea and got ashore somehow with a rain of bullets all round us. I found Jarrett and a lot of men but very few not hit.'[21] Nightingale was sent back to the *River Clyde* by Jarret to advise Tizard not to attempt to send any more men ashore in daylight. Wisely Tizard heeded this advice and chose to ignore the division's orders to press ahead, which had been despatched in ignorance of the true situation at V Beach. Nightingale returned to the beach and

> lay all day in the blazing sun and the groans and cries of the wounded and dying were awful. The swines of Turks were picking off the wounded as they tried to crawl up the sand to us. At dusk Jarret, and I got together about 40 men who had not been hit and we pushed up a little and formed what we could of an outpost line with sentries so that we would have some sort of warning if we were rushed. Geddes was too bad to do much and finally had to be taken away. Just as it was dusk

Jarret came up to me to have a look at the sentries I had put out and, as he was talking to me, he was hit in the throat. He died in a few minutes. That left me the only officer.[22]

Nightingale, who despite his youth and relative inexperience, was now the effective commander of the force on shore (later temporarily combined with the Dublins, because of the huge losses, into one unit, the 'Dubsters'), passed an anxious and miserable night, soaked to the skin like the rest of his men who had waded ashore, lashed by a heavy shower of rain, and expecting the Turks to counter-attack and try and push his small force off the beach. Capt. Lane, lying helpless and wounded behind a bank, was almost resigned to the inevitable. 'That night the Turks came so close that on one occasion we could hear them talking and I feared it was all up.'[23] Lane became one of the long-term victims of the war. He was finally evacuated and taken to Malta where surgeons were forced to amputate his leg.

Capt. Geddes was also evacuated. 'Hell it has been, with a vengeance,' he wrote,

and the men who were at Mons and La Bassee say it was sheer child's play to what we've gone through here ... As I write we have only six officers and just over 300 men left, out of 28 officers and 900 men. The Dublins have one officer and just over 200 men, the two regiments are now amalgamated into one. The Turks are killing, torturing and burning the wounded—this is reported on every side. They outsavage the worst savages. Flanders is a picnic to this and its the most inhuman show that has ever been known—its simply downright murder![24]

(His allegations concerning the Turkish treatment of the wounded are, if they have any substance at all, greatly exaggerated.)

Overnight the remaining troops from the *River Clyde* came ashore. Groups of them worked their way across to the fortress on the right hand side of the bay. That night the Turks set fire to some of the houses in Sedd-el-Bahr, probably to create more open sight-lines or 'fields of fire' for their snipers than were afforded by the narrow streets of the village. Tizard, as he surveyed the bay from the *River Clyde*, described his situation on the morning of the 26 April in the following terms.

The enemy were still holding their position. On my left Lt. Nightingale with about ten men had dug themselves in under the cliff on the left. A small party of men were a little way up the nulla from the shore and there was a connecting party at the shore end. They were apparently held up. On the right under the fort and amongst the ruins on the shore were the greater part of the force.[25]

A staff officer, Capt. Stoney of the King's Own Scottish Borderers, offered to go ashore and take command of a detachment of the almost officerless and hopelessly mixed-up troops.

At dawn the ships began pounding the enemy positions. Nightingale assisted in the burial of Major Jarret on the beach and at 7 a.m., in the early morning light of 26 April, the survivors of three companies of the Munsters, two of the Dublins and one of the Hampshires took the Sedd-el-Bahr fortress with a bayonet charge and moved into the village beyond where they were held up by well concealed Turkish snipers.

> The village was an awful snag. Every house and corner was full of snipers and you only had to show yourself in the streets to have a bullet at your head. We spent from 9 a.m. till 2.30 before we finally cleared them all out, we lost a lot of men and officers in it. It was rotten fighting, nothing to be seen of the enemy but fellows being knocked over everywhere. I got one swine of a Turk with my revolver when searching a house for snipers but he nearly had me first.[26]

Once the village had been cleared of snipers by the force now led by the delightfully-named staff officer Lt.-Col. Doughty-Wylie, the next target was the hill beyond (Hill 141). The hastily improvised plan was to take it from two sides. When Doughty-Wylie's troops were ready, those led by Stoney emerged from their shelters and both forces stormed the hill with supporting fire from offshore from HMS *Albion*. Though Nightingale claims this assault didn't take place until nearly 4 p.m. Tizard puts the time much earlier.

> By about 1.30 p.m. Capt. Stoney had collected the men and the attack started and it was now that Cpl. Cosgrove R.M.Fusiliers, greatly distinguished himself in clearing a way through the wire entanglements and leading a charge after Sgt. Major Bennett had been killed. For this he was awarded the VC.[27]

Tizard's typically military and stylistically-laconic account does scant justice to William Cosgrove's courage. Cosgrove, a huge man for that era, 6' 5" in height, from Aghada in Co. Cork, had enlisted in the Munster Fusiliers in 1910. Finding the wire in front of the Turkish positions was still intact, despite the bombardment, the attackers took cover. Cosgrove rushed forward, with some others, to attempt to dismantle the wire, right under the noses of the Turk defenders, who opened fire. The wire, however, could not be cut with the equipment available, so, instead Cosgrove grabbed one of the poles buried in the ground which bore the wire and heaved. He managed to uproot it and one or two others, creating a gap through which the Munsters poured on their way to taking the Turkish trenches.

A rather florid description of the incident is ascribed to Cosgrove himself as he recovered from wounds on his family's farm in Cork:

> Some of us having got up to the wires we started to cut them with the pliers, but you might as well try to cut the round tower at Cloyne with a pair of lady's scissors. The wire was of great strength, strained like fiddle strings, and so full of spikes that you could not get the pliers between. Heavens! I thought we were done; I threw the pliers from me. 'Pull them up!' I roared to the fellows; and I dashed at one of the upright posts, put my arms around it, and heaved and strained at it until it came up in my arms, the same as you would lift a child ... We met a brave, honourable foe in the Turks, and I am sorry that such decent fighting men were brought into the row by such dirty tricksters as the Germans.[28]

Cosgrove's action, being entirely voluntary (he was not acting under orders), qualified him for the Victoria Cross, which he was duly awarded. Later, in a bayonet charge which took the trenches at the top of the hill, he was hit in the spine by a bullet and invalided home.

On the other side of the village the attack led by Doughty-Wylie (who wielded nothing but a cane throughout) was also successful in scattering the Turks from Hill 141. He did so with troops who, as Lt. Henry Desmond O'Hara pointed out, had 'had no food for about 36 hours after landing, as we were fighting incessantly'.[29] Guy Nightingale, having survived the snipers in Sedd-el-Bahr, experienced a rush of adrenalin as he raced to the top of the hill.

> My company led the attack with the Dublins and we had a great time. We saw the enemy, which was the chief thing and all the men shouted and enjoyed it tremendously. It was a relief after all that appalling sniping. We rushed straight to the top and turned 2000 Turks off the redoubt and poured lead into them at about 10 yards range. Nearly all the officers had been killed or wounded by now. A Colonel Doughty-Wylie who led the whole attack was killed at my side. I wrote in about him to the staff and he has been recommended for a VC. I buried him that evening and got our Padre to read the service over him.[30]

There were a couple of attempts that night by the Turks to retake the hill but the depleted 86th Brigade held on. A force of almost two thousand men had now dwindled to a bare 700 and O'Hara was the only officer of the 1st Dublin Fusiliers who was not a casualty. The Brigade Major of the 86th, Maj. Farmer, wrote of O'Hara, that he 'rose to every occasion with the greatest coolness and competence, from commanding a platoon at the terrible landing from the *River Clyde* to the command of a company the next day, and after 28 April to commanding the Battalion.'[31] In the days that followed he would be obliged to exhibit all his considerable composure as the Turks counter-attacked mercilessly.

The following morning (27 April) at 7 a.m. 2000 French troops arrived to relieve the Dublins and Munsters who returned to the site of their virtual annihilation two days before.

> We went back to Beach V where we had landed, had breakfast and tried to sleep. It was very hot. The dead lying on the beach wasn't a pleasant sight. There were hundreds of them ... No one can understand how we ever effected a landing when we see the strength of the position. There were 9000 Turks up against us.[32]

The next day the advance began on the town of Krithia with the 29th Division and the newly arrived French working in concert. The Dublins and Munsters had to traverse V Beach on their way to take up reserve positions. Now a safe two miles from the nearest enemy machine-gun, it was an altogether different place.

> The French were already quite at home on Beach V where we had landed and it looked very different with camp ovens and tents in the place of corpses and dying men. The sea was beautiful and the colour was no longer red with blood as it was the day we saw it last.[33]

At the last moment the 'Dubsters' were sent forward as the advance began to falter. But it made no difference: the Turks managed to hold on to Krithia and (though this was not apparent at the time) little further progress would be made by the Entente forces. Bar a further attack on Krithia two months later, the duties of the British and French troops were of a holding or defensive nature.

Lt. Guy Nightingale's diary entry for the night of 1 May 1915 conveys something of the extremities to which the men who had come through V Beach were further exposed when the Turks attacked in huge numbers, often egged on (sometimes savagely) by German officers. The night was cold and

Nightingale was resting under a makeshift canvas tent which he had managed to scrounge from the body of a French officer.

> Woke up at 10.30 p.m. to the sound of firing from a dense mass of Turks advancing on the line, silhouetted against the moon which was rising. They were on the other side of the nullah but on our side they had crept up through the gorse and bayonetted most of the men in their sleep and swept on. Whatever remained of our coy. retired. I ran up the line shouting to them to get back and on joining my Dublin coy. which was on the left of my own coy. found a great scrap going on so joined in myself and stuck a Turk with my bayonet. We drove them back. I spent the remainder of the night with O'Hara and my Dublins. We fought for 5 hours driving back charge after charge of the Turks. At dawn they were in full retreat and we slaughtered them.[34]

Henry Desmond O'Hara was told that as many as 20,000 Turks had been involved in the night attack. The 360 men who remained of the 1st R.D.F. between them fired 150,000 rounds of ammunition. The fight began at 10.30 p.m. when Nightingale was awoken, and continued until 5.00 a.m. the following morning. 'The Turks were simply driven on to the barbed wire in front of the trenches by their German officers, and shot down by the score', wrote O'Hara.

> At one point they actually got into the trenches, but were driven out by the bayonet. They must have lost thousands. The fighting is of the most desperate kind—very little quarter asked on either side. The men are absolutely mad to get at them, as they mutilate our wounded when they catch them. For the first three nights I did not have a wink of sleep, and actually fell asleep during the big night attack.[35]

Writing to his sister about the attack Guy Nightingale does not bother to spare her feelings. His tone is that of a man who has been utterly desensitised by his experiences.

> The Turks attacked again and again shouting Allah! Allah! It was most exciting hearing them collecting in a dip in the hill about 40 yards away waiting for their next charge. We mowed them down and only once did they get so close that we were able to bayonet them. When dawn broke, we saw them in hundreds retiring and simply mowed them down. We took 300 prisoners and could have taken 3000 but we

preferred shooting them. All the streams were simply running blood
and the heaps of dead were a grand sight.[36]

Elsewhere the 1st Inniskillings, of the 87th Brigade, who had come ashore
unopposed on 25 April at X Beach (north of where the Dublins and Munsters
met their nemesis), were getting and giving similar treatment. They were
defending a position guarded only by a single stand of barbed wire and with
long grass in front of their lines which afforded some cover against detection
to the attacking Turks. 'We heard the swish swish of the Turks feet as they
advanced towards us and the voices of their officers as they gave orders.
Somebody sent up a Very light, and they were advancing in a solid mass
towards us.' The Inniskillings let loose a murderous fire against the full
frontal assault of the Turks. 'The effect was deadly. We could hear the shrieks
of their wounded and the shouts of their officers as they urged them on; but
they never reached our line.'[37]

A sort of torpor now settled on both sides and the fighting became spo-
radic and episodic. The troops of two armies were crushed into an area of a
few square miles and ever present were the dead of both forces. Nightingale,
sent forward for a night attack with a contingent of Munsters, found himself
sharing an entrenchment with the bodies of men from the King's Own Scottish Borderers which had lain in the same spot since the landings of 25 April.

> These bodies were still lying there highly decomposed and the stench
> was awful. In the dark we kept tumbling over the bodies and treading
> on them. When it was light I found I had dug in next to the remains
> of an officer in the KOSBs whom I had last seen at the Opera at Malta
> and had spent a most jolly evening with. There were ten KOSBs and
> seven South Wales Borderers lying there but I only recognised a few.[38]

It was not until the middle of May that a four-day truce designed for the
purpose allowed both sides to bury their dead. By then, ironically, the campaign had become a carbon copy of the stasis of the Western Front.

It was only in retrospect that the full enormity of the losses at V Beach
and on other parts of the Gallipoli peninsula became apparent. It took some
time for the name 'Gallipoli' to acquire the connotations of military disaster
and incompetence which it eventually did. The casualty figures were manipu-
lated to give an erroneous impression of the success of the landings themselves. Nightingale noticed this when he was sent a copy of the *Times* in May.

> I see they are breaking the casualties gently to you at home. Out of the
> 14 officers of ours hit on Sunday April 25th the *Times* of the 2nd of
> May only gives Major Jarret killed and five wounded. A lot of the

regiments like the Lancashire Fusiliers who lost 20 officers the first day are not mentioned at all! I think the Dublins are the only complete list. I suppose they'll try and make out its been nothing at all out here, just a scrap with the Turks whereas its been hell and frightfully misman-aged.[39]

Such were the losses that when an officer like Capt. G.W. Geddes returned from having his wounds treated he did so not as a mere company commander but as CO of the battalion. But he was a much changed man.

Geddes is a ripping commanding officer to work with but he is fright-fully worried and his hair is nearly white! I've never seen fellows get old so quickly. This morning I saw a fellow called O'Hara in the Dub-lins whom I hadn't seen for about a fortnight and I hardly recognised him ...'[40]

The constant and vicious fighting of the early days of the campaign had taken their toll. 'Simply tons of fellows are going off their heads from strain and worry—mostly fellows who have been wounded and come back but there are very few now who have gone through from the beginning and are not the worse for it ...'.[41] One such victim of the fatalism induced by war was Henry Desmond O'Hara. He wrote to his fiancee that he didn't think he would survive the campaign. His assumption was correct, but a vacation in Alexand-ria seems to have restored at least some of his shattered spirit. 'You would hardly believe him for the same person, he looks so much better for it. He's an awfully decent fellow and very amusing.'[42] Sometime between his leave and the subsequent transfer of his division O'Hara was hit. Towards the end of August the 29th Division was moved to Suvla for the attack on Scimitar Hill but O'Hara was not with them. He had been evacuated to Gibraltar, where he died of his wounds on 29 August.

Nightingale, in his letters home, while commenting on the fragile psyche of his brother officers, is consistent in his assertions that he himself was suffering no such effects. He continued to eat heartily, draw (he was a talented artist) and take lots of photographs, like a curious if heavily-armed tourist. But the sub-text of his letters belies his claims of psychologicial vigour. He spares his family no details of the horrors of the conflict, and the tone of the letters suggests a man who has become so personally desensitised by what he has witnesssed that he can no longer grasp the difference between normality and extremity. He exhibits a callousness which becomes more pronounced as the (self-censored i.e. uncensored) letters become more graphic.

> We are a very small lot of the original officers now ... All the rest are Territorial Officers and absolute strangers. They know nothing about soldiering and are nearly all senior to me being Captains and Majors! However, they are very keen and are rapidly getting thinned out. One was hit last night during dinner and fell into the soup, upsetting the whole table, and bled into the tea pot making an awful mess of everything and we finally didn't get dinner till after dark ...[43]

The revelation of the extent of Nightingale's personal frailty came twenty years later when he killed himself with his service revolver. The date on which he chose to end his life was significant, 25 April 1935, the twentieth anniversary of the V Beach landing. Some wounds endure!

From mid-May until their move to Suvla in late August (with the exception of the attempt to take Krithia in late June) the 29th Division settled back into a dreary round of mundane trench warfare. Death was everywhere. It was, quite literally, in the very air itself, as hundreds of decomposing, unburied bodies left a stench which men could still recall three quarters of a century later. It was carried, afresh, through the air in the form of shells or bullets which wreaked haphazard havoc on both sides. This daily round of boredom and terror was enlivened occasionally by events such as one described by Geddes:

> A divisional signal wagon with four horses came over the ridge about 400 yds from Pink Farm from the direction of the beaches, with field telegraph poles; it appeared to be a gun. The Turks concentrated their shelling on the wagon; the men in charge left the wagon, the horses, so petrified with fear, never moved. Two horses, having charmed lives, survived. Suddenly, two figures were seen cutting the horses loose— Serjeant [*sic*] Slattery and Private Twomey—who, jumping on their backs amid a hail of shell, galloped the horses out of danger into safety amidst the cheers of their comrades. Bearing charmed lives, they escaped being hit—a miracle. No military decorations could be given for this gallant exploit, but they were awarded a very beautiful medal by the Society for the Prevention of Cruelty to Animals.[44]

There were few enough awards for gallantry for the Dublins and the Munsters on 25 April. This generated considerable bitterness. It was suggested that the Dublins, in particular, were not in favour with the Divisional commander (Gen. Hunter Weston) The 1st R.D.F. received only 14 awards for gallantry of which the highest was that given to O'Hara, although they suffered more than 2000 casualties through the entire Gallipoli campaign and nearly 600 deaths. Of course the awarding of medals is not an exact science. For essentially the same action on the night of 1 May, 1915 O'Hara got the DSO and Nightingale was merely mentioned in despatches.

> I think the reason there were so few awards to the Dublins and our-selves or to all the landing party, was because there were no senior officers left to report on what happened. It was rather amusing that O'Hara got his award for the same thing I was recommended for, but at the same time it must be remembered that he would have got a DSO anyway for commanding his Bn which he did awfully well considering he was such a young officer to suddenly have to take command ...[45]

The attempt to relieve the static trench warfare on the Western Front had ended in stalemate and in a situation which was a facsimile of the fighting in Flanders and Picardy. What was meant to be the opening act in a new work turned out to be merely the overture. The next act in the opera would take place at Suvla Bay. As the ranks of the regular army was thinning this would feature a cast of ingenues, from Kitchener's First 100,000. Suvla was to have traumatic consequencs for the Irish nation. But it would be no more effective than anything which had gone before. The strategists had become like a man lost in a convoluted maze, just as he thinks he has found a way out his path leads him to another dead end, exactly similar to the ones which have already barred his exit.

# 3  Suvla Bay

'Twas better to die 'neath an Irish sky,
Than at Suvla or Sedd el Bahr.'

The separatist sentiments which provide the context for those lines from the traditional song 'The Foggy Dew' might not have appealed to all the Irish troops at Gallipoli, but by the time of their final evacuation from that morass of incompetence, petulance and shortsightedness most would have agreed with the bald statement as expressed. The landings at Suvla Bay in August, 1915 wrote the first page in another military-Gothic horror story, and like most such tales the ending was not happy.

By August 1915 the first of Kitchener's New Army troops (K1—for Kitchener's First 100,000) were ready to test their Byronic notions about war. The initial attacks on the Dardanelles in April had been a failure, and, like the gambler who throws good money after bad, Gen. Sir Ian Hamilton was determined to turn the situation around by becoming ever more deeply embroiled in the peninsula he once described as 'shaped like a badly worn boot'. Kitchener's saplings were expected to extricate the British from the folly of Gallipoli when what was needed was a host of battering rams.

Suvla Bay lies on the western (Aegean) side of the Gallipoli Peninsula some twenty miles due north of Cape Helles and a mere five miles from Anzac Cove, where the troops from Australia and New Zealand, who had joined to fight a war in Europe, had gained a toehold. The notion of landing troops there was not a bad one in itself. The beaches were long, wide and inviting. The area was lightly defended, three Turkish battalions were all that was left to hold Suvla after the troops of the two divisions defending the plain beyond were withdrawn to Helles and Anzac. The possibility of a repetition of V Beach was remote once the element of surprise was maintained.

The strategy was that as the Suvla force (IX Corps, under General Stopford) broke out of its beachhead the Australian and New Zealanders at Anzac Cove would do likewise and between them the two Corps would drive a wedge across the peninsula. To do this the 10th, 11th and 13th Divisions which were to form the IX Corps were required to occupy the heights around Suvla within 24 hours of landing and link up with the Anzacs who would be assaulting the Sari Bair ridge, which rose to almost 1000 ft, and which, with its heavily scored sides had defied their attacks and overshadowed their beach-head since the April landings, However, the plan was compromised straight-away when the 13th Division and the 29th Brigade of the 10th (Irish) Division were separated from IX Corps and sent to assist the Anzacs instead.

The 10th (Irish) Division, bar one battalion—the 10th Hampshires—was overwhelmingly Irish, a product of the recruiting frenzy of 1914. It was the first distinctly Irish division in the British Army. It had a native-born Divi-sional commander in Lt.-Gen. Sir Bryan Mahon. Mahon, a Galwayman, had been a career soldier since joining the 8th (Royal Irish) Hussars in 1883. His chief claim to military celebrity was his leadership of the column which had relieved Mafeking during the Boer War.

> At the time he took over the 10th Division he was fifty-two years of age. His service in Egypt and India had bronzed his face and sown grey in his hair, but his figure and his seat on a horse were those of a subaltern. He scorned display, and only the ribbons on his breast told of the service he had seen.[1]

So wrote Maj. Bryan Cooper, rather overfondly, of his commanding officer. Mahon may well, habitually, have disguised his rank, but he was, nonetheless, highly conscious of it, and of his own dignity. Many would judge harshly what they were to perceive as the placing of his innate sense of self-worth and pride over the well-being of his soldiers in one of the sorriest chapters of Irish military history, the defence of Kiretch Tepe Sirt on the night of 15 August 1915. John Hargrave, who was a sergeant in a Royal Army Medical Corps unit attached to the 10th Division, offers a more colourful description of a Mahon,

> with large aggressively out-jutting ears, and full lips enfolding a secret smile half hidden under a trim but strangely piebald grey-and-(start-lingly) saltwhite moustache. Without doubt one of the 'Black Celts to the West of the Shannon', with deepset, heavy-browed, sullen-brood-ing eyes, as fiercely 'dead' and gloomy as a Fitful Head stormcloud stagnant over Inisheer.[2]

The 10th brought with it to Gallipoli its own, unofficial, historians. It is one of the most exhaustively-chronicled campaigns in which Irish soldiers played a major role in the Great War. Chief among them was Bryan Cooper. Cooper had been a Unionist MP for South Dublin until 1910, the last to be elected to a southern constituency (bar Carson who as MP for Trinity was an excep-tional case). He would later serve as an Independent TD for Dublin County before throwing in his lot with Cumann na nGaedheal in the 1920s (sometime after he had helped save that government in a crucial division, by reportedly getting the 'tiebreak' TD drunk and putting him on the train back to Sligo before the vote). When he died, in 1930, the symbolism at his funeral might have served as an appropriate metaphor for so many of Ireland's World War I veterans: his coffin was draped in both the Tricolour and the Union Jack. A clue to his temperament is provided by Professor Joe Lee who describes him as 'a respected ex-Unionist, respected not least for his formidable capacity for alcohol'.[3]

After seven months of training in Dublin, at the Curragh and in Basingstoke in England the men of the 10th were eager for action. After a few days at Gallipoli the romantic gloss of war, so typical of that era, would wear off quickly. One of the most celebrated units of the 10th Division, D Company of the 7th Royal Dublin Fusiliers, would suffer more than most. It consisted of footballers (mostly rugby players) who had responded to a call to enlist as a 'Pals' unit and had done so at Lansdowne Road. Frank Laird, a member of D Company, had joined out of a combination of curiosity and peer-group pressure (two highly effective recruiting agents). Once their pith helmets had been issued he knew the 10th was not destined for the Western Front. Canny souls decided that tightly cropped hair cuts might make for a more comfortable life in the Mediterranean heat.

> One of the sergeants had secured a hair clippers (some said a mule clippers) and, with several brethren of the three stripes, set about shaving the heads of as many of the men as wished for the performance. When the supply of these failed they chased divers others, laid violent hands on them, and shrove them of their flowing locks. We were given to understand that a Hunnish head was an asset in hot spots like the Dardanelles.[4]

As their transport ship pulled away from Devonport, en route to the Dardanelles, on 13 July 1915, Sgt. John Hargrave of the 32nd Field Ambulance experienced a certain ominous foreboding, undiminished by the Fife Band of the Irish Fusiliers playing 'The Wearing of the Green':

> A Cockney sailor standing by the bow of a coastal sloop cupped his hands and bellowed across the water 'Are we downhearted?' There was time to count seven before a few Irishmen shouted 'No!' At this rather half-hearted response, the cheery Cockney grinned a Seven Dials grin and bellowed: 'Wotcher lookin' so glum abaht?' To which no answer came. Before a month was out there was no fife band. It had perished to a man at Suvla Bay.[5]

While awaiting orders for Gallipoli the 10th was stationed at Mudros on the Aegean island of Lemnos and at Mitylene. Here, Cooper records, their officers got some idea of what might lie in store for their raw troops, most of whom had yet to hear the first shot fired at them. Some officers of the 29th Division, which had been hacked to death at V Beach, were at Mudros, resting; many of them had friends among the 10th.

> Thus we learned from men who had been in Gallipoli since they had struggled through the surf and the wire on April 24th [*sic*] the truth as to the nature of the fighting there. They taught us much by their words, but even more by their appearance; for though fit, they were thin and worn, and their eyes carried a weary look that told of the strain that they had been through.[6]

Such was the understandable level of paranoia after the disaster of V Beach in April that the secrecy surrounding the Suvla landings became a sort of mantra among the higher echelons. It was as if there was some fervent aspiration towards the absoute retention of information. As if the ultimate goal was that *nobody* should know of Hamilton's intentions, bar Hamilton and a few confidential staff-wallahs. In the end this fetish proved counter-productive. Mahon's division suffered more than most as a consequence, never fighting as a single unit and, at one point, operating under three separate commands.

Other units were split off by accident, but the removal of the 29th Brigade from Mahon's command was deliberate. Its four battalions, the 10th Hampshires, the 6th Royal Irish Rifles, the 5th Connaught Rangers and the 6th Leinsters, were sent to assist General Birdwood's Anzacs, who were still stranded at Anzac Cove more than three monhs after the April landings there. Here they served briefly under divisional commander Gen. Sir Alexander Godley, late of the Dublin Fusiliers, cousin of Lord Kilbracken of Killegar and (subsequently) the author of an autobiography entitled *Life of an Irish Soldier* (1939).

The 29th Brigade was landed after dark to avoid the attentions of enemy gunners and to conceal from the Turks the fact that reinforcements were arriving in large numbers for an offensive operation. They had little time to wonder why their resting place on that first night was called Shrapnel Gully before they found out the hard way. Nor had they much opportunity to take in their new surroundings, an arid and deadly environment which had already witnessed the killing and maiming of thousands of young Australians, New Zealanders and Gurkhas. It was a truly inhospitable place.

> Take a sheet of brown paper—say two feet by one—fold it lengthways, a few inches from one side and crumple up the bit below the fold into

innumerable and inextricable miniature valleys and gullies, running in
and out of each other anyhow with razor-edge ridges between them;
but ridges which never seemed able to keep a straight line ... That
gives a rough idea of what the Gallipoli coast line at and near Anzac is
like.[7]

One company of the Leinsters got an early feel for what life at Anzac Cove
had been like. They were sent to relieve a company of Australian troops holding an area called Courtney's Ridge.

It was like hurrying up a steep flight of stairs to an attic passage at a
house top ... The trenches were more like permanently built passages,
with heavy overhead cover, than normal trenches. The first night's
experience was typical of many other nights—tremendous bursts of
rifle and machine-gun fire, kept up for an hour or longer, with short
intervals, but often nothing more developed and one was led to con-
clude that the Turks must have plenty of spare ammunition.[8]

For the 10th Division the 29th Brigade's detachment to Anzac Cove was
a brutal sideshow. The main event was the landing at Suvla Bay on 7 August.
For the first time the sporting 'Pals', D Company of the 7th Royal Dublin
Fusiliers, would go into action as a unit. Jocularly known as 'The Young
Toffs' or 'The Toffs in the Toughs' (the 'Toughs' being the Dublin Fusiliers),
they were a bare week away from annihilation on the rocky scrub-covered
slopes of Kiretch Tepe Sirt, but their morale was high as they approached the
peninsula, first passing by Cape Helles as they made their way north on board
the *Fauvette*. As they passed Achi Baba, viewed from the Aegean side, it was
a mass of bursting shells.

Suvla seemed about as far away as Wicklow Head is from Howth, and
some of them thought the coast looked like Dublin Bay. The large
naval shells bursting on Achi Baba suggested a house going on fire
with a suden blaze and immediately going out again, the noise sounding like one continuous roll of thunder.[9]

Sir Ivone Kirkpatrick, destined for a career in Intelligence, but on this day a
junior officer in the 5th Inniskilling Fusiliers, had no idea where his battalion
was about to land as his troopship dropped anchor a mile or so from shore.
He could hear rifle fire and then,

as the light improved we saw our troops advancing inland. Soon the
guns of the fleet opened fire. We could see huge sheets of yellow and

purple flame on the hill side ... A minelayer appeared and proceeded to lay a line of mines between the shipping and the open sea. They dropped over her stern and bounced some 10 or 15 feet before settling down. They looked like plum puddings of unusual resilience.[10]

The 7th Dublin Fusiliers landed without much incident, though Frank Laird recalled that shrapnel had caused some injuries in the lighters before the shore was reached.

It afforded food for philosophic thought to consider the time, money and trouble expended in ten months training of a soldier who stops a bullet before he can ever set foot on enemy ground ... Our steam barge ran up on a sandy beach without mishap, the hinged gangway in the bow was turned over, and we walked down it on to the soft sand with somewhat of the picnic feeling with which we had often made a landing on Ireland's Eye in the piping days of peace.[11]

Ironically, to Lt. Noel Drury of the 6th Dublins, Suvla at night, lit up by bursting shells, had a sort of compelling, bizarre elegance. 'The scene was very beautiful with star shells going up, and the loom of the early dawn lit up with the beautiful lemon-coloured flash of the naval guns.'[12]

In fact neither side was oversupplied with guns to effect or defend against a landing. The Turks were forced to alternate their fire between the troops on shore and those being landed by the Navy in lighters. The British had only two small-calibre mountain guns to support the landing. 'These two guns were a source of amusement to the men, as every time they were fired they ran backward down the hill with a sweating crowd of gunners chasing after them to haul them into position again.'[13]

The Dublins, along with most of the remainder of Mahon's Division, had landed much farther south than had been originally intended. The northern part of Suvla Bay had been designated A Beach; it was there that the 10th was supposed to come ashore. But inadequate charting and intelligence, constant bombardment and a level of discretion which came in for subsequent criticism had prompted the Navy to put them ashore south of Nibrunesi Point. To labour Hanna's analogy, the Division had been due to land near Howth Head; instead it was put ashore closer to Wicklow. The 5th Inniskillings, along with the 6th and 7th Munsters, were put ashore closer to their original objective. But not, as Ivone Kirkpatrick recorded in his memoir of the landing, until the late afternoon. 'We ran nicely ashore, the drawbridge worked perfectly and we landed. It was just after four o'clock. I assembled my platoon. At the water's edge were several British dead, struck down almost before they had set foot on land ... '.[14]

As they surveyed the landscape of the furnace into which they had been plunged the men of the 10th Division would have been drawn towards the heights around the crescent shaped bay in which they had landed. Close by the southern perimeter of Suvla Bay (Nibrunesi Point) was a low, rolling hillock, 150 ft high at most, called Lala Baba. It had been taken in darkness before the 10th had landed. It afforded some protection from the sightline of Turkish troops who were well entrenched on a more distant hill, which, because of the colouration of the soil on its slopes (or the colouring of the burnt scrub, depending on which version you accept) became known as Chocolate Hill. This hill, about 200 ft in height, was visible on the far side of what the few maps carried by officers characterised as a 'Salt Lake'. In moister seasons a salt lake it may well have been, but on the morning of 7 August 1915, it was little more than a salty marsh of white sticky mud measuring about a mile across. Nonetheless it constituted an obstacle which had to be circumvented. A direct approach to Chocolate Hill from Lala Baba was not possible; the option was to tour the lake by a northern or southern route, thus leaving oneself wide open to shrapnel and shells. Beyond Chocolate Hill was Green, or Burnt Hill, similar in shape and size to its neighbour; beyond that again, less than a mile to the north east was Scimitar Hill. Overlooking a distant plain, dotted with cornfields and olive trees, as well as useless scrub land, was the 900-ft-high Tekke Tepe ridge, the ultimate short term objective of the troops involved in the Suvla campaign. To the south east the land rose to join the Sari Bair ridge which overlooked Anzac Cove.

Physically more imposing, however, and looming far more ominously, was a long humpback ridge to the north which dominated the skyline from east to west and whose craggy, water-scraped slopes ended in the sea at the northern-most limit of the bay, Suvla Point. The ridge—Kiretch Tepe Sirt—rose to over 600 ft in places and featured a peculiar erratic cairn in the centre, which was to become known as the 'Pimple'.

Dry, dusty and fly-infested though it was at the time, the area was not without a stark physical beauty. This has been well captured in the paintings done by an artist who accompanied the invading force, Lt. Drummond Fish. They depict the area in a rather more sumptuous light than do modern colour photographs, but Fish, with the discerning and sceptical eye of the artist, was genuinely impressed with the physical beauty of the place.

> The colours were the most wonderful thing about Gallipoli. There were mornings when the hills were as rose peaches—times when the sea looked like the tail of some gigantic peacock, and the sands looked like great carpets of glittering cloth of gold—the place was an inspiration in itself, and if beauty could have stopped a war, that scenery would have done it.[15]

The Irishmen would have been conscious of a number of other things within minutes of landing. The smell of thyme pervaded the foreshore. It had not yet been obliterated from their nostrils by the stench of putrefying bodies which would be another lasting sensory memory of those who survived Gallipoli. A constant irritant would have been the large and persistent flies. These, however, were merely issuing their calling cards, a brief prelude to more unwelcome return visits. Loaded down with packs weighing upwards of sixty pounds, the men would also have been conscious of the extreme heat, especially as the morning wore on. A heavy shower in the early afternoon offered some welcome relief.

But the overwhelming impressions borne in on the first of 'Kitchener's 100,000' to go into action were that soldiering was thirsty, dangerous and rather chaotic work. John Hargrave, with the Royal Army Medical Corps, had made an astute choice, as it turned out, while still on board his transport vessel. He had been offered some sweet, reviving tea but would have had to hand up a pint from his own water issue for boiled water for that tea: 'I decided that a pint of cold water later on might be a better asset than a pint of hot tea now. I was right—a shade too Boy-Scoutishly prudent in spirit perhaps, but eminently practical'.[16] When they boarded the lighters which took them ashore each man carried one and a half pints of water with him. They were told not to drink it unless it was absolutely necessary and then only to take a sip or two at a time. It was one of the many ironies of the Suvla debacle that the lighters themselves actually carried extra water rations but,

> so far as the lightermen were concerned, speed! speed! was the essence of the operation. Therefore, as soon as each lighter was empty of troops it put about and went back for the next load *and that reserve of water was never distributed.*[17]

Frank Laird noted that the killing had started before his battalion arrived.

> On our right were pitiable groups of wounded and dead men, stretched under shelter of the head of the beach. Overhead the shrapnel burst continually. A long continuous procession of stretcher-bearerss passed us, carrying inanimate forms to the beach, with pith helmets placed over their faces to save them from the blazing sun.[18]

Edgar Poulter was a comrade of Laird's in the 'Pals' Company. 'They said "Look out for land mines" and we saw the odd fellow coming back, leg blown off or wounded with stick bombs or land mines. For the first time we all began to be a little funny in the pit of the stomach.' The 7th Dublin's corpulent CO Lt.-Col. Downing seemed unconcerned by the Turkish shrapnel.

He promenaded along the shore with a long staff in his hand muttering, 'Oh don't mind anything you hear lads, it's not near you, it's over your head, carry on.'[19] James Cahill, another Dublin Fusilier, spoke to the author a fortnight before his death in 1990 at the age of 96 and still remembered his apprehension on reaching the beach. 'It was a muddle up to get there, because you're under shellfire and men were lying around dying and roaring and the order was "Form up in three lines". '[20]

Most of these fresh untried troops would have been too inexperienced and too preoccupied with their own thoughts and fears to have paid much attention to the confusion and disorder which blighted the Suvla operation. In part the claustrophobic chaos on the beaches can be ascribed to the obsession with secrecy and the pusillanimous and unimaginative approach of those in command. In retrospect it is clear that, even before the Irish landed, the entire Gallipoli campaign had been seriously compromised by egregious mismanagement. By the time they had been ashore for twenty four hours it had been well and truly lost beyond recapture.

Contemporary photos showing hundreds of troops packed into small areas waiting to be told what to do next tell the story adequately. Nobody seemed to know who exactly was in control of events. They knew who was in command: there was a military chain which led to the Corps commander Gen. Stopford, who spent 7 August off shore in a yacht, the *Jonquil*. Stopford may have been in command but he certainly never exercised control. That chain, theoretically, extended beyond Stopford to the Commander-in-Chief of the Mediterranean Expeditionary Force, Gen. Sir Ian Hamilton. But it was equally clear that Hamilton was not in control either. In fact he was completely starved of information as Stopford failed to communicate with him for some hours after the landings went ahead.

Stopford, as Corps commander, was privy to Hamilton's strategy. The Divisional commanders Hammersley (11th) and Mahon (10th) knew what part their troops were expected to play in the execution of that plan. But Mahon, ludicrously, had failed to inform his Brigade commander Hill about the role the 31st Brigade was expected to play. After its dismal failure the conduct of the Gallipoli campaign was investigated by a Commission which revealed that Mahon had been given his orders on 28/29 July, but couldn't get a ship to take him from Lemnos to Mitylene, a distance of 70 miles, where the 31st Brigade (and half the 30th) was stationed, to convey those orders to Brig.-Gen. Hill. Unable to give the orders personally, he attempted to do so by cypher telegram. His efforts failed. 'When Hill arrived with 6000 men under his command,' wrote John Hargrave,

> he not only had no idea what the operation was in which he and his
> troops were supposed to take part—he did not even know where he

was! He could see, as we all could, a landing was in progress, but it might have been at Walvis Bay or Botany Bay for all the information he had been given. He had no map of Suvla, had never seen a map of Suvla, did not know where Suvla was, and had no instructions what to do now that he was there![21]

A much-quoted anecdote which illustrates the level of ignorance among senior officers of even their *destination*, let alone what was expected of them when they got there, involves Lt.-Col. F.A. Greer, Commanding Officer of the 6th Royal Irish Fusiliers. On board the destroyer taking them to Gallipoli he was informed by the ship's commander that he was prohibited from giving the colonel any information about his destination until midnight. 'At twelve midnight', according to Greer, 'I went up again to the bridge and repeated my request. He said, "I have orders to put you ashore at Beach C." I said, "Where on earth's that?" "Suvla Bay", he said. "Where on earth's that?" I asked. He showed me a chart.'[22]

At 6 a.m. on the morning of 7 August, Brigadier General Hill, commanding the 31st Division, reported to Stopford on board the *Jonquil*. The original plan had been for the entire 10th Division to take the heights of the Kiretch Tepe Sirt. This would have meant landing on the most northerly of the beaches, within Suvla Bay itself, designated A Beach. But, according to John Hargrave, 'near panic' overtook the naval transport authorities.

Having had enough of A Beach and finding themselves faced by the fearful hazards of landing troops there in broad daylight, they decided to put Hill's 6000 Xth Division troops ashore at C Beach, below Nibrunesi Point—on the *wrong side of the bay*. This was fatal.[23]

Hargrave blames the Navy for not finding an alternative to A beach which was closer to Kiretch Tepe Sirt. Ironically (that word again) they did so shortly after sending one and a half brigades miles out of their way. They discovered a safer landing place, closer to Suvla Point and called it 'A West'. It was on that beach that the last of the 10th's battalion, the 5th Inniskillings, came ashore. Stopford's instructions to Hill were that, as he was going to have to land near the troops of Gen. Hammersley's 11th Division, he might as well put his men under Hammersley's command 'until the arrival of his own divisional general'. Mahon had, in fact, already arrived from Mudros, but Stopford was not aware of this. When Mahon did announce his presence he was given three battalions to take Kiretch Tepe Sirt, instead of an entire Division. He is reported to have 'nearly resigned his command there and then'.[24] By the end of the day his unified command had been scattered across three different battle zones.

Though abetted by the Navy in fouling up the actual landings, the subsequent displays of incompetence by the Mediterranean military hierarchy was all its own work. Chronic delays and indecision followed the arrival of the troops. Much of the procrastination had its origins in the lassitude and ineffectual leadership of the Generals but some was undoubtedly due to the change in military culture brought about by almost a year of static trench warfare on the Western Front. Historian Martin Gilbert puts it thus:

> The generals hesitated: surprised by such a swift advance. Their minds, fashioned by the warfare on the Western Front were attuned to 'victories' of a hundred yards. A virtually unopposed advance of half a mile bewildered them. The hesitation was decisive and disastrous. The bulk of the force stayed close to the beach, where many men enjoyed an unexpected and relaxing swim. These aquatic pursuits could be seen from Anzac Cove. The tired and dirty Australian and New Zealand troops were not impressed.[25]

It was this dilly-dallying which, according to the German commander in Gallipoli, Liman van Sanders, proved crucial in the campaign that followed. Even junior officers on the ground, like Lt. Noel Drury of the 6th Dublins, could not understand the delay in moving inland.

> There has been no fighting all day and the Turks haven't fired a shot, and are probably rushing up reinforcements and digging new trenches. The men are all talking about the waste of valuable time. We have quite a lot of old soldiers who know a good deal about this sort of war and they are all grousing like blazes, saying we are throwing away any chance and will pay for it later.[26]

Drury's assessment was unerringly accurate. The Turks were, indeed, rushing reinforcements to Suvla where, on the day of the landing the British had a numerical superiority of at least 10:1. British inertia began right at the top. Stopford, on the evidence available, was (understandably) delighted that most of his troops had got ashore without mishap. He doesn't seem to have addressed himself sufficently energetically to what they were expected to do once the beachhead had been established. As John Hargrave observed, 'forty-one hours after the landing the troops had not reached the hills—*but they were ashore*. The Corps commander himself had not ventured as far as that.'[27]

They were indeed ashore and doing what came naturally on the *Western* Front, digging in. Their commanding officers (at various levels) decided to strengthen positions which were under no threat of attack from the retreating Turks. (In the following days, when it was already too late, attacks would be pressed home but in clearly inadequate numbers by parched troops.) During the course of that first day, orders had been issued at the top of the hour, countermanded on the half hour and then reinstated at the top of the next hour to the confused and thirsty tourists on the beaches. Finally a move was made against Chocolate Hill (though the aptly-named Brig.-Gen. Sitwell, a Brigade commander 11th Division, declined to allow his troops to participate). The 6th and 7th Dublins, the 6th Inniskillings and the 5th Irish Fusiliers, were despatched to join the assault (the 6th Dublins in reserve). However, their landing on C Beach meant they were forced to undertake a ridiculous trek around the northern perimeter of the Salt Lake before they could get into position for the attack. They were instructed to ditch their heavy packs after a mile or so. 'We never saw them again, and of all the possessions we had so anxiously packed in Basingstoke there now remained to us only what we had in our haversacks and pockets.'[28] Most of the march was over exposed terrain where they were subjected to shelling. This was at its worst around the area known as 'The Cut' where the sea entered the lake itself.

Capt. Paddy Tobin was a popular young officer with D Company of the Dublin Fusiliers. In a letter to his father he described the experience of running hard through heavy sand before reaching,

> a little sheltered bank like the Alps at Dollymount, only not so high, where we rested. Here were collected great numbers of troops huddled together. Well, across that neck of land I expected every minute to fall ... Shrapnel and high explosives were bursting as frequently as the tick of a clock ... I found myself under the bank in a paroxysm of fear, and chattering my prayers between my teeth.[29]

The CO of the 7th Dublins, Col. Downing led by example, frequently exposing himself to shell and shrapnel fire while ushering men across the 'Cut'. The relative lack of Turkish artillery came to their aid. The Turks did not have enough artillery pieces to maintain a constant barrage on one particular spot for any length of time. The shelling settled into a predictable rhythm, a measurable interval elapsing between blasts. Taking advantage of this, the men were sent scurrying across in the gap between shell bursts. Some of the Dublin troops, in blackly humorous vein, unofficially renamed the area. 'Owing to the many casualties this spot was cheerfully dubbed "Dunphy's Corner" after the place of that name in Dublin where the many funerals of old and young pass on their way to Glasnevin.'[30]

The bottleneck at 'Dunphy's Corner' had caused a major delay in the movement of the three Irish battalions earmarked for the assault on Chocolate Hill. The hold up did little to enchance the state of mind of tired, hungry, thirsty and inexperienced troops:

> Except for a cup of tea about 3 a.m., and a mouthful hastily swallowed
> before moving off, they were fasting, and already many of the more
> improvident had emptied their water-bottles. In addition, these young
> soldiers who had never seen war before, had been since four in the
> morning exposed to shrapnel fire, with but little chance either of tak-
> ing cover or of retaliating. They had seen their comrades fall stricken
> at their sides without the consolation of knowing that the enemy was
> suffering to an equal extent.[31]

This was true, up to a point, but the Turks, with access to the wells in the
area, were not suffering from thirst. The shower of rain at about one o'clock
in the afternoon had cooled the area down and provided some short term
relief but the soldiers advancing on Chocolate Hill were already thoroughly
dehydrated.

The Turks were well entrenched on Chocolate Hill, which, although a
mere 160 ft high, rose steeply from the surrounding plain and commanded an
excellent view of the advancing Irish battalions. At the outset of their movement, closer to the beach a German officer noted that they had marched 'bolt
upright as though on parade without using cover'.[32] As they neared their
objective, intense rifle and shell fire made this unwise.

> The rushes were by platoon after platoon. They had to cross ground
> which was very open and exposed to machine-gun and rifle fire from
> Chocolate Hill. It was uncultivated, with a few bushes here and there
> affording no substantial cover. The troops on the left, however, were
> able to advance over better ground, as it was much more closely cov-
> ered with rocks and scrub, resembling the lower slopes of Ticknock.[33]

It was heavy going for inexperienced troops who had gone rather soft after
five weeks on board transport ships or awaiting orders on the Aegean islands.

Frank Laird was not involved in the charge that finally took Chocolate
Hill but he was still required to inch his way across the plain towards the
outcrop: '... we heard for the first time the gentle whisper of enemy bullets
over our heads ... A young Dublin chap near me at one stopping place gave
a sudden choke, stiffened, and lay dead, shot through the throat.' Laird had
made an agreement with Charles Frederick Ball, Assistant Keeper of the
Botanic Gardens in Glasnevin, that they would stick together. They managed
to keep the compact. Others, however, got separated from their units. As the
'Pals' dived in and out of gullies and ditches to avoid shrapnel bursts one of
their number, identified only as 'John Willie' by Laird, was knocked unconscious. When he came to he dutifully continued to advance on his own, in a
straight line. His battalion, however, had wheeled right while he was uncon-

scious so he found himself between British and Turkish lines. He didn't manage to extricate himself until after dark![34]

Among the officers ducking and diving through the scrub was Major Tippet of the 7th Dublins, a man who had served for years in the old Dubln City Militia and who, latterly, had been employed as a political agent in an English constituency. Alongside him was Paddy Tobin, who was slowed down by a bullet in the triceps: 'I had to stop for a minute or two to put on my field dressing, and here I'm sorry to say the Major went on ahead, and I lost him *pro tem.*'[35] As Tobin found out later he had, in fact, lost Tippet permanently. The latter was killed as he went forward, shot in the head. Another significant casualty was Lt. Ernest Julian, the Reid Professor of Law at Trinity College. He died on 8 August, of wounds received in the Chocolate Hill assault.

It was almost dusk by the time the Irish were ready to assault the hill in strength. From the sea the Navy guns began a ferocious bombardment. When this was lifted, A and D companies of the 7th R.D.F. went straight for the Turkish trenches scored across the slopes of the hill. The charge was led by Major R.S.M. Harrison. 'He had a green handkerchief tied to a stick, waving it above his head'. As they waited for the final assault which came around 7.50 p.m. shells from their own navy landed close to their positions. 'Before making a final rush to the trenches we cheered for about a minute like madmen, and then the final rush—only to find one wounded Turk in sight.'[36] By the time Capt. Paddy Tobin reached the top of the hill it was all over. 'We slept or tried to, in the trenches, but got very little, as we were expecting a counter-attack which never came—thank God.'[37] In a letter to his wife Col. Downing claimed the right to rename the eminence 'Dublin' Hill: 'Major Harrison led the final attack and capture, and I came after with the reserve. (he is the bravest of the brave.) We have gained a great name for the capture and for the splendid regiment which I have the honour to command.'[38]

After the success of Chocolate Hill, Edgar Poulter had a single obsession, to celebrate with a long drink of water.

> From the time we landed to the time we took Chocolate Hill we'd had nothing to drink and the temperature was in the hundreds. So two men were detailed to go and draw water from a well, a little pipe out of the side of a hill. We walked up to this and found there were dozens and dozens of fellows all shot by snipers who had it well covered. We lost an awful lot of men getting water.

Snipers or not they took their chances and got their water: 'We brewed our iron rations, the cup of tea and the biscuit. That was the first drink we had. I remembered it was the nicest cup of tea I'd ever tasted. No sugar or milk but it was grand. The tongue was sticking out and it was half black and swollen.'[39] According to Poulter, as they retreated the Turks contaminated the local wells by dumping bodies in them. As the bodies decomposed the wells became unusable.

Among those who witnessed the taking of Chocolate Hill was an Australian officer, Capt. Thornhill. He offered a colourful account of the event, quoted by John Redmond in Michael McDonagh's glorified recruiting pamphlet, *The Irish at the Front*.

> The Empire can do with a heap more 'freshies' of the Irish brand. Their landing at Suvla Bay was the greatest thing you will ever read of in books by high-brows ... The way they took that hill (now called Dublin Hill) was the kind of thing that would make you pinch yourself to prove that it was not a cheap wine aftermath. How they got there Heaven only knows. As the land lay, climbing into hell on an aeroplane seemed an easier proposition than taking that hill.[40]

The taking of Chocolate Hill, with a full frontal bayonet charge, was the first major achievement of the untried battalions of the 10th. Most of the rest of their sojourn in Gallipoli would be characterised by a series of half-victories or 'glorious' defeats. At least some, and possibly all of those could have been avoided if a diffident and overly cautious Command had not decided to rest on its laurels. Granted, the troops were exhausted and thirsty, but they were also exhilarated at their own achievement. The Turks were in retreat. A few hundred yards in front of Chocolate Hill lay 'Green' or 'Burnt' Hill. Even a mere private like Edgar Poulter wondered why they didn't push forward and occupy its slopes, 'which would have been commanding'.[41] After the taking of Chocolate Hill a message had been sent to the CO of the 11th Division, Gen. Hammersley informing him of its capture and seeking further orders. None were forthcoming![42]

On 8 August, the 7th Dublins, after a largely sleepless night spent fortifiying their captured trenches against a counter-attack which never came, and burying their dead, were instructed to take Burnt Hill. Edgar Poulter took part in the unsuccessful attack on a position the Dublins probably could have strolled through the previous night.

> The minute a man moved there was machine gun and artillery fire. They could see everything you were doing, you hadn't a chance. One particularly horrible thing was you couldn't go for your wounded. Eventually the gorse caught fire, your wounded and dead were just cremated. Attack after attack was launched but we never took it.[43]

The following day (Monday 9 August) a haphazard plan to take the heights was put into effect at the insistence of Hamilton (who had arrived at Suvla). It failed. It also ended Frank Laird's interest in the Gallipoli campaign.

> I was proceeding in stooping fashion behind a hedge, when a sudden pang in the shoulder and a frightful thump in the back caused me to execute a sort of high dive on the stony ground, and there I lay with a singing in my ears and a feeling as if my whole body was strung up to its highest tension. My first thought was 'The beggars have got me at last' and my second a kind of irritated surprise, irrational enough, considering that I had been wading through bullets for some hours.[44]

Laird fainted, was dragged to safety and was found to have been shot through the right shoulder and lung. His fall, thanks to bandoliers of extra ammunition, had fractured three of his ribs. He was stretchered to the beaches and evacuated.

Elsewhere the other battalions of the Tenth's *diaspora* were having similar experiences. At Anzac Cove the attack on Sari Bair which had coincided with the Suvla landings had been stalled. The Turks still held the heights, and a counter-attack by them on the night of 9/10 August threatened to engulf the 6th Leinsters. The battalion was positioned to the right of two battalions of the Wiltshires and the North Lancashires on the inappropriately named Rhododendron Ridge (in fact it was dotted with wild oleanders) below the Turkish positions on Chunuk Bair. The Turkish attack overwhelmed the two English regiments and they pressed forward against the Leinsters. But the Irish battalions had better luck. As the enemy crested the ridge, surging forward with cries of 'Allah, Allah', they came within sight of the guns of the fleet off Anzac Cove. They were shelled mercilessly and cut to pieces.

> They fell by thousands, and as the few survivors struggled on, they were met with the fire of a concentrated battery of New Zealand machine guns. Line after line fell, and those who had the good fortune to escape hastened to place themselves in safety on the further side of the ridge.[45]

The annihilation of the Wilts and North Lancs meant a Leinster withdrawal to readjust the line. As they dug into their new positions they were harrassed by constant shrapnel and sniper fire. Having no desire to tangle with the guns of the fleet again so soon, the Turks waited until nearly dawn to attack. But the Leinsters, rather than wait, attacked first, 'The Turks faltered as the charge swept against them, and the Leinsters were at last able to take their revenge for the losses of the night'. Some enthusiasts, unfortunately, carried the pursuit too far; two officers Capt. D'Arcy Irvine and Lt. Willington, and many of their men in D Company were cut off and never seen again. 'Probably they were surrounded and killed, and their bones still lie with those of many another brave soldier on the slopes of Chunuk Bair.'[46]

In a distant corner of the Suvla area, a corner which many of the men who had taken Chocolate Hill would have ample cause to remember, the 5th Inniskillings were on the extreme left of the landing force, near Suvla Point and underneath the slopes of Kiretch Tepe Sirt. They had come ashore during the late afternoon with instructions to relieve the 11th Manchesters, who had gained a tenuous foothold, and to dig in. Ivone Kirkpatrick passed an uncomfortable night:

> The soil was hard and rocky; our digging implements were entrenching tools. We dug all night and when dawn broke had little to show for our labours. Most of the men had succeeded in digging shallow graves with a parapet of loose earth and flints, but some who had struck rocks had not even that. It was indeed fortunate that we were not shelled in the morning.[47]

But two of the three battalions left to Gen. Mahon to carry out his mission, the 6th and 7th Munsters, pushed forward up the steep (in places almost precipitous) slopes of Kiretch Tepe Sirt. They had got to within about 100 yards of the crest before darkness forced them to abandon the attempt to make further progress. They waited, tired and thirsty, for dawn. As the sun rose behind the Turks' backs, the 6th Munsters charged up the slopes, led by their second-in-command Major Jephson. (The main position captured by the Munsters and known as Jephson's Post is roughly half way between the western crest of the ridge and the Pimple.) Unlike the 10th's experience at Chocolate Hill, the Turks, who knew the area they were defending intimately, did not retreat in disarray but contested every inch of the crest. The Munsters drove them off the western extreme of Kiretch Tepe Sirt, but the uneven terrain and the lack of water exhausted them in this process. Now would have been the time to bring up reinforcements, fresh troops who would not have had to fight their way to the top of the ridge. But Mahon had none to introduce. As military historian Tom Johnstone has pointed out,

> The presence of Hill's battalions or 29th Brigade (soon to be destroyed at Anzac to little gain) would have been decisive. Just behind the enemy lines, plentiful water gushed from a spring. At the end of this ridge was the main Turkish ammunition dump for the Gallipoli Peninsula; its capture would have been disastrous to the enemy. Both prizes went begging.[48]

John Hargrave of the 32nd Field Ambulance witnessed the fatigue and frustration of the Irish battalions:

> If these thirst crazed troops could have got water—if they could have been reinforced without delay—if Hill's battalions had not been switched to C Beach—If—If—If. But the troops were staggering in a daze, the rocks rolling before their eyes ... I recall their haggard faces, their cracked lips; for we were bringing out their wounded along with the wounded of the night before. Some of them came limping painfully towards us; unkempt, scarecrow-figures, their voices husky-low like whispering grass—'We have the heathen Turks on the run, by the holy!—why don't they send us some wather?'[49]

Water, finally, did come ashore, sent from the destroyer *Grampus*, but there were insufficient receptacles to get it up to the front line.

Some of the blame for the failure of the 'rump' of the 10th to achieve the objective assigned to the entire division must accrue to Gen. Sir Bryan Mahon. As his battalions were going into battle he was still smarting at the manner in which he had been stripped of two-thirds of his fighting strength. 'In fact he fumed and fretted and did little more than that,' according to John Hargrave, 'for he was convinced that it was impossible to advance along the Kiretch ridge without adequate artillery support. He was convinced of this because he believed there were—yes the same old bugaboo!—strong enemy entrenchments in front of him.'[50] Hargrave is convinced that Mahon actually had enough troops to take the entire ridge. He had his own insight into the strength of the Turkish defences. Over a ten-day period he pulled, carried and dragged wounded out of almost every gully, dere (dried-up river) and trench on the ridge. But Mahon informed Stopford that the Turks were strongly entrenched in front of his positions and sat back to await developments. It must also be said, in defence of Mahon, that his troops had, at least, made some progress in the taking of the heights around Suvla. The same could not be said for the other generals. Indeed, Hargrave is critical of Hamilton for ignoring Mahon (the senior general, in terms of rank) when he came to see for himself what was going on.

For the next week or so the campaign settled into a sort of routine, one familiar to veterans of the Western front, but with consistently warmer weather (a mixed blessing, as we shall see). Men found time to write home. A letter from Paddy Tobin to his father, written almost a week after the landings, captures some of the mundanity and minor privations as well as the hazards:

> Water is our difficulty here. There are two wells about a quarter of a mile from here and all the water has to be carried in jars to us on the

hill. The Turks have snipers and guns trained on these which make it an unpleasant and difficult operation. We've not been able to shave or wash since our landing, and you can imagine the objects we look. The flies too are a devil of a nuisance—thousands of them buzzing around you all day, especially at meal times. The food though plentiful is monotonous. Bullybeef, dog biscuits, a little tea and sugar, no milk and little water is all we've had since our arrival. We expect to get a few days 'rest' soon, which consists of remaining on the beach and getting shelled. Still it also means a wash, and I hope a change of clothes, which is worth anything.[51]

A young private, Billy Richards, wrote in a similar vein to his father on 10 August:

In the last five nights I have had about 5 hours sleep but still feel fairly fit in body but my heart is broken for all those fellows I liked so much ... After yesterday I have a feeling I shall get through this 'job'. I would like to see some of the young lads who are staying at home get a few days of this. If they weren't killed they would or should die of shame.[52]

Both Tobin and Richards were to die less than a week later on Kiretch Tepe Sirt!

Water remained a problem throughout the early days of the Suvla campaign. Getting it onto the beach was a job in itself, it had to be transported from Port Said or Alexandria. Getting it to the front lines was a complicated, uncomfortable and potentially dangerous logistical operation. Ivone Kirkpatrick took a detachment of 30 men to A Beach to collect supplies for the 5th Inniskillings in what quickly became a gruelling and hazardous ritual.

It took us well over an hour to cover the three-mile-journey. On arrival I paraded the men in front of a large iron tank the shape of a trough into which water had been pumped by a hose from a ship. Each man advanced in turn, filled the water bottles he was carrying and then put his head in the tank to drink until he could drink no more ... Our return to the line took longer even than the outward journey. The men weighed down with the weight of their water bottles could do little more than crawl up the rocky paths and gullies which led back to the battalion.[53]

What water they got was usually warm and muddy and insufficient to combat the dehydration of a Turkish summer spent in unshaded trenches. The allocation per soldier per day was a single gallon, for drinking and washing. This at a time when the average daily consumption of water in London was 30 gallons per person. The pursuit of water became a primary consideration for the parched soldiers: 'Men lied to get water, honest men stole it, some even went mad for want of it; but it was cruelly hard to obtain'.[54] John Hargrave, escorting a crazed and wounded Irish soldier named Kelly to the beach, ended up having to punch him to keep him away from a poisoned well from which, in his delirium, he insisted on trying to drink.[55] Men carrying water to their colleagues would, almost inevitably, steal some for themselves and blame the loss on natural spillage.

> Some men became hardly responsible for their actions; the heat was intense, the biscuit was dry and the bully beef very salt, while many men were suffering from dysentery or enteritis and were parched with fever though they were unwilling to report sick in the face of the enemy. In such times surface civilization vanishes, and man becomes a primitive savage.[56]

Some developed techniques to combat thirst. Kirkpatrick devised a practice which sounds quite stomach-churning. Instead of drinking his ration directly, he actually

> spat it back into a small collapsible tin mug and kept rinsing my mouth at constant intervals, always spitting what remained back into the mug. Even so I must admit that I had a perpetual craving for a drink and envied the people at home who have only to turn on a tap to get as much as they want.[57]

Others used what was, apparently, an old Indian Army trick of gathering smooth, rounded pebbles and keeping them moving around the mouth generating saliva.

Because of the intense heat (and the risk of attracting unwelcome Turkish attention) most duties involving physical labour were carried out in darkness. This meant that troops 'slept' during the day. In fact they slept as best they could in this almost shadeless environment. During the day, as the sun sank behind the hills patches of shade would appear and as this occurred there would be a rush by men to claim it for themselves.[58] Little cognisance seems to have been taken of climatic conditions when it came to the relaxation of the British Army uniform code. According to Major Bryan Cooper 'Officers and men were dressed alike in thin, sand-coloured khaki drill. Shorts were forbidden, and the men wore their trousers tucked into putties of the darker khaki shade that is worn in England'.[59] Amongst the less-disciplinarian Anzac forces nearby shorts were commonplace. The proximity of the azure-blue sea often merely added to the general frustration. Bathing, though desirable as a means of cooling down and washing, was often dangerous and discouraged. Bathers tended to attract shellfire.

Another irritating phenomenon, which added to insomnia and general discomfort, was the secret Turkish weapon, the fly. 'It is not that we have merely more than one', wrote one disgruntled soldier, 'we have myriads of flies. And such enterprising flies. They visit everything from dead Turks down. They light on your face. You knock them away, and, just as if they were attached to your face with elastic, they bump back again ...'.[60] Only those who had had the prescience to provide themselves with mosquito nets could hope to ward them off when sleeping during the day. Ivone Kirkpatrick viewed them with particular distaste:

> It was almost impossible to get a piece of food into one's mouth without swallowing a fly, which had probably only just left one of the putrefying corpses with which the hillside was strewn. I used to cover the top of a box with sugar and kill flies en masse with a sort of home-made ping-pong raquet, but though I often went on killing till I was tired, it never seemed to make any difference.[61]

Not that what the troops had to eat for the first few days (at least) of the Suvla campaign was a lot better than a mouthful of flies. For most it was the staple field rations, bully beef and biscuit, the latter

> ... possessing the appearance of a dog biscuit and the consistency of a rock. It was no doubt of excellent nutritive quality, but, unfortunately, no ordinary pair of teeth was able to cope with it. Some spread jam upon it, and then licked the surface, thereby absorbing a few crumbs; others soaked it in tea (when there was any); while a few pounded it between two stones, and found that the result did not make bad por-ridge. After a week of this regimen, it is easily imagined how glad men were to put their teeth into something soft again.[62]

Suvla provides an interesting contrast to Flanders or Picardy in studying how people cope with varied physical conditions. On the face of it Gallipoli should have been a more convivial place in which to kill one's fellow human beings, but then these things are relative. Is mud, ice, rain and rats more enervating than dust, thirst, rocks and flies? 'Sitting was exceedingly uncomfortable' for Ivone Kirkpatrick,

> sharp flints stuck out at every angle and induced a feeling of feverish restlessness and dissatisfaction. During the long hours before dawn a

heavy dew fell and wet us to the skin ... Each morning I dreaded, needlessly as it turned out, the prospect of having to make an attack in these conditions. When dawn broke the morning sun steamed us dry and we faced more cheerfully the heat, thirst and flies which made up the day before us.[63]

Though Kirkpatrick was not subjected to any there were, nonetheless, surprise attacks:

These Turks are not at all considerate of one's comfort; a few days ago when I was enjoying another bath in a biscuit tin, the Turks had the audacity to make a surprise attack. Now it is bad enough to be clothed and in one's right mind on these occasions, but to be in one's birthday costume with one's thoughts in Dublin, well, then it becomes, to say the least of it, rather awkward.[64]

Fatigue duty was as much a feature of Gallipoli as it was on the Western Front, but in Suvla the discomfort was reversed; digging trenches and saps was often extremely difficult but, at least, they didn't become inundated and start to float out to sea. The Turks weren't nearly as enthusiastic as the British Army about this sort of defensive excavation. Listening patrols were frequently sent out. Their job was not just to wait quietly in no man's land and eavesdrop but to meet any Turkish incursions and hold them up until their own lines were alerted. One unfortunate member of Edgar Poulter's battalion spoke Turkish. 'The ticklish job was to go up these saps and listen ... he always got the job of being stuck at the head of the sap to hear what was going on. So he said he was sorry he ever knew anything about it.'[65]

Because, in some places, it would have required days of work with pick and shovel to penetrate the stony soil, trenches (some only 30 yards distant from the Turks) were often shallow. Soldiers developed the 'Gallipoli stoop', a sort of crouching walk, which protected those moving about from the attentions of the canny, accurate, courageous and ubiquitous Turkish snipers. They seemed to inhabit solid rock and scrub vegetation which would scarcely provide cover for a jack-rabbit. (Many of them took to painting their faces green as camouflage.) Some of the best Turkish marksmen, as it turned out, were markswomen. 'Among those discovered was a peasant woman—the wife of a Turkish soldier—who lived with her old mother and her child in a little house near the Irish lines.'[66] This particular woman was a good shot who specialised in hitting stragglers on the many trails between the front lines and the beaches. Having made sure her targets were dead she would then rifle their bodies. When she was finally identified and captured her house was searched. A large quantity of money was found, but more surprising was the

discovery of a number of identity discs. Either she was proud of her achieve-
ments or she was getting paid a piecework rate for the job! What price,
therefore, the rumoured Turkish or German 'spies' who, supposedly, donned
British Army uniforms and wandered through trenches unchallenged. Myths
arose about suave, authoritative but unfamiliar officers who had thus managed to avoid detection while gaining valuable intelligence.

Gradually Mahon got his missing battalions back and prepared for an
assault in greater numbers (and with proper reserves) on the daunting slopes
of Kiretch Tepe Sirt which swept down to the Aegean on the Turkish right
flank. This whaleback ridge, which rose to a height of over 700 ft, was rarely
less than 600 ft high and dominated the skyline, in an east to west direction,
near Suvla Point. Mahon, despite having the elements of his command restored to him, was 'still smouldering-dark in the chambered mood of his
soul's resentment'.[67] The stage was set for what Bryan Cooper has aptly called
'a little-known fight in an unlucky campaign'.[68] The plan was for a simultaneous attack, on Sunday 15 August, from the seaward side by the 30th Brigade
and on the inland slopes by the 31st Brigade. The 6th Munsters and 6th
Dublins of the 30th conducted a highly successful operation as they cleared
the Turks with a wild bayonet charge from most of the northern slopes of the
ridge at about 6 p.m. They were watched by Sgt. John Hargrave.

> It was uphill for the first few yards. The Irish seemed to have been
> shot like rocket-men out of the sun itself ... All that seemed to bother
> the Irish was that so few of the retreating troops would turn and fight.
> One Irish soldier—this is well authenticated—was heard to cry out to
> a fat Turk who fled before him 'I don't want to stick ye behind. Turn
> round now, and I'll stick ye in the belly dacent.'[69]

On the southern slopes, however, the 5th and 6th Inniskillings of the 31st
Brigade were not quite so fortunate. Supported by a single, small, mountain
battery they were sprayed with highly-effective machine gun fire from their
target Kidney Hill. The Turks defended the southern side of the ridge in far
greater numbers because their troops there had not been exposed to shell fire
from the naval vessels, like the *Grampus*, off Suvla Point. Before going into
action Ivone Kirkpatrick and the other officers of the 5th Inniskillings dined
from a Fortnum and Mason hamper.

> During the meal we discussed the coming attack and arranged what
> was to be done with our effects if we were killed or wounded. I esti-
> mated for three casualties but was hooted down as a prophet of evil.
> No one guessed that by evening no survivors would be left to carry out

our complicated testamentary dispositions. Three were to be killed and three wounded and of the latter two lucky to escape with their lives.[70]

Kirkpatrick's platoon was on the extreme left of the assault force. They came under immediate fire from an invisible enemy and were hampered by difficult terrain,

> ... the scrub and the broken nature of the ground made it impossible often to see more than two or three men on either side of one. Secondly the rate of advance varied necessarily in various parts of the line. Whilst a section were racing across a bare sandy patch, the men on each side of them would be slowly pushing their way through dense clumps of scrub. It was only by dint of much labour and running hither and thither that it was at all possible to keep in touch with one's platoon let alone the rest of the company.[71]

Kirkpatrick was finally hit, and after dragging himself to the crest of the hill was picked up by a party of stretcher-bearerss from the Dublin Fusiliers.

The Meath-born poet Francis Ledwidge, also with the 5th Inniskillings, was seeing action for the first time.

> A man on my right who was mortally hit said: 'It can't be far off now', and I began to wonder what it was could not be far off. Then I knew it was death and I kept repeating the dying man's words: 'It can't be far off now' ... It was Hell! Hell! No man thought he would ever return. Just fancy out of D Company, 250 strong, only 76 returned.[72]

The two Inniskilling battalions, unable to take Kidney Hill and secure the southern slopes of Kiretch Tepe Sirt, were ordered to withdraw. Under cover of darkness stretcher parties and a medical corps detachment brought back more than 100 wounded men. One of those was Robert Christie of the 5th Inniskillings, a close friend of Ledwidge: 'On that open ground, I remember going up into the air—and that was that. When I came to, I found that one of my legs had been hit and I could not get to my feet.'[73] Christie was one of the lucky ones picked up in the dark. Ironically it was only as the four men carrying his ground sheet deposited him where the Medical Corps could deal with his wounds that he recognised one of his rescuers as his friend Ledwidge. It was the last time they saw each other in uniform. The bullet which had hit Christie's left leg had severed the sciatic nerve in his thigh. After fourteen months in hospital he was discharged from the army and sent back to Belfast in crutches. He never fully regained the use of his left ankle.

This half success of the 15 August operation was to turn to disaster for the 7th Dublins. They were moved up from reserve positions to secure the advances made on the seaward side by the 6th Dublins and 6th Munsters (losing their CO Lt.-Col. Downing, wounded, to a sniper as they did so). But they faced an undefeated enemy on the far side of the ridge. The situation has often been compared to that of two groups of men on opposite sides of a roof, sitting in the gutters and fighting across the apex. The enemy, on the inland slopes, were protected from the navy guns out to sea. The pale light of the August moon shone from behind the 7th Dublins, silhouetting them on the skyline if they presented themselves as targets to the Turks. The crest was also dotted with large boulders behind which the Turks crept and secreted themselves as snipers or, even more effectively, bombers. Rifles were useless as a defence against such tactics. On the night of the 15th and the morning of the 16th the Turks picked apart the 7th Dublins and, in particular, the much vaunted D company, as Edgar Poulter recalled vividly:

> Johnny Turk used to come up to attack your position and he'd have a cigarette in his mouth and these round grenades like cricket balls with a fuse out of them and he'd put a cigarette to the fuse and he'd come up and lob these over and we used to lob them back again. We never saw any grenades till we got to Serbia and then Mills grenades came out. The lads were the inventive kind and used a lot of the empty jam tins and filled them with gunpowder and made home-made bombs.[74]

But on Kiretch Tepe Sirt that night the 7th Dublins didn't even have improvised jam jar grenades to hand.

Some of the Dublins took astonishing risks in picking up the short-fused Turkish bombs and hurling them back. Private Wilkin, of D Company, caught and returned five grenades successfuly but was killed when a sixth exploded in his hand. His actions were deserving of the Victoria Cross but, as only one of the officers of his company survived to recount his exploit he was merely 'mentioned in despatches'. Others, through sheer frustration, picked up stones and threw them at the well-concealed Turks:

> The unceasing noise of the bursting grenades, the smell of death, the sight of suffering, wore their nerves to tatters, but worst of all was the feeling that they were helpless, unable to strike a blow to ward off death and revenge their comrades. It is by no means easy to realise what the men felt during this ordeal. Perhaps the strongest emotion was not the sense of duty, the prompting of pride, or even the fear of imminent death, but blind, helpless rage.[75]

D Company were coming in for the brunt of the Turkish bombing raids and that sense of rage and frustration prompted the call for a bayonet charge. As rifle fire was utterly useless it was the only alternative to staying put and soaking up the Turkish grenades. Major Harrison, now in command, sent out Major Poole Hickman, the eminent barrister, with elements of D Company in a fruitless charge. Hickman was killed almost immediately. Seeing this, Harrison attempted to replace him at the head of the attacking party but was shot and killed also. Soon it was every man for himself. One of the few survivors of the raiding party found himself stuck between both lines surrounded by dead and dying comrades:

> I was lying quite close to a chum called Cecil Murray (from the Bank of Ireland); he was badly hit. I asked him where he was hit. He showed me his left hand, which was in pulp, and, while speaking to him, he was hit three times in the body. The groans were heartrending. Then a young chap called Elliot, who played 'footer' [Thomas Elliot, from Strabane, Ulster Rugby interprovincial] was shot in front of me when running out; he jumped about three feet when hit; he started to crawl back to our lines and just got above me when he was hit again. He died in a few minutes. Then came my dash for safety. I made two rushes of it, and had to shout to our fellows to stop firing to allow me to get in.[76]

Capt. Paddy Tobin, one of the few officers left in the 7th Dublins, was now in command of D Company. In a letter to Tobin's father, his friend Lt. Ernest Hamilton, a Trinity College medical student, described how Tobin became the next victim of Turkish snipers:

> Our men at this time were getting badly knocked down. Paddy and I took up a position on the top of the knoll from where he controlled the fire and steadied the men. Such gallantry and coolness I have never witnessed. We fought like demons against three times our numbers and held on too. Our knoll came in for at least six attacks. During one of these your son was killed, shot through the head. He caught me by the shoulder and when I turned round he had passed away. I carried him back some distance and placed him under shelter but had to get back to my position and try and follow his magnificent example. His death affected the men so much that I thought all was finished, but spurred on by his example they fought for another hour as they never fought before.[77]

Also killed at this stage of the fighting was Lt. Michael J. Fitzgibbon, son of a nationalist MP. Hamilton survived the ordeal (the only officer of the 'Pals' company to do so), but his spirit was broken by the experience. Subsequently he began to drink heavily and was later 'dismissed the service'.[78] Despite the death of most of their officers, 'The Irish did not give in. The line still held. The scruffy troops clung to the crestline, more like warmed up corpses than living men.'[79]

One survivor of that night was hit by three separate bombs and left unconscious for nearly eight hours. When he came to he was unable to move and watched the 7th Dublins being relieved. He was unable to follow or even to call out:

> I decided to lie in the scrub all night and at dawn to make good my escape. I had no water, as my water bottle had been smashed by a bomb. Next morning, after much trouble and excitement avoiding hidden snipers, whose bullets often whizzed unpleasantly close, I found water, and then safety, by getting down the cliff to the beach—travelling along the latter waist deep in water sometimes, and then swimming round the headland ... [80]

Abandoned by the General Command (as we shall see), deprived of leadership, the 7th Dublins, and the 'Pals' in particular, suffered another 'glorious' defeat:

> They were all young soldiers—though they looked old and worn now— all volunteers with less than a years training in Kitchener's much sneered at 'civilian army'. A week ago none of them had been under fire. They did not flinch. They did not budge. They used their bayonets. They flung stones. They got no help. They stayed where they were because they had been given no order to retire.[81]

By the time they were relieved D Company had lost 11 officers and 54 men killed or wounded and 13 missing. The 'Pals', which included the cream of the Irish intellegentsia, had landed 239 strong. After the attrition of the night of 15/16 August on Kiretch Tepe Sirt the company was reduced to 108 officers and men. Some days before this debacle Lord Granard, the CO of the 5th Royal Irish Regiment (the Pioneers), had written about the huge losses already sustained by the 10th (114 officers and nearly 3000 men killed or wounded) and had claimed that 'Ian Hamilton is entirely responsible ... and the sooner he is recalled the better. He has run the whole show like a madman.'[82] At least some of what transpired on Kiretch Tepe Sirt can also be attributed to Hamilton, but a significant share of the blame must lie with General Mahon himself.

Dissatisifed with progress at Suvla, Hamilton, on 15 August, decided to seek heads (the better to protect his own). Stopford, Hammersley and Sitwell were sacked. Stopford was replaced by Maj.-Gen. de Lisle as Corps Commander. As de Lisle was of inferior rank to Mahon, the latter ascended his high horse, refused to waive his seniority and serve under him, and resigned, despite the crisis being experienced by his division. Hamilton's diary entry for the following day smacks of understatement, or subsequent amendment: 'a Lt.-Gen. in the British Army chucking up his command whilst his division is actually under fire—is a very unhappy affair.'[83]

Although not attached to the 7th Dublins, John Hargrave of the RAMC writes about the fate of the battalion with unconcealed anger:

> After nearly five hours of stone-throwing—the ranks thin, the living in a daze of exhaustion, the mangled bodies of the dead lying beside them—Brigadier Nicol felt compelled to make an urgent appeal for reinforcements. It reached divisional and corps headquarters at a bad moment to ask for anything. Mahon had gone—and neither Hill nor anyone else knew what to do. Stopford was busy packing up. De Lisle was busy taking over. Nothing happened. There was, literally, *no one in command*.[84]

The 7th Dublins, unlike their Divisional commander, did not have the option of taking umbrage at the Turkish grenades, quitting and setting sail for a distant Greek island. They remained at their posts and sustained heavy casualties. Many of the men who died were of a calibre the country could ill afford to be without in the years ahead.

Less than a week later, on 21 August, with de Lisle established and Mahon having polished up his pride and recovered his command, the 29th Division, luckless victims of V Beach, were shipped in to Suvla and aimed at Scimitar Hill, which had been taken and then abandoned on the first day of the campaign. Lt. Guy Nightingale wrote to his mother, on 25 August, about the fighting which, ultimately, failed to take the hill. Continuous shelling had set the undergrowth blazing.

> Many of our wounded were burnt alive and it was as nasty a sight as I ever want to see ... Our doctor and one of the stretcher-bearerss went out under a murderous fire and brought in one officer and 3 men, who were lying out with broken legs, with the fires creeping up to them. They have been recommended for the VC and I hope they get it.

The 29th's Divisional HQ was quickly surrounded by flames which were so intense they blotted out the sound of the bursting shells and shrapnel.

We had to lie flat at the bottom of the trench while the flames swept over the top. Luckily both sides didn't catch simultaneously or I don't know what would have happened. After the gorse was burnt the smoke nearly asphyxiated us! ... The whole attack was a ghastly failure. They generally are now ... Barret, my old servant who had only rejoined from hospital a short time ago, is still out there; dead, I hope, for his sake, for those who are still alive and wounded must be suffering agonies from thirst and exposure.[85]

The 1st Inniskillings, of the 29th Division, managed to reach the crest of Scimitar Hill but were left unreinforced and were beaten back. Capt. William Pike of the Inniskillings called for volunteers and they rushed toward the Turkish entrenchments. None was ever heard of again. Another Inniskilling, Capt. Gerald ('Micky') O'Sullivan, who had won the Victoria Cross in the aftermath of V Beach two months before, called for another attempt to reach the crest. 'One more charge for the honour of the regiment', he is reported as having shouted. Fifty men followed him and only one, a wounded sergeant, returned. O'Sullivan's body, like that of William Pike, was never found. Lord Longford, commander of the 87th Brigade, was also killed on Scimitar Hill. His body, too, was never recovered. Out of an assault force of just over 14,000 troops targetted at Scimitar Hill more than 5000 ended as casualties!

In a simultaneous and co-ordinated attempt near Anzac Cove to take the area around Hill 60, to the south of Scimitar Hill, the Connaught Rangers had been badly mauled in capturing the Kabak Kuyu wells. They suffered more than 250 casualties in the initial assault and even more defending their gains. Among the survivors was an old soldier, Sgt. Nealon from Ballina, who had re-enlisted on the outbreak of war. Nealon was a rotund, ungainly man who took over command of his platoon when his officer, Lt. Blake, was killed. He and his men held on, along with some New Zealanders, to a line of trench which was being constantly bombarded, until they were relieved. Another sergeant, John O'Connell, who had returned from America to take part in the war, crawled out under heavy fire to rescue a wounded New Zealander, for which act he was awarded the DCM. By the end of August the 5th Connaught Rangers had less than 100 men not on the casualty list, and many of those were suffering from enteric fever or gastric illness.

The failure of the attack on Scimitar Hill effectively ended any pretensions the British might have had to the taking of the heights around Suvla. From September Gallipoli became something of an offensive backwater with both sides settling into their trench routine. The expedition which had been intended to help break the inertia of the Western Front had become just as bogged down in its own right. During this period the 10th was rebuilt with drafts of new recruits. Most, but by no means all, came from Ireland. 'As a rule, a draft is a comparatively small body of men,' wrote Bryan Cooper,

> which easily adopts the character of the unit in which it is merged. In Gallipoli, however, units had been so much reduced in strength that in some cases the draft was stronger than the battalion that it joined ... As a result after two or three drafts had arrived, the old battalion had been swamped.[86]

The survivors of the 'Pals' company now found themselves further broken up because of the urgent need to recruit men experienced in combat who were officer material. The company was paraded and volunteers were called for. Many preferred to stay in the ranks, but eighteen were promoted to 2nd Lieutenant, six from the rank of private. Seven were commissioned to the 7th Dublins, including the brother of Poole Hickman, Thomas.

Long before the Entente powers had given up on Gallipoli the 10th Division had been transferred to a new theatre of operations in Salonika. 'We got word that we were to pack up, which we did, and we moved away silently like the Arabs in the night.' Edgar Poulter recalled:

> ... just before we left the peninsula a boat arrived with 70 or 80 bags of mail for the battalion. They told us, 'You can't land in Greece like a Christmas tree carrying parcels draped round your neck.' We didn't want to dump everything and leave it behind. But that was the order. 'What you can put in your pack you can take but you're not to carry anything in your hand except your rifle and ammunition.' So off we went and we had to leave all our mail behind us, [though we] took the letters of course.[87]

'As the 29th Brigade filed down the long sap to Anzac in the darkness, as the 30th and 31st Brigades retraced their steps past Lala Baba and over the beaches at Suvla, it was impossible to avoid retrospect', wrote Bryan Cooper.

> We had passed that way less than two months before, but going in the opposite direction full of high hopes. Now we were leaving the Peninsula again, our work unfinished and the Turks still in possession of the Narrows. [The narrowest part of the Dardanelles—on the far side of Gallipoli from Suvla Bay]. Nor was it possible to help thinking of the friends lying in narrow graves on the scrub-covered hillside or covered by the debris of filled-in trenches, whom we seemed to be abandoning. Yet though there was sorrow at departing there was no despondency.[88]

The 29th Division, however, remained. On 12 September Sir Ian Hamilton visited the 1st Munsters, Guy Nightingale observing wryly in his diary that, 'It was a very different Bn [sic] to the one he saw in Egypt last. He was nice and insisted on being shown all the men and officers who had been here since the day of the landing, barely 40 in all, out of 1037.'[89] Three weeks later the division got news of the death, of his wounds, in Gibraltar of Henry Desmond O'Hara. Nightingale had come to know him well, in extremis, in the hours and the days following the V Beach landing. He noted that 'Poor O'Hara's death was great blow to us all. He was so very much a part of our regiment too.'[90] As the winter began to set in Nightingale's mood became more pessimistic. He saw no prospect of progress and his letters home record the effects of weather, disease and 'wastage' on the remnants of the battalion. By October it was down to 292 men! Most of those were from drafts sent out subsequent to the V Beach disaster. Nightingale himself succumbed to enteric fever and was evacuated from Suvla in late October to the Number 17 General Hospital in Alexandria. When the final evacuation of Gallipoli took place he was back in England recuperating.

That final step was dictated by the lack of any possibility of a successful offensive action without the committment of thousands more troops. With stalemate inevitable it was decided not to try and maintain and supply the Gallipoli forces through a difficult winter. It would have been a horribly difficult logistical operation. In October Hamilton was recalled and replaced by Gen. Sir Charles Monro. He advised that the campaign be brought to a speedy end. Kitchener paid a visit and came away in agreement. It was decided that evacuation was the preferable option, though fraught with its own hazards.

Had as much ingenuity and imagination been put into the Gallipoli landings and subsequent campaign as into the withdrawal of the troops they might never have had to pull out in the first place. An obvious and blatant evacuation would have invited dire consequences once the Turks realised they were facing a defeated and vulnerable enemy. Various subterfuges were used to disguise the fact that, little by little, forces were being withdrawn. The evacuation began at the end of December 1915, and within 11 days over 35,000 troops had departed, without much remorse though with a multitude of regrets. 'In a final effort to challenge the Turks they left behind booby traps, land mines, dummy sentinels, and 'clockwork' rifles which would fire when water dripping through a tin of sand dropped through to a lower tin that would then fall on the trigger mechanism.'[91] The Mediterranean Expeditionary Force left behind 66,000 Turkish dead, 28,000 British, 7595 Australian, 2341 New Zealand and 10,000 French. A sizeable percentage of the 'British' dead (around 10 per cent) were, in fact, Irish. 'The story of Gallipoli was one of lost opportunities, which became one of the world's classic tragedies.'[92] Over 400,000 British troops had been used, at one time or another, in the eight-month Gallipoli campaign. Of those more than half became casualties of one kind or another. Out of 214,000 British casualties 145,000 were due to diseases such as enteric fever or dysentry (though, astonishingly 15,000 suffered from frostbite). Nearly 70,000 men were killed or wounded as a direct consequence of military actions.

The 10th Division, which had given up so many of its men to Gallipoli (and so many of those had been sacrificed needlessly) heard about the final evacuation not long after they had beaten a retreat of their own, from Serbia, while involved in the new Salonika Front. Lt. Noel Drury wrote in his diary on Friday 31 December:

> ... we heard that no forward movement was made there since we left. Now they are gone! Well, well. I suppose it was better to clear out if we could not progress, but it is hard lines when you think of our fine fellows buried there. They did their best anyhow and I suppose that's all that matters. It must have been a wonderful bit of work getting everybody away.[93]

Despite the tone of his writing (that of a literary recruiting sergeant) Michael McDonagh is only one contemporary observer who lashes the feeble performance of the generals at Gallipoli. He says, 'It was a soldier's campaign, in which the bayonet and the man behind it counted for everything, and the brains of the generals—if there were any—for nothing.'[94] Later, Hamilton would become the scapegoat. The efforts of journalists like the Australian Keith Murdoch (father of Rupert) and Ellis Ashmead-Bartlett, of the *Daily Telegraph*, to expose the truth about Gallipoli (which had been shamelessly concealed by censorship and the careful management of casualty figures,) discredited him. Murdoch, in Gallipoli to do a series of articles, agreed to smuggle an uncensored despatch from Ashmead-Bartlett to England which was the first article to tell the true story. Without the benefit of hindsight (or a particular overview) Lord Granard, one of Hamilton's subordinates on the ground, damned him in his own writing. Granard was the CO of the 5th Royal Irish Regiment.

> Our losses in the fighting after the landing have been very heavy and I attribute this to the stupidity of Ian Hamilton in starting operations before he had sufficient troops and, what was more criminal, starting the fighting without any artillery whatever. If this campaign had been properly run we ought to have gained the position we are attacking and cut off a great portion of the Turkish army.[95]

This was written before the fiasco of Kiretch Tepe Sirt on 15/16 August.

Hamilton, however, blamed his generals for the failure of the Suvla landings and their aftermath. He wrote, 'Driving power was required, and even a certain ruthlessness, to brush aside pleas for a respite for tired troops. The one fatal error was inertia. And inertia prevailed.'[96] There is both an element of special pleading and an element of truth in that statement. As we have seen the long-term prospects for success at Suvla were irrevocably prejudiced by the failure to take advantage of vastly superior numbers on 7 August and the willful failure to seize uncontested ground. Some of the generals, of course, blamed the troops. Despite lavishing praise on the 29th Brigade which had served with him at Anzac Cove, the New Zealand Army General Alexander Godley (late of the Dublin Fusiliers) was unimpressed by the rest of the troops whom Kitchener had despatched. He wrote to Lord Kilbracken, his cousin, about the failure of the attempt to take Hill 60 on 21 August.

> The reason for our comparative failure was the slowness of the 9th Corps which landed at Suvla Bay. Who was to blame it is of course difficult to say. Sir F. Stopford and Generals Mahon (who relieved us in Mafeking) and Lindley have been made the scapegoats, but they had a very difficult task, and I am afraid the quality of the troops (New Army and Territorial) that they had at their command had something to do with it.[97]

Bryan Cooper in his book on the Suvla episode offers some points in mitigation where the generals (like Stopford and Hammersley) were concerned. He explains their inaction and reluctance to advance by reference to tired troops, lack of knowledge of the enemy's strength, Turkish command of the high ground, the effect of the enemy barrage and lack of water, little of which really qualifies as extenuating circumstances for what the military historian A.J. Smithers has called 'the greatest chance of the war ... thrown away by the most abject collection of general officers ever congregated in one spot.'[98] Granted the troops were tired but much of their fatigue was due to their having spent a hot day, without water plodding aimlessly about the landing beaches awaiting instructions from the generals. The barrage all through the 7th was not as severe as Cooper suggests. Shells were dropping on the landing beaches but the Turks had insufficient artillery to do much severe damage. It has been described by many as a virtually unopposed landing and bears no comparison to that at V Beach four months earlier. That Hamilton and Stopford had no idea of the numbers of Turkish defenders is their own fault. Intelligence was in its infancy but a better effort could have been made to ascertain the size of the enemy force. The lack of water was a function of lack of imagination and (as was so often the case with generals and staff planners), lack of empathy with ordinary soldiers.

What of the suggestion that the New Army soldiers were not adequate to the task. Certainly the men of the 10th division were not the Spartan heroes portrayed by contemporary apologists like Cooper, MacDonagh and Kerr but neither were they romantic dillettantes scared into febrile panic by 'Johnny Turk'. The separated elements of Mahon's division accomplished much in a lost cause in Gallipoli. Ironically, most of its successes were achieved in his absence. The Leinsters and the Connaughts were under Anzac leadership on Chunuk Bair and at the Kabak Kuyu wells. Brigadier Hill led almost half the division into the tilt at Chocolate Hill and Mahon failed to finish what he started on Kiretch Tepe Sirt. In defeat (and there were many of them) it can be said of the 10th that they did what they could and died in numbers doing so. Dead men cannot pull triggers!

In his memoir Sir Ivone Kirkpatrick debates the pros and cons of Gallipoli, with himself and with Sir Ian Hamilton. He accepts that it seemed like, and was, a good idea at the time because,

> With the forces at our disposal we could not hope in 1915 to carry out a decisive operation in France ... That the operation was feasible is shown by the fact that the attempt nearly succeeded despite serious tactical mistakes and the error of the home government in treating the expedition as a mere side-show.[99]

He selects a dearth of information from among the long list of candidates as the principal reason for the failure of the enterprise. Ten years after the events described here he wrote to Hamilton and, *inter alia*, noted a rather begrudging attitude towards the role of the 10th and 11th divisions at Gallipoli. He then returned to his theme

> The cardinal mistake was surely to leave the rank and file in ignorance of our objective. You stress in your diary 2 or 3 times the imperative need for explaining the position to officers and men. This was never done. I personally was in complete ignorance and I think my experience was fairly general. Of course everyone knew in a general way that a quick advance was desirable, but if the desperate need for haste had been explained on the 8th, I am sure the men would have moved with alacrity. However, instead of this the troops got their tone from their commander and the feeling was 'to-morrow will do as well'. I really wonder whether Generals Stopford and Hammersley did not unconsciously use the weariness of the troops as a pretext for their inertia.[100]

Kirkpatrick received a reply from Hamilton on 1 October 1925 in which he talks about the problems over water supply. His attitude betrays a mindset common among the generals of World War I, an inflexibility in coping with real rather than carefully contrived situations, 'this is how the world should wag, if it does not then it is scarcely my fault' sums up the philosophy. Referring to the troops who had landed at Suvla he notes

> Of course they were not experienced warriors. Otherwise they would have had no water difficulties, water being at 10 to 12 feet below the surface all over the whole plain and the digging easy. They ought of course to have had with them a seasoning of either Indian or other experienced troops. But their gallantry was altogether outstanding.[101]

Kirkpatrick's response to that needs no further decoration from me. 'If the troops did not know that water was to be got by digging, the experienced warriors in GHQ and Corps Headquarters should have known and imparted their knowledge to them without delay. They did not do so.'[102] To which one might add that it would have been an interesting and rewarding sight to have witnessed some of the 'experienced warriors' in GHQ roll up their sleeves and try to dig ten or twelve feet through the rock of the Kiretch Tepe Sirt

In his writings Hamilton pays scant attention to the attack launched against those heights on 15 and 16 of August. He seemed to have been barely aware of the attack. Which is interesting given the importance that the German commander in the area, Liman von Sanders, ascribed to the assault.

> Had the English on August 15th and 16th occupied the Kiretch Tepe, the whole of the 5th Army would have been outflanked and success might then have attended the operations as a whole. The crest of the Kiretch Tepe and its southern foothills commanded the whole of the wide Anafarta plain from the North. From the Eastern slopes a deci-sive attack could have been made ...

Von Sanders' view was clearly not shared by Hamilton and others on his staff who saw the exercise as a mere 'straightening of the line'.

Unionist Ulster remembers the first day of the Somme. Australians and New Zealanders are still obsessed with the mismanagement of Anzac Cove. Had nationalist Ireland taken a different political direction perhaps Gallipoli might occupy a place in the Irish psyche similar to that of the Australian. The name should be far more evocative for the Irish than it is, that it is not is due to the decision of many Irishmen that it was indeed 'better to die "neath an Irish sky than at Suvla or Sedd el Bahr" '.

# 4    The Drury Diaries

Largely ignored by historians, and, indeed, underrepresented in contemporary personal accounts are the wartime experiences of the 10th (Irish) Division after the termination of the Gallipoli campaign. From the Suvla landings to the evacuation there is a glut of material (Cooper's *The 10th Irish Division at Gallipoli*, Henry Hanna's *The Pals at Suvla* for example) but after that very little. However, the 10th Division did have among its ranks an inveterate diarist, Dublin-born Capt. N.E. Drury of the Royal Dublin Fusiliers. His unpublished journal runs to four volumes, 577 pages of manuscript, some typed, mostly written in a neat compact hand, totalling about 170,000 words. It tracks his own progress during the Great War from its outset, through most of the Eastern campaign, to the arrival of his battalion in France and ends shortly after the Armistice.

Drury was gung-ho for the war right from the declaration of hostilities, and although he was one of Kitchener's First 100,000, and a non-professional soldier, he remained so and became highly attuned to the ways of the Army. Not even the experience of Gallipoli had dampened his enthusiasm. On 31 December, 1915 he was able to write in his diary 'so here's the end of another year, and it seems extraordinary to confess that I have enjoyed it thoroughly and wouldn't have missed it for anything.'[1] As will be clear from his writing, he was also a convinced unionist. He was a conscientious officer who became steeped in the history and traditions of the Dublin Fusiliers. His diary (in reality more of a memoir) was occasionally tedious, frequently revealing, often grumpy and unfailingly honest. It confirms most of what others have written about the Gallipoli experience and adds greatly to our knowledge of the activities of the 10th Division in Salonika and Palestine, campaigns greatly overshadowed by the Gallipoli catastrophe and the slaughter of the Western Front.

Shortly after the outbreak of war Drury joined the Trinity College Officers Training Corps. He applied for a commission within two weeks and was eventually sent to the 6th Battalion of the Royal Dublin Fusiliers. He trained as a Signals Officer and was then returned to the battalion, initially taking command of No. 16 Platoon, D Company with the rank of lieutenant. The battalion left for the Eastern Front in May, 1915 but, to the chagrin of Drury and the other officers, did so without 'exercising the old right of the Dublins to march through the city with fixed bayonets and show ourselves off a bit to the delight of the onlookers and our own secret satisfaction. We thought ourselves devilish fine fellows and forgot that pride goes before a fall.'[2] That honour instead went to the rival 7th Battalion and it would be uncharitable to suggest that their subsequent experience might bear out Drury's observation.

Most of the first volume of his diaries relates to his Gallipoli experiences which closely parallel those recalled by others in the previous chapter. He writes of the confusion which surrounded the entre operation and the lack of basic information on what was expected of officers and men. His account of the 15 August attack on Kiretch Tepe Sirt offers an interesting perspective, one of a man with ambivalent feelings towards D Company of the 7th Dublins, whom he viewed as an elite corps of intellectuals. He was, nonetheless, dismayed at their fate. The build-up to his own involvement at Kiretch Tepe Sirt (with the successful assault of the 6th Dublins) included a period in an area known, euphemistically as 'Rest Camp' after five consecutive days of intense fighting.

The name 'Rest Camp' prompted Drury to

> suspect the division of having a subtle wit. Anything less like a rest camp you couldn't imagine. It was a bare slope cleared in the scrub and having traces of a 'hay' crop of hard wiry burnt grass. The sun was beating down with a heat such I [*sic*] have never felt before. There was no shade. After having been as long without food (15 hours) everyone lay around limp and sweating and unable to sleep for the flies.[3]

Forty-eight hours later a much needed trip to the beach for a wash meant that Drury could be parted from the clothes he'd been wearing for ten straight days. It was a tranquil prelude to the attack which began that same afternoon (15 August) on Kiretch Tepe Sirt. The 6th Munsters and 6th Dublins were to take the ridge from the seaward side. 'It seemed to me' recorded Drury,

> a pretty tough proposition to take the ridge including the climb up. The advance was naturally slow owing to the dense scrub and precipitous hill side, seared with gullies but the men were magnificent, and they worked up the hill through the scrub with fixed bayonets and in open order. When about fifty yards from the top we charged and reaching the top drove out the Turks with the bayonet sending them rushing down the other side ...[4]

The 6th Battalion, as we have seen, was not to bear the brunt of the Turkish counter-assaults but still suffered heavy casualties in holding their reserve positions. He is scathing about the lack of support for the troops who were expected to hold the Kiretch Tepe Sirt ridge. He notes that 'It became obvious in the evening that we could not go on losing men at the rate we were, to hold the end of the ridge. The rotters in the plain [an English Territorial division—Drury had no time for these] have not advanced at all and we are attacked from both sides.'[5] Col. Cox, CO of the 6th Dublins, sent Drury to 30th Brigade HQ where General Nicol upbraided him 'and practically accused us of having the wind up, and for no reason. Afraid I was a bit insubordinate and I invited him to accompany me up to the knob to see for himself. He did not go.'[6] But Drury's insolence was rewarded; after a consultation with his Brigade Major, Nicol ordered a withdrawal to be supported by naval shelling. Over the course of the night the battalion lost seven officers and sixty-two other ranks, not as severe as the casualties of the 7th R.D.F. but not inconsiderable and, with proper leadership, avoidable.

Drury's Suvla sojourn ended on 1 October 1915 when the 30th Brigade left Gallipoli to return to Mudros. By then Drury had been promoted to Captain (in charge of B Company) and the 6th Dublins had become a far less Irish unit after drafts of non-Irish troops. The evacuation, which should have been a relatively leisurely nocturnal ramble from the front lines, across Lala Baba to the beaches, was to turn into a frenetic race against time. Relief should have come from the 5th Wiltshires. However they contrived to get lost and didn't arrive until 4 a.m. The brigade was now faced with the prospect of a march across open ground in broad daylight, where, inevitably, they would be spotted and shelled. Relying on the remaining hours of darkness and the omnipresent early morning autumnal mists to mask their departure they set off on a forced march. So exhausting was the trek that at one point the Brigadier General, Nicol was carrying a machine-gun for a gunner who had collapsed with exhaustion, his Brigade Major was carrying the man's ammunition and the CO of the 6th R.D.F. was toting the rifles of two soldiers who had also collapsed. The battalion made it to the beach just as a light sea breeze blew the last of the morning mist away and opened up the plain to the binoculars of Turkish spotters. The first campaign of 10th Division was over.

However, the division did not have long to wait before it was reassigned. After a brief stop at Mudros, where Drury found himself disconcerted by the quiet of the night after the constant noise of Gallipoli, it was despatched to Salonika in Greece. Bulgaria, after blandishments from both sides, had finally decided to ally itself with the Germans and Austrians in the hope of wresting Macedonia from the Serbs. The Greeks had been persuaded to make common cause with the Allies but only after an assurance that 150,000 British and French troops would be sent to Salonika to defend against a Bulgarian invasion. As luck would have it, by the time the 10th Division finally got to Salonika the complexion of the government had changed and Greece had opted to remain neutral (a very pro-German neutrality dictated by King

Constantine, who was related to the Hohenzollerns). This Greek hostility ensured that instead of a force of 150,000 barely 30,000 were sent to resist the Bulgarian invasion of Serbia. In addition there was a reluctance on the part of the British to rush to the aid of their Serbian allies. The French crossed into Serbia to assist but the British spent more than a fortnight awaiting orders to cross the Greek border. According to John King, from Waterford, who served with the Royal Irish Regiment, 'We hadn't the equipment at the time. We weren't fully organised so they held us there for a hell of a long time.'[7] King had been in the army since 1907, mainly serving in India. He spent the first year of the war in France before being transferred to Salonika, 'a God-forsaken place.'

Drury's introduction to Salonika came on the 10 October, 1915. 'I woke up early and saw the most magnificent morning with Mount Olympus on our Port hand. The top was covered with snow which was tinted salmon colour with the morning sun. No wonder the old Greeks thought and wrote such a lot about it.' He found the city of Salonika fascinating: 'Beautiful slender minarettes, pure white in colour, spring up here and there from the general level of the houses.'[8] At night, viewed from off shore, the town reminded him of Douglas, in the Isle of Man. He was conscious of the delicacy of the political situation. A hostile reception had been anticipated because of the change in administration: 'I can't imagine what we are going to do here,' he observed, 'unless the Greeks have come in on our side or we are going to bluff them to do so. Up to now Greece has been neutral and we ought to be interned if we land.'[9] The following day the troops landed and moved through the western part of Salonika to a spot about five miles outside the town, without opposition or any overt hostility from the local population. However, the town was full of Greek troops and, as a precaution, extra guards were placed in the 10th's camp and officers always carried side arms when walking about the town. A week or so after the arrival of the 10th Division in Salonika reinforcements arrived in the form of eight officers and 388 other ranks from the Norfolk regiment, continuing the process of 'diluting' the Irish regiments.

Not that the Norfolks appear to have been that pleased at their fate either. Col. Cox had insisted that most of them be accommodated together in D Company and in their own platoons in other companies. Drury felt they were 'a bit "uppish" ' and

> I have overheard a few remarks about their 'hard luck' in being at-tached to an Irish Regiment. By the Lord, I'll make them have sense. It isn't everyone has the honour to be in the oldest Regiment in the Army, making Empire history since 1641. I have a little booklet which I must read them extracts from on parade, and make them learn our battle honours.[10]

He was not being 'tongue in cheek' either: later that week, sensing a 'jealousy between the Norfolks and the others' he issued instructions to his Company Sergeant Major to

> take the greatest care that all duties and fatigues are evenly divided ...
> I have given CSM Atkins my history of the R.Dub.Fus and told him
> that all NCO's must learn it, including those of No. 8 Platoon[11] [the
> Norfolks in Drury's Company].

By the end of his second campaign Drury was prepared to allege that 'in fact all these "foreigners" seem to be rotters'.[12]

Drury might have taken a leaf from his own book in examining his attitude towards his regimental brothers in the 7th Royal Dublin Fusiliers. He emphasises throughout the early part of the diary that the 7th R.D.F and, most especially, the famous D Company, was his least favourite unit in the 30th Brigade. While expressing solidarity with their tremendous losses at Suvla (though underestimating their contribution on Kiretch Tepe Sirt ridge in mid-August) he takes pleasure in many of their other discomforts. Guilty of *schadenfreude* in the third degree! Noting that, for example, on 23 October,

> The 7th R.Dub.Fus officers had a dinner today in a private room at
> the Hotel Roma. They had two G.S. [General Service] wagons to take
> them in and bring them back. It was pouring rain on the way home,
> and at a very bad part of the road a wheel came off!—Curtain![13]

On Friday 19 October the 30th Brigade entrained for Serbia, reaching Gjevgjeli, near the Greek-Serbian border, in the early afternoon. Then, escorted by a Serbian officer they trekked along a rutted, muddy and pot-holed road, little better than a mule track, which was typical of the surfaces which would make the Salonika campaign a logistical nightmare. As well as having to contend with water-filled holes in the road which could develop into pools capable of drowning an entire team of mules, the brigade also encountered groups of refugees moving south to escape the Bulgarian army. Serbia, and particularly the infamous Struma Valley, is not recalled fondly by veterans such as John King:

> It was an awful place. It was deadly in every way ... there were two
> extremes in it. It was very very cold in winter and very hot in summer
> and it was rotten with malaria ... We hadn't roads or anything else we
> had to go along old goat tracks.[14]

Like King, Capt. G.H. Gordon, also with the 10th Division, and with experience of Picardy, preferred France: 'All our moves here have been done in
inky blackness and usually under rain and on very ill-defined tracks in the
hills.'[15] Drury, without any personal knowledge of the Western Front, still
preferred Salonika: 'I would rather be humping my pack about here, and
leading the open-air life in a strange and interesting country, than floundering
in the bogs of Flanders ...' .[16]

The next month was an uneventful period of consolidation during which
Drury, against his wishes, became adjutant (administrative assistant to the
commanding officer) and was moved away from command of B Company.
The wheel also turned for Gen. Sir Bryan Mahon. His nemesis, Sir Ian
Hamilton, had probably agreed to the removal of the 10th from Gallipoli to
Salonika so that he could get rid of Mahon (who, purged of his pique had
reassumed command of the 10th). Now Mahon was promoted from command
of the Division to lead the entire Salonika force. (Hamilton, meanwhile, was
replaced as Commander-in-Chief of the Gallipoli operation.) This change
meant that the sexuagenarian Gen. Nicol, a capable leader of whom Drury
was extremely fond, was given temporary command of the 10th, while Col.
Cox took over the 30th Brigade. Major W.H. 'Bill' Whyte took over the 6th
Dublins from Cox.

In one diary entry in mid-November Drury, unwittingly, anticipates the
two main enemies of the 10th Division while in Serbia, the weather and the
inadequacy of communications.

> Wednesday, 17th November. It has become bitterly cold and I was
> going about with gloves, wooly waistcoat and muffler ... There is great
> delay here in the telephone working and important messages are taking
> hours to get through. The trouble is that the distances are so great and
> our wire (D.I.) is in bad condition  ... The cable has to be laid across
> the bare mountain, and as there are no roads, the ration convoys take
> their own course and often mules break the wire in the dark.[17]

Both the bitter cold and the inability to communicate adequately with Divisional and Army Headquarters, with their French allies, or even with other
battalions at Brigade level dogged the 10th Division throughout their second
campaign.

Edgar Poulter, of D Company, 7th Dublins, a survivor of the heat and
mayhem of Kiretch Tepe Sirt, was less concerned with communications than
with the raw and freezing conditions that came with the first November
snows: 'You went to bed, lay down on the blanket at the side of the rocks and
the next morning woke up covered with snow.'[18] (Poulter eventually suc-

cumbed to typhoid and was evacuated to Malta, like so many of his colleagues in D Company he ended up with a commission on his return to action.)

As is often the case when an army takes on an enemy accustomed to the terrain and conditions the 'home team' was far better prepared.

> The Bulgars all wear heavy underclothing. Some have sheepskin shirts, but most have a sort of quilted cotton shirt stuffed with cotton wool. Many of these Bulgars had well-made knee boots of excellent leather and some had leather sandals or moccasins strapped over the boots.[19]

This was written, by Drury, on 15 November before the weather had turned really cold. Less than two weeks later he added:

> Very bad night—no shelter from the cold and the wet. I had a rotten passage round the line, falling and stumbling about in snow drifts up to my shoulders in some places. The snow kept on falling yesterday evening and part of the night, and then changed to the most intense frost. This morning everything is frozen hard and every track is too slippery to walk on. There are now about 2 feet of snow everywhere and much more in places where drifts have formed. Our overcoats are frozen hard, and when some of the men tried to beat theirs to make them pliable to lie down in they split like match wood. The men can hardly hold their rifles as their hands freeze to the cold metal.[20]

Towards the end of November captured prisoners, under interrogation, began to tell French and British intelligence officers of a possible Bulgarian offensive which would fall first on the town of Kosturino. This part of the line was manned by the Irish battalions. It froze heavily for the days prior to the major Bulgarian attack. Two feet of snow covered the ground, far more where drifts had formed. Men slid all over the trenches as they froze. Dozens reported sick with frostbite. Some, in order to alleviate the worst of the cold, tightened the puttees round their feet. This had the opposite effect and brought a greater risk of frostbite. Risking Bulgarian shelling fires were lit as temperatures dropped to 10 degrees below zero. It was a particular nightmare for stretcher-bearers, whose job it was to negotiate the frozen, rocky ground between the front line trenches and the field ambulances. Lt. L.C. 'Stuffer' Byrne, the 6th's resourceful Quartermaster—Byrne had received a Military Cross for his ingenious efforts in getting water up to the front in the early days of the Suvla landing[21]—provided the only relief sending up two woollen cardigans to each man in the battalion. Their entitlement was one, but Byrne had, adroitly, managed to misappropriate those of the 6th Munsters as well.

During this period the Bulgarians were exceptionally quiet. Probably aware that General Winter was softening up the enemy they saved their shells.

When the Bulgarian offensive began on 6 December, the 6th R.D.F. was in reserve. As with most such situations confusion reigned, added to, in this instance, by the inadequacy of communications. Throughout the day the 6th R.D.F. was getting reports that the French and British positions at Kosturino had been overrun. It soon became clear that the 10th Division was fighting a force which outnumbered it by a factor of ten or twelve to one. Withdrawal was the only realistic option but even an organised retreat would be a risky business. The French forces occupied positions to the left of those held by the 10th Division, and as to the support available on the right, 'What comes then I don't know. Let's hope there's someone there!'[22]

With the Bulgarians making inroads on Allied positions and a withdrawal decision anticipated the tone of the journal becomes more agitated. Drury bemoans the lack of proper communications even at company level. With no phone lines and visual signalling impossible he was forced to send out order-lies to transmit messages, none of whom returned. He is critical of the lack of leadership at all levels, reserving his most scathing comments for the second-in-command of the 6th Dublins, Capt. E.T. Horner, lately arrived from the Norfolks. Offering some excuse about the Brigade Transport section needing an experienced officer to look after things, Horner had left the line. As usual Drury doesn't mince his words:

> He had the wind up properly and the dirty blighter went off at a most critical time, when he was most wanted as second-in-command of the battalion. If I had anything to do with it I would have him courtmartialled for cowardice—and I told him so. What must the men think of him?[23]

By 8 December the 10th's position was becoming untenable. They had been ordered to hold their positions to allow time for the French forces to withdraw equipment which had, rather optimistically, been brought up to the front line the previous week. But faced with the onslaught of up to 7 Bulgarian divisions (a Bulgarian division being about twice as large as a British one) the 10th stood a good chance of being swallowed up by a vastly-superior force.

The 6th Dublins managed an orderly retreat on the night of 8 December after first having had to deal with a Bulgarian attack which, under cover of a fog, had made it to within fifty yards of their trenches. But as they got closer to the Greek-Serbian border it was clear that the situation was becoming chaotic. Thousands of British and French troops were converging on the roads and passes to the south without any semblance of order and organisation. Once again 'Stuffer' Byrne stepped in. According to Drury he created some order from this chaos at the village of Dedeli where the evacuated troops stopped to rest. 'That man ought to get the DSO. He rises to the occasion,' wrote Drury admiringly, 'and no job is too big for him to run when the need arises.'[24] He even managed to produce a hot meal for the troops with an entire Bulgarian army only a matter of miles away. (The Bulgarians, content with their initial successes had failed to press home their advantage by pursuing the retreating British and French armies more vigorously.)

The priority now became damage limitation, the objective to get safely from Dedeli to Doiran. 'The Greek-Serb frontier is at DOIRAN and there seems a doubt if the Bulgar will cross this, as he has not declared war on Greece— in fact I think he expects the Greeks to join with him. In that case we may have to mishandle the Greeks somewhat to get back to Salonique'.[25] Subterfuge was used to persuade the Bulgarians that they were still facing a functioning defensive army. Fires were lit behind crests which would shine in the seemingly permanent mist and convince the enemy that troops were camped in large numbers. Twenty men from each battalion were left behind for twelve hours on 10 December to loose off occasional rifle fire with the same purpose in mind. As the column moved south on a surprisingly good road bridges were blown up behind them by the Royal Engineers to slow down the Bulgarian advance.

The 10th Divison crossed into Greece early in the morning of 11 December to be faced by a barracking from the 64th Brigade of the 22nd Division, based near Doiran. They were subjected to taunts like 'look at the Balkan runners'. 'I really thought the men would break ranks and go for them,' Drury records:

> Our fellows had stood all sorts of hardship and trouble and were still a fine fighting unit, and here were these pampered blighters calling them cowards. These people had tents to sleep in and huge fur coats with the fur outside, and heavy gloves and mufflers, and everything to make them warm and comfortable. All their wheeled transport was there and their cookers were going full blast with their breakfast. These fellows had never seen a Bulgar nor probably any other enemy and that's the way they behaved to our veterans.[26]

Later Drury heard that a company from the 64th Brigade were sent out on patrol and none returned. One senses little sympathy for their fate as he records this fact. From Doiran the 10th Division entrained for Salonika. The Bulgarians stopped at the Greek border, respecting (a very partial) Greek neutrality. Drury's postscript to the entire experience being 'Here endeth the 2nd spasm and for the second time the battalion has been saved by the fog.'[27]

The 7th Dublins had shared the fate of Drury's battalion. Edgar Poulter, of D Company, was one of those assigned to the rearguard. Before the withdrawal began

> ... we were told, 'Any man who drops out don't bother about him. It'll be just too bad.' We had our pouches full and fifty rounds in our bandoliers slung over each shoulder. That's where we got the name the Balkan Harriers. We retired in three days when it took us three or four weeks to go up. Running like hell for a couple of hundred yards, turning round, blazing away and then going round again. Eventually we arrived back at Lake Doiran and the Division that was relieving us was equipped with the short fur jackets, sheepskin coats and winter equipment. We were still in our shorts, pith helmets, no winter clothing of any sort. Fellows were frost bitten and in a rotten mess.[28]

For the entire 10th Division the next six months was a period of relative inactivity. They encamped at various points around the port of Salonika, took on new drafts of men, built up their strength and, more importantly, built up defensive positions against a Bulgarian invasion or the victory of the pro-German side in the struggle for power in Greece. No offensive action of any kind was taken against the Bulgarians. This display of lethargy drew the scathing comment from the French Prime Minister Clemenceau that Mahon's Army be known as 'The gardeners of Salonica' when he inquired once what they were doing and was informed that they were 'digging'.[29] Towards the end of June the 10th Division began to return to the line, north to the Struma Valley in Macedonia. The move came during the hottest part of the year to an area where the mosquito was king. The division would suffer horrendously from malaria, with many of those struck down by the disease dying from its effects.

In the middle of July, Drury, who had so far escaped injury at the hands of the enemy, went down with a fever, which turned out to be malaria. At first he refused to leave camp for a field hospital but spent an entire week in an almost comatose state.

> I don't remember much about this week. Seem to recollect intervals of violent shivering and then sweating until my blanket was soaking. I seem to have spent most of the time dreaming most awful dreams and vague sensations of some terrible doom impending.[30]

Drury was evacuated, eventually, to the 4th Canadian General Hospital at Kapujilar. That particular journey was a nightmare. He was carried by stretcher

into a transport vehicle and placed on the top tier, his face a few inches from
a roof which was baking hot.

It was a terrible journey over awful tracks and I had to keep my hands
jambed [*sic*] against the roof of the waggon [*sic*] to prevent my head
from being battered. What on earth happens to wounded men is hard
to imagine. Here was I with nothing wrong with me and I could hardly
stick out a few hours of it.[31]

Within a week he was on hospital ship to Malta. So, while his battalion
ventured into the heat, humidity and disease of the Struma Valley the last
entry in the second volume of Drury's diary reads 'The M.O. says I must
land at Malta and go to hospital for a while as I couldn't possibly be let back
to the Battalion for some weeks. Damn!'[32] And he meant it. The expletive
carried with it not a trace of irony.

Had Drury known then exactly how long he would remain away from his
battalion his language might have been stronger and his depression more
severe. There follows a gap of almost exactly a year in his diary and when it
resumes in July 1917 we find him on his way back to Salonika to rejoin the
6th Dublins. He had not finally been released from hospital until May 1917
and had then spent a month in Victoria Barracks in Cork on light training
duties. He petitioned the War Office to be allowed go back to Greece and was
permitted to do so. But his enthusiasm outstripped the state of his health.
Malaria has a nasty habit of recurring and no sooner had he returned to
Salonika than he was hospitalised again. Worse still, from his point of view,
was that his unit was on the move soon after he arrived, bound for Egypt and
service in Palestine. Only the collaboration of a friendly Medical Officer who
looked the other way, ensured that he was discharged from hospital and
allowed to rejoin the 6th Dublins.

Had he been absent from a Western Front battalion for an entire year he
would probably have recognised few faces upon his return. But even after a
campaign in the intensely hot, disease-ridden Struma Valley in Macedonia the
10th Division was still, relatively speaking, intact. Many of the officers with
whom Drury had served were still in place. He saw the last of Salonika on 9
September, 1917. Looking back at the city from the *Aragon* as he sailed away
he noted the contrast in the appearance of the place from his first view of it.
Almost two-thirds of the city had been destroyed in a fire the previous year
and it was a sad, much reduced sight. The destination of the 10th Division,
after landing at Alexandria, was Ismailia Junction on the Suez canal. There
the troops were to be allowed a brief acclimatisation period, which involved
getting accustomed to the difficulties of movement in the soft desert sand and
to the heat. This Drury found to be far more to his liking than that of

Salonika. 'The air here is extraordinary, because it is hotter even than up country in Salonika, 1000 miles north of here and yet it is dry and bracing and everyone feels fit for work.'[33]

The 10th had become a part of the Egyptian Expeditionary Force, led by Gen. Sir Edmund Allenby, whose job it was to improve on two previous attempts and expel the Turks from Palestine. Allenby was atypical of Great War generals and one about whom there are critical divisions. Coming from a cavalry background his period as commander of the Third Army in France was unremarkable. He was an opponent of Haig's profligate waste of human life. At Arras in April 1917 his troops had made an almost unprecedented four-mile-advance but suffered appalling casualties (in a cemetery near Arras there is a monument to 36,000 British soldiers killed at Arras who have no known grave). Allenby protested to Haig about the extent of the losses and within weeks was sent back to England. It was thought at the time that his career was over and the posting to Egypt was definitely a backward step. But he took literally the instructions he received from Lloyd George before being despatched to the Middle East, 'Jerusalem by Christmas' (though his state of mind was hardly improved by the news that his son had been killed on the Western Front in July 1917).

He arrived in Egypt at the end of June 1917 and took over a force which had already tried, and twice failed, to take Palestine. Allenby was quick to realise that morale among the troops was low. He set about a series of 'raids' on his own units, visiting each in turn and creating an impression of vitality and highly visible leadership. He became renowned for his outbursts of temper, but in the minds of his troops these were translated into attacks on those enemies of the ordinary soldier, the 'staff-wallahs'. Inspired rumours began to circulate about his affection for the ordinary soldier. According to one such story he saw beer being unloaded for the use of staff officers at El Kantara. He ordered it reloaded and sent to the men at the front.[34] Drury, who tossed praise about like a man trying to shift a heavy weight, gave him a vote of confidence after a few weeks in Egypt:

> I like this Egyptian Army as there seems an air of life and activity about it which I'm told is entirely due to the energy of Gen. Allenby. Everyone seems to know his job and does it efficiently, and the slackers seem to have been weeded out and sent to the line.[35]

Allenby took quite a risk in deciding to put the 10th into action sooner rather than later. Hundreds of its members were suffering from malaria. General Longley, the 10th Division's CO, had served with Allenby in France and Allenby relying on his judgement, rather than that of medical staff, decided to include the 10th in his plans rather than leave them in the rear recovering from the effects of disease. Ismailia certainly suited Drury and many of the officers of his battalion. They made use of the facilities of the French Club and the town itself was

> a most lovely spot ... the whole town is thickly planted with trees, many of them being the 'flame' trees with their wonderful bright red blossom. The houses are well built on the bungalow style with verandahs and sun blinds. The delightful effect of the whole is increased by the fresh feeling in the air owing to the fresh water canal which passes through.[36]

One of the few drawbacks was that swimming in the canal could lead to a potentially-fatal disease known as bilharziosis, where one of the local residents, a flatworm, would penetrate the skin and lay its eggs in the human hosts.

Towards the end of September the 10th moved out of Ismailia and marched north to El Kantara. Unlike other punishing route marches this one, conducted in the crisp chill of a desert night, enchanted Drury: 'It was almost like a night in fairyland with the brilliant stars shining overhead and being reflected in the still waters of the canal', he wrote.[37] From Kantara the division entrained to Rafa, at the southern end of the Gaza Strip to await the beginning of Allenby's offensive.

The Third Battle of Gaza began on Wednesday 31 October with the 10th Division in reserve, guarding against a Turkish counter-attack on what was a wide front, stretching from Gaza on the left flank to Beersheba on the right. (Beersheba was half way between Gaza and the Dead Sea.) The 10th had strict orders not to reveal their presence near Beersheba. Allenby had concentrated his forces there but wanted the Turks to believe his main target was the city of Gaza. He had hatched an imaginative plan to mislead the Turks. A British officer 'stumbled' across a Turkish guard post, allowed the guards to chase him and dropped a bloodied haversack from his horse as he disappeared from view, inside were details of the proposed 'attack' on Gaza. Allenby's cunning was in marked contrast to the mulishness of most of his peers on the Western Front.

Drury's diary, for perhaps the first time since the beginning of the war, took on a frenetic air as the tempo of events increased. The Third Battle of Gaza, unlike anything experienced by the 10th at Gallipoli, or even in Salonika, was to become an engagement of rapid movements. More ground was covered in a day than many units on the Western Front would have advanced during the entire war. The mood was one of elation as well laid plans actually began to work, the only drawbacks being the torrid heat, periodic sandstorms known as 'khamsins' and the difficulty in keeping units supplied with water.

By 6 November, with Beersheba taken, the fight on the 10th's flank had developed into something reminiscent of the open warfare of the 19th century. Once again cavalry was being employed to good purpose, a fact which suited a general with Allenby's background. Artillery batteries were operating with the mobility of machine-gun units. From some high ground Drury had a perfect view. War as spectator sport.

> It was the most magnificent sight and I will never bother to look at a military review again ... I had a great view of two batteries of 18-pounders galloping up under heavy shrapnel. They tore along at top speed over the desert and, when they got to 50 yards of where I was, they wheeled round and got the guns into action like a flash.[38]

The 10th was mainly employed in the taking of the Hureira Redoubt, a strong defensive position on the Gaza-Beersheba road. It was seized with relatively few losses. Afterwards Drury inspected it and 'found it immensely strong, and it is extraordinary how few casualties we had. *We* would never have been pushed out of it by the Turk.'[39] By 8 November thousands of prisoners had been taken and the Turks were in retreat, leaving behind anything from nails to intact artillery batteries. For the 10th Division, who had suffered heavily under dubious leadership and disadvantageous conditions up to that point, it was a relief to be the pursuers rather than languishing amongst the ranks of the permanently beleaguered.

Allenby's next major objective was Jerusalem. A local Arab tradition suggested that success was inevitable. It held that a prophet of God would come from the West and take Jerusalem from the Turks. In Arabic the phrase Allah Nabi was used for a 'prophet of God'. It was close enough to the conquering general's name to be seen by more than the Arabs as some sort of omen. The 10th division was transferred from the right to the left flank of the attack, moving to Gaza where, for three weeks or so, the division was 'trained to staleness and bored to tears ... a lot of natives are gradually returning to Gaza and the villages near. They seem a very unwarlike, mercantile lot, who just want to be left alone to rob and cheat the troops.'[40] Clearly, inactivity of any sort allowed Drury plenty of time to hone his tart and jaundiced literary observations.

Other Irish troops shared Drury's lack of regard for the native Arab population. John King of the Royal Irish Regiment preferred the Turks to their sometime-allies: 'I'd describe the Turks as very good men but the Arabs I didn't care much for them. You knew you were up against it when you saw the fellow with the red fez. He'd fight on but the other ... would move when he saw trouble coming.'[41] Lt.-Col. F.E. Whitton, in his regimental history of the Leinsters, adopts a casually racist attitude to the native population among whom they were accommodated.

> The habits of the Palestinian being as bad as those of any other Orien-
> tal, a considerable amount of work was necessary before the village was
> fit for billeting. Fortunately, however, nobody knew a single word of
> Arabic—(or whatever language the inhabitants spoke), so they soon
> realized the uselessness of argument.[42]

The task of taking Jerusalem fell, in the main, to the divisions on the right flank advancing northwards from Beersheba, through Hebron and Bethlehem. The 10th worked its way up along the coastal route into the hills to the east of the city. News of what was happening elsewhere was sparse and it wasn't until two days after the capture of Jerusalem (achieved, as Allenby had de-sired, without a shot being fired and with no damage to the city) that the 10th became aware of the fact. 'It is hard to imagine the Holy City in Christian hands after so many hundreds of years', wrote Drury, sounding like some latter-day Knight Templar,

> I hope the politicians won't botch up matters after the war and let the
> Turks come back to it again. That's the sort of thing we are all afraid
> of, as history shows that the troops win the wars but the politicians
> nearly always loose [*sic*] the peace.

His illusions about the holy city itself were shattered by his first visit, on the 19 December. 'I think Jerusalem is the dirtiest place I have ever been in, and the whole atmosphere stinks with rotting matter thrown into the streets and alleys.'[43] The ancient religous sites were more to his liking though.

Cleverly pushing all the right buttons Allenby's entry into Jerusalem (which, naturally enough, predated that of Drury) was that of the humble pilgrim, *sans* pomp, triumph or ceremony. 'He just walked in on the 11th at noon, unarmed and carrying a cane.'[44] His forces had advanced 60 miles, along a 30-mile front in 40 days. He was now faced with a number of dilemmas, some brought about by his own successes. After heavy rains the coastal plain was causing transportation and supply difficulties and there were serious logistical problems being faced in keeping up with the advances of Allenby's forces. On 16 December Drury noted that 'there is nothing doing yet and we seem to have run clean away from our supplies as the country is almost impassable for wheels and camels are useless in mud.'[45] In addition a Turkish counter-attack could be anticipated north of Jerusalem. The British had ambitious plans themselves to push northwards towards Nablus, but these were almost ne-gated by the Turkish counter-offensive which came at the end of December.

The job of the 10th was to move north east while engaging the Turkish offensive. The going was rough, the terrain mountainous and there was little hope of artillery support as it was virtually impossible to haul guns up the narrow mountain passes. Drury's notes give the impression of obectives attained with surprisingly light casualties but this particular part of his diary was lost in transit and his account lacks any detail. 'Our principal concern', he notes,

> was that we hardly ever saw a sign of a Turk and it was perfectly hopeless to capture either prisoners or M.G.s [machine-guns]. Whenever they found that we had turned the flank of a position or even got unpleasantly close frontally, they just packed up and slunk back quietly.[46]

It was not until March, when the 10th were involved in another push that culminated in the Battle of Tel Asur, that Drury expressed misgivings about the task they faced. He reconnoitred the area a few days before the offensive and wrote: 'Tel Asur will be a tough job to tackle as its height is 3318 feet and the sides precipitous.'[47] The 6th Dublins were to take a natural obstacle called Wadi Jib. Progress was slow as the climb was steep, though, fortunately, there was little accurate shelling from the Turks. 'I'll never forget that climb', he wrote,

> It was impossible to see over any terrace to the one above, and every moment we expected a shower of stick grenades on our heads. We pushed up in as uneven a formation as possible, every man either pushing up his pal first or pulling him up from above.

When the Dublins got within striking distance of their target they jettisoned their packs and fixed bayonets.

> When the whistle blew, away we went with a 'screech' like only Irishmen can give (it reminded us of the 15th August, 1915 on the 'K.T.S.' [Kiretch Tepe Sirt] ridge at Suvla Bay, Gallipoli). When the Turk saw us coming, he never waited till we were within range, but just bunged every grenade he could lay hands on, in our direction, and even some of their rifles and FLED!! What a scene! ... We were sure Johnny Turk would have waited for us and put up some scrap, and everyone was disgusted to find we had only to say 'Boo' and he ran away.[48]

The casualties suffered by the 6th Dublins were unusually light, one dead and twelve wounded.

Progress in Palestine that month was being accompanied by near disaster in France for the British and French armies as the German March offensive forced the British and French back over ground dearly won in the preceding three years. Drury hinted himself at what was to be the battalion's next major assignment. 'We are all debating if we will get a shift to France, but I don't want to get stuck in trenches again. These open fights here are much finer business with plenty of elbow room, and a chance to work out your own little show.'⁴⁹ The move to the Western Front didn't come for a couple of months and not before Drury, on leave, encountered one of the legends of the desert war.

He was travelling by train towards Ismailia, on his way to Cairo for a week, when he noticed

> a peculiarly shabby looking fellow mouching [*sic*] along in an officer's tunic but without badges or regimental buttons, unshaven and with long hair. He looked such a disgrace that I was on the point of speaking to him when one of the 10th Div. staff with whom I was sitting said to me 'Don't you think you might think first before blazing at him, and do you know who it is?' I said I didn't and he replied 'That's Colonel Lawrence.' He was probably just back from one of his wonderful stunts with the Arabs and had picked up any old gear to take him to Cairo.⁵⁰

Coincidentally, at the end of his leave, driving back to the front he had a close encounter on a hairpin bend with that other legendary figure of the campaign. General Allenby, nicknamed 'The Bull', was being driven in his Rolls, 'which took up nearly all the corner and was going fast. What an escape. We shot out of sight round the bend and down the hill one side while "The Bull" buzzed down the other and no time for recriminations.'⁵¹

The 6th Dublins, as will be seen elsewhere, were transferred in July 1918, to the Western Front and when the end of the war came Drury's sense of disappointment is palpable and not necessarily to be wondered at. He undoubtedly shared the sentiments of his soldiers who, having been subjected to three years of mayhem, harrassment and premature death by the Germans and their allies, now wanted to exact some retribution. But it is clear from his writings over a four-year-period that the Army had come to fit Drury like a warm, practical glove. He enjoyed the life. With the exception of his time at Gallipoli his experience of war had not been unlike that of many of the veterans of World War II. The risks and the discomforts were constant but not overwhelming. He believed himself to be fighting for a just cause against a malevolent enemy and he never experienced the static attrition of the Western Front which ground the spirits of so many young men just like him.

While serving with the 6th Dublins he had become imbued with the military tradition of the Royal Dublin Fusiliers. His diary concludes on 11 March 1919 with the unsentimental observation 'Doffed uniform and turned civilian again'[52] but the fourth volume of his memoirs then continues with a lengthy account of the history of the Dublin Fusiliers, which he constantly refers to as the 'oldest regiment in the British Army'. It is a source of pride for him that he was a member of the first Fusiliers 'Service' Battalion to join the first Division of 'Kitchener's 100,000' (the role of the 7th Dublins being, as usual, ignored or undervalued). His pride in his own unit can quickly turn to tribalism or chauvinism as he disparages other battalions, divisions, and nationalities. Although he is a Southern unionist, and a protestant, he has little time for the English or indeed for anyone other than the Irishmen of his own Battalion. All others are 'foreigners' or occasionally even 'dagoes'.

Within the confines of his diary he displays all the snobbery, prejudice and bigotry of his class and 'race'. But it would be pointless to judge him against the 'politically correct' standards of our own times. He was an honest, conscientious, hard working, brave man who possessed in abundance what Napoleon required of his generals, luck. Men standing beside him were killed by bomb and bullet; he was never touched. His hat, his water bottle and his pack were all, at different times, on different fronts, rent or shattered by bullets or shrapnel, he remained unscarred. He did become a victim of malaria and who knows what discomfort that would bring him throughout the rest of his life, but, despite being in the firing line in Gallipoli, Salonika, Palestine and the Somme, he emerged from the Great War otherwise unscathed.

And he has left behind him a fascinating account of the terror, horror, ennui, humour and pathos of a seedy war fought by decent men for the threadbare ideals of the European ascendancy.

# 5   The Battle of the Somme

> We beat them on the Marne
> We beat them on the Aisne
> We gave them hell
> At Neuve Chapelle
> And here we are again!

The song sung by many British troops as they prepared for the cataclysm of the Somme was an inappropriate anthem for the men of the 36th Ulster Division. They had anthems of their own which had helped instil a formidable *esprit de corps* and they were relatively untested volunteer troops for whom the Marne and the Aisne held no particular resonance. There was no unit quite like them in Kitchener's Army and certainly none amongst the well pruned ranks of the 'Old Contemptibles'. The closest equivalent were their southern counterparts in the 16th Irish Division, as overwhelmingly (though not exclusively) nationalist as the 36th was unashamedly (though not uniformly) unionist. Although of divisional strength only, this was not a mere divison. This was an army, a homogenous unit of covenanters, based on a politically motivated militia, pledged, ironically, both to defy the authority of the British Empire if necessary while determined to prove its atavistic loyalty to that same Empire. The division was 'unparalleled for its kind since Cromwell's "Ironsides" in enlisting stern religious fervour and political enthusiasm in a fighting phalanx.'[1] Its mettle and motivation would be tested in the searing kiln that was the Somme battlefield on 1 July 1916. Though many other Irish units were in action on that hideous day no story has quite the poignancy of that of the Ulster Division.

The Somme offensive was a product of the 'body-count' battle of Verdun in which the Germans and the French were bleeding each other white. To relieve pressure on the French the British Commander-in-Chief, Field Marshal Sir Douglas Haig, began planning a summer offensive in January 1916. The Fourth Army, based in Picardy, would provide the attacking force using five corps, with help from the French Sixth Army on its right. The plan was based on the concept of *force majeure*, with advances to be made along a wide front brought about by sheer weight of numbers and overwhelming artillery fire. Enthusiasm for the offensive was heightened by assurances from the Royal Artillery that it now had the resources to annihilate the German front lines and so shatter the morale of the few remaining defenders that the infantry could, so to speak, walk the ball into an open goal. Unfortunately such a concept contained within it the virus which would devastate the entire plan. The Royal Artillery overestimated the effectiveness of its own poorly mass-produced ordnance, underestimated the strength of the German defences and the mental toughness of the defenders. Additionally the nature of the assault itself, 'stereotyped attacks and robbed commanders of initiative'.[2]

When the 36th arrived in the Somme sector in the Spring of 1916 it was one of the quietest on the entire front. An aggressive policy of raiding followed their arrival as the British sought as much intelligence as possible on the strongpoints which would threaten the summer offensive. The division was allocated a front, approximately 3000 yards wide, which was bisected by the River Ancre and by marshy ground on either side. (It is one of the ironies of Unionist Ulster's evocative commemoration of the 'Somme' that the division never actually fought near the river itself.) The Ancre meandered lazily through the low-lying land which fronted and flanked the Ulster positions. Immediately behind their front line lay Thiepval Wood, which offered both an inviting sanctuary for concealed troops and an obvious target for German artillery. To the south of the Ulster sector lay the village of Thiepval itself, in front of lines occupied by the 32nd Division. Directly in front of the 36th's own lines was the tiny hamlet of St Pierre Davion, on the southern banks of the Ancre. To the north of the 36th's positions the British lines were occupied by the men of the 29th Division, recently evacuated from Gallipoli, and including the 1st Dublins and 1st Inniskillings; the 1st Munsters had been transferred to the 16th (Irish) Division.

The Ulstermen had ample time to study what could be seen of the impressive edifice they were being asked to capture. Not that there was that much to admire in the overpowering Schwaben Redoubt which was visible from the British lines. Like a menacing and destructive iceberg, its secrets and its strengths were largely subterranean. The Germans had built the Redoubt to last. It was a series of underground caverns which linked machine-gun emplacements. Liberal use had been made of concrete in its construction and the accommodation provided in its dugouts was so far below the surface (20–30 ft in most cases) as to be virtually impervious to even the most awesome artillery barrage. The German positions in the Ulster's section (and all along the front) overlooked and dominated those of their opponents. The Ulster advance, when it came, would be over rising ground and towards well protected positions.

Among the men of the 36th, under Maj.-Gen. Sir Hugh Nugent, waiting for the beginning of 'the Big Push' were larger-than-life characters like Lt.-

Col. Percy Crozier (later Brigadier). An intensely disagreeable and mean-spirited man, he commanded the 9th Royal Irish Rifles, a battalion which derived its complement from the streets of working-class West Belfast. Crozier called them 'my Shankhill boys'. A small pudgy figure with a thin wispy moustache, he was, in many respects, the epitome of the cartoon-British officer class. He had been too short and too underweight to join the Army in 1896. By 1914 he was still too short but not even a distorting mirror could have altered his well-fed appearance. He would gain a reputation as a martinet (he was also a reformed alcoholic) who delighted in 'knocking the beer and politics' out of his Belfast unionists, although he was a convinced loyalist himself. Crozier survived the war and would go on to write about his experiences, memoirs which included one of the most tastelessly titled books ever to pass through a printing press, *The Men I Killed*. During the War of Independence Crozier saw service with the notorious 'Auxiliaries' but, to his credit, resigned from this gang of glorified murderers in protest at the policy of official reprisals.

Crozier's batman and connection to the real world was Cpl. David Starret, a wily Northerner whose own (far more entertaining) memoirs remain. It is often interesting to compare the perspective of the two men on the same set of jointly-experienced events. Starret's recollections are probably far more in tune with the emotions of the men of West Belfast than the subjective and self-serving utterances of his commanding officer.

The 9th Rifles were part of the 107th Brigade (the 36th Division encompassed the 107th, 108th and 109th). One of its brother battalions in the Brigade was the 10th Rifles (mostly recruited from South Belfast and based, like the other battalions of the Division, on the UVF unit from that area). It was led by Lt.-Col. N.G. Bernard, a cousin of the Church of Ireland archbishop of Dublin. Crozier and Bernard were to be unique amongst the commanders of the 36th during the forthcoming battle. An order had been issued for the CO's of those Fourth Army battalions taking part in the 1 July assault to remain at battalion HQ and not to lead their troops into action. It was an edict which was bitterly resented by many senior officers and, as the second-in-command of most battalions also, habitually, remained behind, it meant that many units going into battle (and these were raw troops!) had no one above the rank of captain leading them. Crozier would have none of it: 'The "indecent" order had come from high up in the hierarchy—and well back from the front line. The rule of clerks was being employed where battlefield rule should have prevailed.'[3] Crozier and Bernard however, both agreed to ignore the order and proceed as if it had never been issued. The gesture cost Bernard his life. Crozier survived and was recommended for a VC. He was told, through channels, that it was touch and go whether he would get a VC or a court martial for insubordination, a compromise was reached and he got neither!

Among the other ranks of the 36th was a typically mixed bag of individuals, of different social and geographical backgrounds. There were farmers from the Glens of Antrim and merchants from Armagh cheek-by-jowl with rural labourers from Donegal. Bob Grange was a twenty-year-old from Ballyclare, Co. Antrim who was not greatly pleased to have been attached as a signaller for Forward Observation Officers to a French artillery brigade. He had joined up along with 53 comrades from the Mid-Antrim UVF on the first day of recruiting in Northern Ireland. Most of his friends from Ballyclare were members of C Company, 12th Royal Irish Rifles. Jack Christie, a Belfast man, was a stretcher-bearer. His family was reasonably wealthy, owning a public house and a confectionery shop on the Shankhill Road. He had found life in the retail trade drab and soulless and joining the army seemed like an adventurous alternative. Tommy Jordan, also from Belfast, was a sixteen-year-old when war broke out. His youth had frustrated his attempts to join the UVF who told him 'they wanted men not boys.' The army was not so choosy and he was barely eighteen years old when he found himself on the Somme with the 16th Royal Irish Rifles, the 36th Division's Pioneer Battalion.[4] Tommy Ervine, a shipyard worker from East Belfast, was a private in the 8th Royal Irish Rifles Though small in stature he was a keen amateur boxer and had already proved himself handy with a bayonet, when the need would arise, on night patrols and raids.

For the purposes of the assault on 1 July (postponed by two days because of heavy rain) the 36th's front was divided in four. The area north of the Ancre river was primarily the responsibility of the 108th Brigade. The section of the line south of the river was not to be frontally attacked and the marshy area which interrupted the 36th's trenches was flooded with gas shells to make it unusable by the enemy. The principal onslaught would come from the 109th Brigade, and elements of the 108th on the Schwaben Redoubt and a landmark on the road between Thiepval and Grandcourt called the Crucifix. The 107th Brigade (which included Crozier's and Bernard's battalions) was to be held in reserve. The German lines were to be pummelled by an artillery barrage of awesome destructiveness for days before the final assault. This already concentrated bombardment would be further intensified an hour before the 'off'. Then, as the first wave of troops approached the advanced German trench line (the A line) the barrage would lift and move forward to the next line (B) and so on, through C until it would finally pulverise the German reserve trenches (D)

Altogether some 170,000 shells were expended during the preliminary bombardment, though far too many on 1 July, from a British point of view, were duds which failed to explode. For five days and nights the Germans were subjected to the kind of treatment they had meted out to the French at Verdun. 'As one watched the big shells bursting, sending up huge columns of earth, day after day, it appeared as though no life could continue in that tortured and blasted area.'[5] Years later, his writing flavoured with a tincture of hindsight, another Irishman, Pte. Anthony Brennan (2nd Royal Irish Regiment) stationed near Mametz to the south, an area remote from Thiepval, wrote in much the same terms,

> ... a seemingly endless line of big guns—wheel to wheel almost—sent out a continuous chain of projectiles towards the trenches of the long suffering Boche ... it seemed as if we had completely silenced him and our job on the morrow promised to be an easy walk over ... Rations and 'rum issues' were plentiful that evening. We were being fattened for the slaughter. Some of us may have guessed it, but few could have thought that the Somme was to call for such a ghastly toll in human lives.[6]

Gaps had been cut in the British barbed wire to allow access to no man's land, and it was assumed the shelling would have ripped apart the formidable German wire defences. The troops, went the cocksure official line, would have a relatively easy task of mopping up the few shell shocked and demoralised Germans who had not been blown to pieces by the barrage. At this stage in the war the men of the Ulster Division were unused to being lied to by army propagandists, but not all the men accepted the confident prediction that they were destined for little more than a lively summer stroll. One soldier, a former teacher, wrote to the Secretary of his Orange Lodge.

> There is no doubt that when you receive this note I will be dead. There are all the signs that something bigger than has ever taken place before in this war is about to be launched. The more I brood on what may happen the surer I am I shall not survive it. All of us say 'It'll be the other fellow who'll be killed'. I feel that I am one of those other fellows.[7]

The night before 'The Big Push', Col. Percy Crozier came upon one of the men in his battalion, named Campbell, 'showing a light' against specific instructions. He ordered the young soldier to put the light out. Campbell explained that 'I am writing a letter home, Sir, it will be my last, and I just feel like it ... I am very sorry, sir, I shouldn't have done it.' Campbell gave his letter to Crozier to post and, sure enough, was killed the following day.[8]

And the bombardment was, of course, not all one way. In the Ulster's sector one of the favourite German targets was Thiepval Wood, which they supposed, correctly, was being used to conceal and shelter troops. On an hourly basis troops in the front line trenches were coming under German retaliatory bombardment. William John Lynas was a 27-year-old UVF man from the staunchly loyalist Tiger's Bay area who had joined the North Belfast Volunteers. In general the established UVF battalions had simply transferred *en bloc* into the British Army and his unit had become the 15th Royal Irish Rifles. Two weeks after the offensive he wrote to his wife Mina about the fighting and its prelude. He had been wounded but cheated death in what he called a

> miraculous escape. It was on the night of a big bombardment and a shell paid us a visit in our dug-out. As soon as I realised what happened I scrambled out of the debris as best as I could [and] made for the door to feel if it was blocked up as we were choking, the gas from the shell near suffocating us ... I was a little bit shaken at the time but I had a bit of work in front of me so I got stuck into it and forgot about my calamity. It was for work done on that night that I was commended to my Colonel and Company Officer. For what ever little bit of good work I done I consider I only done my duty the only thing I can say is that I hope I will be spared to do many a little turn for our boys in the trenches.[9]

Lynas was promoted to Lance-Corporal on foot of the commendation. He survived the war and was demobilised in 1919 but by then his lungs had been permanently damaged by gas and he died in the early 1920s.

For many of the men of the 36th what they faced was more than a mere offensive conducted at the behest of faceless generals many miles to the rear of the front lines. The loyalists of the 36th were imbued with a sense of mission. They were fighting, as a race apart, to prove their loyalty to King, Country and Religion. Who knows how many had felt cheated of a fight with the menace of Irish nationalism by the suspension of Home Rule on the outbreak of war. The coincidence of the anniversary of the Battle of the Boyne, to a people so much in thrall to their history, would have been just another positive omen. This *ex post facto* defining event in the canon of unionist shibboleths had taken place exactly 226 years before (owing to a change from the Julian to the Gregorian calendar in 1752 it has been celebrated in modern times on 12 July). As far as Lt. Cyril Falls of the Inniskillings was concerned 'the extra strain of waiting was more than counterbalanced by the coincidence of the date.'[10]

There have been many recent arguments, prompted by the mould-breaking Frank McGuinness play *Observe the Sons of Ulster Marching towards the Somme*, as to whether or not Orange sashes were worn into battle. McGuinness has the men of his fictional unit adorn themselves with their sashes before going over the top. Journalist and historian Kevin Myers has argued vehemently that the men of the 36th did not wear their Orange finery into battle. McGuinness, of course, does not claim that they did. The action of *his* soldiers in so doing was purely symbolic. But some men undoubtedly did adorn themselves with the colour orange. Rifleman Edward Taylor of the West Belfast Volunteers, Crozier's 9th Rifles, recalled that the battalion's second-in-command Major Gaffikin 'took out an orange handkerchief and, waving it around his head, shouted, 'Come on, boys, this is the first of July!' (Crozier's own memoirs, in part, confirm this.) Another observer noted that 'One Sergeant of the Inniskillings went into the fray with his Orange sash on him. Some of the men provided themselvs with Orange lilies before they went up to the assembly trenches.'[11]

Calvinistic influences and the resulting high percentage of teetotallers among the ranks of the 36th meant that when the rum ration was issued many were able to consume so much that they were anaesthetised going into battle. As they waited, in the dank mist of the early morning, for zero hour many of the men prayed, some wrote final letters home, some made out their wills. Maj.-Gen. Nugent, in an inspired moment, had ordered that the men leave the trenches before the barrage finished, to be that much closer to their objective when the guns lifted and moved onto the next trench line. This order was to prove crucial in the almost unprecedented gains made on 1 July by his Division.

But the first major mistake of the day had already been made. The British and French commanders had argued long and hard over the timing of the first assault wave. Many of the British commanders (though not Haig) favoured the period just before dawn; the French, reliant on their powerful artillery, wanted the opening raids to be in daylight to allow for better targetting by their forward artillery observers. The French won the argument. It was already broad daylight as the Ulstermen filed through the gaps in the wire watching the ground shake a few hundred yards in front of them, some experiencing an empathy that passes understanding for the Germans they believed to be dying miserably by the score under the British shells. The whistles were scheduled to sound the advance at 7.30 a.m. A short time earlier the pre-dawn twilight and a heavy early morning mist would have made it difficult for the German defenders to see their adversaries. By 7.30 a.m. the only visual protection afforded the attacking troops was the smoke and mud being thrown up by the bombardment. By the time they started moving forward the shells would be dropping elsewhere.

Then came the second major mistake of the day. At approximately 7.20 a huge mine, dug by sappers in the 29th Division's sector and packed with high explosive, was triggered near Beaumont Hammel. All around the nearby countryside the earth shook. The Germans took this as a clear signal that the main event was about to begin. They readied themselves for the lifting of the barrage and the arrival of the troops who would follow the shells.

The Ulstermen assembled, watched by their senior officers. Some, already burdened enough for a gallop across a thousand yards of rising ground, carried rolls of barbed wire, which would be used to secure the gains they were confident were going to be made. Lt.-Col. Ambrose Ricardo, CO of the 9th Inniskillings, one of the majority who obeyed the instruction not to accompany his troops into battle, wrote that he would

> never forget for one minute the extraordinary sight. The Derrys, on our left, were so eager they started a few minutes before the ordered time, and the Tyrones were not going to be left behind, and they got going without delay—no fuss, no shouting, no running; everything orderly, solid and thorough, just like the men themselves. Here and there a boy would wave his hand to me as I shouted 'Good Luck' to them through my megaphone, and all had a happy face.[12]

Lt.-Col. Macrory of the 10th Inniskillings watched 'lines of men moving forward, with rifles sloped and the sun glistening upon their fixed bayonets, keeping their alignment and distance as well as if on a ceremonial parade, unfaltering, unwavering.'[13] Just before zero hour a solitary German, probably suffering badly from dugout fever after five days of shelling, jumped into one of the 36th's forward saps and offered to surrender. He was fortunate, as Tommy Ervine recalled, that he was not shot by troops who were wound taut.

> I made him turn round and searched him all over in case he had any weapons but he'd nothing of that kind. I even took his pocketbook out and I saw his children's and his wife's photograph. I patted him on the shoulder and told him to 'Go down that way' ... How he got there I don't know.[14]

Sergeant Jim Maultsaid of the 14th Royal Irish Rifles, an American citizen, born in Pennsylvania of Irish parents (he had returned to live in Donegal at the age of six), and a talented artist, was waiting in shallow trenches in Aveluy wood in the hours before the offensive began. German retaliatory bombardment had begun to denude the wood. Fires had broken out all around. Maultsaid found it impossible to talk to his comrades, amid the incessant din. He tried to remain composed during the hours before dawn but found his thoughts becoming more and more morbid as he dwelt on the horrors that might occur when the attack began. Another Ulsterman compared the tumultuous vigil to

> waiting for someone to die. You know it's coming and you wish to God it was over and done with. You smoked fag after fag, took sips of water, oiled the rifle, did everything over and over again. Even above the shelling you could hear small noises like a man sucking air in between his teeth and this got on your nerves more than the shelling.[15]

As dawn broke Cpl. David Starret brought Col. Percy Crozier hot water for shaving. The Belfast corporal had lain ' ... waiting for dawn. Not an easy thing to do at best of times and hell then, when all nerves were keyed up.'[16] As he shaved Crozier listened to the men offering words of encouragement to each other. Then, 'The whistle blows. The men fall in, in fours, in their companies, on the Hamel Albert Road. The battalion is reported present! Zero hour is at 7.30 a.m. All is quiet in the Western front. It is now 6.45 a.m. A pin could be heard to drop.'[17] Crozier's second-in-command, Maj. George Gaffikin, was aware of the Colonel's plans to go over the top with his men.

> 'Stick close to the Colonel, Starret.' he told the batman. 'He's one in a thousand. Too good to be lost. Good luck!' He went about his duty, and that was the last sight I had of him and word from him, for he was among the killed ... Quiet everywhere—you would have thought the war had ended. We fell in and moved off, woodbines in mouth, across the Ancre swamp. A couple of shells fell. 'Jerry has woke up!'[18]

The men of the 36th Ulster Division, in common with so many other units that day, won a bucketful of gallantry medals (including four VC's). Before the division even ventured into no man's land the incident which would earn the Ulsters their first Victoria Cross had already taken place and led to the death of young Lurgan man Billy McFadzean, of the 14th Rifles. He had been handing out grenades from a pile of wooden boxes while German shells rocked the ground around the trenches. A sudden blast shifted one of the boxes from the unsteady pile and two of the grenades shed their pins as they tumbled to the ground. Their proximity to the rest of the grenades made it certain that when they went off a fearsome explosion would rip through that section of trench and kill dozens of the men packed into it. McFadzean must have known he was going to die but, in less than the time it took for the grenades to explode, decided that he would die alone. He threw himself on top of the grenades and muffled the blast. Only one of his comrades was injured. As his broken body was stretchered away many of the men who owed him their lives took off their steel helmets as he passed, despite the incessant German barrage. Some wept openly. By the days' end, they would have few tears left to shed.

Undoubtedly Billy McFadzean had simply saved many of the men of the 14th Royal Irish Rifles so that they could stop German machine-gun bullets instead. That was to be the fate of hundreds of Ulstermen on 1 July. As the British bombardment of the first line of German trenches lifted and passed on to the B line beyond, north and south of the river Ancre the men of the 108th and 109th Brigades began to move across no man's land. In another of the symbolic ironies of that day the 9th Royal Irish Fusiliers, mostly recruited in Armagh, Monaghan and Cavan, were attacking between two points called William and Mary. They were accompanied by the men of Mid-Antrim, the 12th Royal Irish Rifles. Their ultimate target was Beaucourt sur Ancre, more than a mile away from their trenches, north of the river. A few hundred yards in front of their positions was a ravine which slowed their progress considerably. The first wave of the attack (said to have left their lines shouting 'No Surrender') must have been convinced that the optimistic forecasts about an unopposed advance were actually true. They found the wire sufficiently well cut to allow them through. They met little opposition as they charged forward. One platoon even made it all the way to the railway station outside Beaucourt. Most were never heard of again as the mouth of the Venus fly-trap closed behind them.

The reason for the initial lack of opposition was probably the length of time it took the Germans to confirm for themselves that the barrage had moved on and to get out of their well-protected dugouts and into position. Because the second wave of attackers met a hail of machine-gun and rifle bullets. They were lucky. The last two waves were almost totally annihilated by fire coming from the trenches in front of them and from Beaumont Hamel further to the North. In that sector the 29th Division had failed to make any progress. 'The bullets literally came like water from an immense hose with a perforated top' recalled one Ulsterman, while another could see 'the bullets in the air and it looked like a fine shower of hail, you know the way hail looks as if it's thinning out and the sun behind it.'[19] Many of those who made it as far as the German barbed wire funnelled through the few openings, relieved that they had found them, only to be hosed by machine-guns which were trained on those breaches. Bob Grange's friends from Ballyclare died or were wounded almost to a man in that charge. 'They had about the longest part of no man's land to cross over of any of the other battalions that were attacking.' Grange, even at the age of ninety, clung to the belief that his friends should have been moved up to the sunken road which crossed no man's land in their sector and been asked to attack from there: 'That would have been half the distance to cross ... In Ballyclare alone that day, out of the small community that we had there, there were over thirty men killed and over one hundred wounded ... an awful total for such a community.'[20]

The attack north of the Ancre was abandoned by 8 a.m., those who had made it across to the German front line and beyond made their way back as best they could. Right across no man's land men lay dead, unconscious or writhing in agony and wishing for unconsciousness. Some had the courage to leave the relative security of the trenches and bring in the wounded. Lt. G. Cather of the 9th Irish Fusiliers did so repeatedly under fire from machine-guns. Finally his luck ran out and as he was carrying in another wounded man he was killed himself. He was awarded a posthumous Victoria Cross. Pte. Robert Quigg of the 12th Rifles lived to receive his VC personally. He was the servant of Lt. Sir Harry Macnaghten of Dundaraye. Macnaghten had twice managed to reorganise his company for an attack on the German trenches before he was killed going through a gap in the wire. Nine times Quigg left the British trench line to go out into no mans land and look for his officer. He spent, in all, seven hours crawling and stumbling amid the churned-up ground, the shell holes and the countless corpses. Each time he came back he brought with him a wounded man, the last one he dragged on a waterproof sheet from within a few yards of the German wire. Sometimes ordinary men can do extraordinary things.

Just as the carnage north of the Ancre was exacerbated by the failure of the 29th Division, on the left of the 36th, to make any progress around Beaumont Hamel, so would the failure of the 32nd Division, on the Ulster-men's other flank, have horrendous consequences for the attack on the Schwaben Redoubt and the Crucifix. The latter, however, was characterised as a 'success', at least in military terms. In human terms it was catastrophic. For the historian of the 36th, 'Elsewhere for all its losses, the attack was a complete success. Every objective was reached. Had it been possible to attain the same results all along the front, the day would have ended with the greatest British victory of the war.'[21] But no other unit along the Somme achieved as much as did the 36th, and given their losses that is, perhaps, just as well. The gains made by the Ulsters, against terrifying odds, were of no military consequence as they could not be exploited, so widespread had the failures been elsewhere. The 36th reached its objectives south of the Ancre 'though with such dear sacrifice of men that there was won nothing but glory'.[22]

The 9th and 11th Inniskillings and the 14th Rifles were among the first groups into action. As they advanced up the slope towards the Schwaben Redoubt they were hit by enfilading fire (fire from the right or left flank) from the guns in Thiepval. Gaps began to appear in the ranks as men fell but the first line of trenches was taken on schedule. What puzzled the Ulstermen was the sight of hundreds of German soldiers scattering to their positions as the Irish advanced, first at walking pace, then trotting and finally at a canter as they neared the German wire and charged forward. What had become of the 'token opposition'? The millions of pounds of high-explosive expended on the German lines should have killed everything but the rats.

Jack Christie was a stretcher-bearer with the 36th. The busiest and most hazardous day of his young life lay ahead of him. He shared the surprise of many of his comrades when

> ... to the amazement of everyone, the German machine-gunners appeared on their trenches and started to mow our fellas down ... really the Germans were very brave people, they're great soldiers, because it was bad enough for us hanging behind the bombardment, but we weren't getting the same shelling as they were getting. They were getting, as we thought, cut to pieces, but their dug-outs were so good, so strong that we weren't breaking through the dug-outs at all, we were only ploughing up the surface of the trenches, it was a shambles.[23]

The huge casualties taken by the Ulsters that day were, as we shall see, a function of their success in seizing their objectives. Because of Nugent's policy of placing his men in no man's land they did not share the experience of other Northern Irish units of the Regular Army who were involved elsewhere in the line. The 1st Inniskilling Fusiliers (along with the 1st Dublins) wasted their strength at Beaumont Hamel in the sector adjoining that of the Ulsters. On the other flank of the 36th the guns of Thiepval claimed the lives of hundreds of troops of the 32nd Division. Among them were men of the 2nd Inniskillngs. Charles Miller had the job that day of liasion between the battalion and Brigade Headquarters as the attack went forward. Except that the attack didn't go anywhere.

> It might have been a pretty hazardous job but actually it was a complete sinecure. There was no need to tell the brigade where the 2nd Inniskilling Fusiliers were that day. Three companies of them were lying like swathes of corn within twenty yards of our line. Mortal man cannot get through a sort of tier of machine-gun bullets knee high, breast high and head high so they could only go as far as possible and then die because the Higher Command had under-estimated the skill of the Germans in building concealed concrete machine-gun emplacements. The Brigadier stopped the fourth company from attacking and was very nearly Stellenbosched for so doing by the Divisional General.[24]

As another observer put it 'only bullet-proof soldiers could have taken Thiepval that day.'[25]

Despite heavy losses the Ulstermen of the 36th Division beat enough of the Germans to the trench parapets to make their way, as per timetable, through the first three lines of trenches. It is hard, even for those who were involved in the mayhem and murder, to convey the impression of the chaos and slaughter of the early minutes of that ultimately futile assault. Many, to their dying day, resolutely refused to talk about it. Some (incuding a disproportionate number of medal-winners) suffered their own private hell in the years that followed. Men watched their friends, quite literally, die screaming, torn to pieces by shells. Some talked of standing outside themselves in an ethereal daze and watching as they, in their turn, were hit. All around the earth was being churned up by German shells or British 'unders' [shells which fell short, onto one's own troops], it didn't matter, they were equally deadly whatever the source. Bullets 'fizzed' and 'hissed' past some before finding a target, any target, in the lottery of battle.

As well as coming under fire from their flanks and from the front the men of the 108th and 109th Brigades were also hit from the rear. The job of the first waves of attackers was to take a trench line and move on. It was left up to others coming behind, particularly bombers, to ensure that the trenches were properly secured. This they often failed to do, for a number of reasons. Those bombers who survived the death-race across no man's land to reach the Redoubt were to toss grenades into German dugouts. But they didn't always manage to get to the entrances before the Germans emerged. And some German dugouts had spiral staircases which prevented the bombs from dropping into the chamber where the troops were sheltering. Some bombs simply failed to go off. The upshot was that as each wave of Ulstermen passed through the first trenches German riflemen and machine-gunners kept popping up behind them to shoot them in the back.

Long before he made it to the A line, Pte. Robert Monteith, of Lislap, near Omagh, Co. Tyrone, had his leg blown off above the knee. Using his rifle as a crutch he continued to advance. Lt. William Arthur Hewitt, also of the 9th Inniskillings, was killed on his own dash to the Schwaben Redoubt. His brother, Lt. Holt Montgomery Hewitt, a machine-gun officer, would also die on 1 July. Their brother, Lt. Ernest Henry Hewitt, had been killed the previous year. All three brothers were prominent rugby players. John Kennedy Hope of the 14th Rifles witnessed the appalling fate of another Inniskilling as a bullet penetrated his steel helmet:

> He rolls over into the trenches at my feet. He is an awful sight. his brain is oozing out of the side of his head and he is calling for his pal. An occasional cry of 'Billy Gray, Billy Gray will you not come to me?' In a short time all is quiet, he is dead. He's the servant to an officer

who is lying in the trench with a fractured thigh and won't let anyone touch him, and he is bleeding badly. They die together.[26]

Capt. Eric Bell of the 9th Inniskillings, a trench mortar officer, seemed less fazed than most by 'the Devil's Dwelling Place'. He took out a German machine-gun emplacement single-handedly with the aid of only his service revolver. Later he cleared a trench with hand grenades and when these ran out tossed in trench mortars instead. As the 9th's attack ran out of steam later in the day and the Germans were counter-attacking, he stood in an exposed position picking them off with a rifle he had managed to find among the dead. He died defending the 36th's gains and was awarded the Victoria Cross. His namesake Leslie Bell of the 10th Inniskillings (who died in February 1995) was with 13 Platoon, in D Company of his battalion. 'We were hit in no man's land when a shell landed on 13 platoon and wiped them out. I was hit in the leg and back. I lay out all day and night. That finished my war.'[27] But only as an infantryman. Bell did not completely recover from his wounds but finished the war as a driver for the Army Service Corps.

Lt. Henry Gallaugher, of the 11th Inniskillings, a man from Manorcunningham, in northern Co. Donegal probably deserved a VC as well, but the military is jealous of its awards and so many were given to others that his actions were 'merely' considered worthy of the Distinguished Service Order. To describe Gallaugher (whose name is often incorrectly spelled as Gallagher) as a 'Southern' unionist would be something of a misnomer. Geographically, his stamping ground was much further north than that of most 'Northern' unionists, but the nomenclature of partition now places Donegal in the 'South' and, for example, Fermanagh in the 'North'. The Orange tradition in Donegal took much longer to wither than in other 'Southern' border counties. Gallaugher was simply a pre-partition unionist. He was educated in Derry and Letterkenny and was a Company commander in the Manorcunningham branch of the Ulster Volunteer Force at the outbreak of war. Soon after he joined the 11th Royal Inniskilling Fusiliers he became Battalion Transport Officer. But Gallaugher, as his letters show, wanted to be more involved in the action than his status would allow. He volunteered to go over the top with his battalion on 1 July 1916 and was given charge of a platoon. He was the most fortunate officer in the battalion that day, the only one to survive the encounter uninjured, despite placing himself in the thick of the fighting. (Another officer of his battalion, critical of some men of his company's tardiness in reaching the German lines that day, recieved the riposte, 'Sorry, Sir, but we were delayed coming through Hell'.)[28]

After early casualties among the officers Gallaugher took charge of the attack on one of the Inniskilling's objectives, the Crucifix. On the way he killed six German snipers who were inflicting serious casualties on his platoon. By the time he got to the Crucifix he had only nine men left. They organised a flimsy defensive barricade and Gallaugher went back to the German trenches to the rear, which had already been overrun, to round up some more support. A regimental account of the battle indicates baldly that

> in carrying out these details he came in contact with several parties of Germans, which he killed or took prisoners. On arriving at the Crucifix he found Major Gaffikin, 9th Royal Irish Rifles, in command, and he returned to the B line, where his Battalion was.

Gallaugher also managed, along with a Lt. Austin from the 10th Inniskillings, to rescue a subaltern from the enemy barbed wire and carry him back to the British trenches. Two nights later Gallaugher was back in action again, having volunteered to accompany a party of 20 others to rescue wounded in no man's land. They succeeded in bringing in 28 between 10 p.m. and 2.30 a.m. After the first day of the Somme battle he wrote to his father, 'I am sorry some of our boys are missing. I don't think Ulstermen have betrayed the trust, and I think the Inniskillings led the way. We are all proud of our old 109th Brigade; it was the first Brigade complimented by the Army Commander.'[29] Gallaugher lived through the fighting of 1 July 1916 but died in the 36th's next major offensive at Messines the following year.

The plan for the 36th had been to hold the 107th Brigade in reserve for the final push against the furthest line of German trenches. But within an hour of the 'off' it became clear to Nugent that this move would be pointless. With the 29th and the 32nd having made no forward progress on either side the Ulster division had already created a dangerous salient or bulge in the lines which could be exploited by a German counter-attack. He asked for permission to delay the 107th's advance, at least until the 32nd had made some inroads on the guns of Thiepval village. Permission was denied as the intention of the planners was to try and push both the 29th and 32nd forward again. So the 107th was ordered up shortly after 8.30 a.m. Three-quarters of an hour later that decision was rescinded and the 107th was told to wait. But the order had come too late. The brigade was already on its way across no-man's-land to the trenches held by the Ulstermen in the Schwaben Redoubt.

As they moved off some of the men of the 9th Rifles picked up coils of wire and iron posts which they were expected to carry with them into battle. Their CO Percy Crozier was dubious; he didn't anticipate any of the hardware reaching its destination. He said goodbye to Major George Gaffikin, his second-in-command, who carried an orange handkerchief with him into battle. Gaffikin had had an accurate premonition of his own death and asked Crozier to 'tell them I died a teetotaller, put it on the stone if you find me.'[30] As his men moved into forward positions Crozier spotted the 10th Rifles (led

by Lt.-Col. Bernard) in front. He then looked to his right and watched the
32nd Division being mangled at Thiepval, still held by the Germans. He
described the '... heaped up masses of British corpses suspended on the
German wire in front of the Thiepval stronghold, while live men rush forward in orderly procession to swell the weight of numbers in the spider's
web.'[31]

Tommy Ervine of the 8th Royal Irish, the East Belfast Volunteers, was hit
a few yards after the whistle sent him into action.

> I was looking about and I spotted the fellow that done it, I could just
> see him moving, he was in round hole. The men had to go down into
> the water to get to the line and as they were coming up through that
> water the German must have had his sights trained on them and he
> was shooting them. He spotted me and that's where he hit me. But
> then I fired back at him later on and I hit him on the face.[32]

Corporal David Starret moved, with Crozier,

> into [an] inferno of screaming shells and machine-gun bullets. Crouch-
> ing, we slowly moved across no man's land. The Colonel stood giving
> last orders to his company commanders, and I beside him. Bullets
> cutting up the ground at his feet he watched the advance through his
> glasses. Then he went off the deep end and I danced everywhere at his
> rear. Something had gone wrong. When the fumes lifted we saw what
> it was—a couple of battalions wiped out. Masses of dead and dying
> instead of ranks moving steadily forward.[33]

Crozier, despite his girth, began a frenetic dash forward to retrieve the situation. By his own admission Starret makes

> a bad second in the race. 'The Tenth Rifles are wiped out!' he shouted.
> We reached our own men. They had taken what cover the place af-
> forded. Bernard had been killed. Crozier rallied what was left of the
> Tenth. 'Sound the advance!' he yelled. 'Sound: damn you: Sound the
> advance!' The bugler's lips were dry. He had been wounded. His lungs
> were gone. A second later he fell dead at the colonel's feet.

The bugle is given to someone who can play and Crozier continues forward.
'He walked into bursts, he fell into holes, his clothing was torn by bullets, but
he himself was all right. Moving about as if on the parade ground he again
and again rallied his men ... without him not a man would have passed the
Schwaben Redoubt, let alone reach the final objective ...'.[34] But when the 9th

Rifles and the other battalions of the 107th went beyond the Schwaben Redoubt and reached the German D line (the limit of the 36th's advance that day) they found it full of reserves and were forced to backtrack:

> Of that last wild and desperate venture across a thousand yards of open country, few returned to tell the tale. Those that did tell of an entry into that last entrenchment, of desperate hand-to-hand fighting, and then, when the odds were too great ... of a stubborn retirement to the next line.35

They were harrassed all the way as they attempted to regroup in the C line.

As Tommy Ervine and his comrades of the East Belfast Volunteers (8th Royal Irish Rifles) made their way into action, Ervine noticed a man beside whom he had slept the night before come staggering back. He had been hit in the head and as he opened his mouth to speak blood poured from it in rhythmic spurts. He did what he could for him and continued towards the German lines to assist the men of the two brigades who had already taken them. A burst of shrapnel, however, immobilised him and a half dozen of his comrades.

> There I was. I couldn't move very well because I didn't know exactly what my leg was like, I thought it had burst everything and that my leg was no good. But then I held onto something and found I could walk a bit. So I went along with the rest of them but I only got about twenty yards when a shell burst over my head. They were all behind me and there were about five or six of them blown to bits. I was lucky again because I got shrapnel all over me, the back of my neck and my shoulders and I knew nothing more after that.36

Tommy Ervine was found by stretcher-bearers and brought to safety. His injuries were so serious that he never rejoined his (shattered) battalion.

Now a new problem became apparent, that of resupplying the troops holding out in the Schwaben Redoubt. They needed ammunition and water, not just to slake their fearsome thirsts but to keep their machine-guns operational. 'But Thiepval's guns were still firing, and no man's land was a land of death',37 so re-supply was a hazardous and potentially deadly job. Efforts were made by bands of men to bring supplies forward, but these groups were mostly shot to pieces. No man's land was not a place where the wise would raise their heads, so a decision was taken to dig, there and then, a communications trench to help the resupply effort. A start was made, but that plan too had to be abandoned. It was a case of waiting until dark or braving the shrapnel and bullets being targetted at anything which moved among the dead and the dying.

An unidentified private, who was fortunate to survive the day, wrote to his parents about no man's land as it had appeared to him during his spells on sentry duty before 1 July: 'How calm and peaceful it looked then; how fresh, green and invitingly cool looked that long, blowing grass! Now what a ghastly change! Not a level or green spot remained. Great, jagged, gaping craters covered the blackish, smoking ground ...'. When he made it, unscathed, to the German trenches he told his family how he had looked back over the ground which he had just covered and saw the men behind him still advancing:

> You couldn't hear them for the noise of the guns and the exploding shells. Everywhere among those fearless Ulstermen burst high explosive shells, hurling dozens of them up in the air, while above them and among them shrapnel bursts with sharp ear-splitting explosions. But worst of all was the silent swish, swish, swishing of the machine-gun bullets, claiming their victims by the score, cutting down living sheaves and leaving bunches of writhing, tortured flesh on the ground.[38]

Sgt. James Maultsaid, of the 14th Rifles, whose sketches capture as much of the reality of war as many a photograph, left a graphic account of his own misadventures in no man's land:

> The slopes of Thiepval run red with the blood of Ulstermen—dead in heaps, dying in hundreds. God above us this is glorious war! Huddled together, surrounded, the end is near. Rifle flashes stab the half darkness. Friend and foe are now almost unrecognisable. All is utter confusion. Every man for himself. We are fighting back to back, a last hope. Bullets nip and zip around us. The gunflashes of the Germans are not 30 yards away. We yield ground as little parties are simply wiped away, clean away. Survivors crawl back, turn around, fight, then retreat again, but still facing their front, dying in their tracks.

Finally Maultsaid too was hit by what felt like a 'thousand ton hammer'.

> Anger and annoyance struggle for mastery. Then blood, blood, blood everywhere. All over me. I can feel it. I sink down. It rushes in a hot quick gush from my mouth. It streams over my breast and the back of my neck. In the name of God where am I hit? I try to lift my right arm up to my head. It refuses to act. Thoughts run through my brain. My

right arm gone! Will I never be able to box again, or sketch? Hell, I'm finished.

But Maultsaid was fortunate, found by two infantrymen (whose names he never discovered) he was carried to safety.

For the Royal Army Medical Corps and battalion stretcher-bearers, dealing with the returned wounded was becoming intolerably difficult. Their work had begun early, with the men who hadn't even made it past their own parapet. As one medical orderly put it,

> We were soon busy for a burst of machine-gun fire caught a lot of men as they climbed over and some of them fell shot at our feet. The ones we knew were dead we put in a dugout and started carrying the wounded to the posts. Some of the men were whistling Orange songs and now and again you'd get a few words from 'Dolly's Brae' or 'The Sash'.[39]

The whistling didn't last long. Jack Christie and his colleagues were part of a chain of bearers who worked until they collapsed with exhaustion:

> You were carrying day and night. There was no difference, you just walked up and down, and you were in a sort of sleep, you know, half conscious of what was going on. It was a terrible shambles ... we never again had anything like the casualties we had on the Somme.[40]

Davy Starret of the 9th Rifles watched ' ... our women workers, nurses and drivers, working at terrific speed, under fire, but working, and doing their job magnificently. I shall always remember that when I think of that Battle of the Somme.'[41] He had been despatched by Crozier to Battalion Advance Headquarters to bring up ammunition. His return journey was a harrowing one: 'Trenches and tops were blocked with the dead, but on days like that there's no sympathy in your heart. Over them you go ... twas hard passing men in terrible pain—men you knew.'[42] Jack Christie's friend Billy McCormick, from the Shankill Road, also a stretcher-bearer on 1 July, found it impossible to leave men in such a condition, even though he was in severe pain himself. He spent twelve straight hours ferrying the wounded to the Regimental Aid Post and did so with a lump of shrapnel in his arm. 'It was enough to get him honourably out of the way, he could have went [*sic*] back, got a dressing on it and been sent back ... but he didn't ... he went on carrying for another twelve hours and he got his medal for devotion to duty'.[43]

Even amid the carnage north and south of the banks of the Ancre individual acts of bravery did not go unnoticed. Like that of Cpl. Thomas McClay of Laghey, Co. Donegal, who led twenty German prisoners across no man's land single-handedly and then returned to the battle. Or Cpl. John Conn, of Caledon, who found two British machine-guns out of action. He repaired them and used them both to fend off a German flanking attack. Then, during a withdrawal he tried to carry both guns back but their sheer weight got the better of him and he had to abandon one of them. L/Cpl. Daniel Lyttle, from Leckpatrick, near Strabane, attempted a similar feat but found himself cut off. He fired off all the ammunition in one gun then destroyed both and used his bombs to get back to the rest of his group which was at the Crucifix. Cpl. Daniel Griffiths, from Dublin, L/Cpl. Lewis Pratt, from Cavan, and Pte. Fred Carter, from Kingstown (now Dun Laoire), together bombed or shot nine Germans and prevented them from mounting a machine-gun which would have inflicted even heavier casualties on the Ulsters.[44]

But not all the men of the 36th were quite so willing to risk their lives. Many, with their officers dead and with no hope of making any forward progress, broke under the constant shelling and strafing and cut for the British trenches. Crozier, one of the officers least disposed to sympathise with this sort of behaviour, came across such a group in full retreat.

> I go out to meet them. 'Where are you going?' I ask. One says one thing, one another. They are marched to the water reserve, given a drink and hunted back to fight. Another more formidable party cuts across to the south. They mean business. They are damned if they are going to stay, its all up. A young sprinting subaltern heads them off. They push by him. He draws his revolver and threatens them. They take no notice. He fires. Down drops a British soldier at his feet. The effect is instantaneous. They turn back to the assistance of their comrades in distress.[45]

A complicating factor on the day was the number of German prisoners who had been taken (more than 500 over the course of the day). These had to be taken back across no man's land before being handed over. Some were shepherded across individually, others in large groups. 'One man whose name we shall never know, could be seen waking across the open behind about sixty prisoners, some of them apparently wounded, holding them together as jealously as a sheepdog holds his flock, urging along the laggards, keeping ever behind the last man of his party.'[46] On occasions nervous or trigger-happy troops would spot detachments of men in grey uniforms advancing towards the British-held trenches and open fire. One group of the 10th Rifles, who had been with Col. Bernard when he and many of his men had been annihilated, opened fire at a range of 600 yards on 'an advancing crowd of field grey'. Crozier stood beside them as they fired, thinking they were about to be overrun.

Their nerves are utterly unstrung. The enemy fall like grass before the scythe. 'Damned — —' shouts an officer, 'give them hell'. I look through my glasses. 'Good heavens,' I shout, 'those men are prisoners surrendering, and some of our own wounded men are escorting them! Cease fire, cease fire for God's sake,' I command. The fire ripples on for a time. The target is too good to lose. 'After all they are only Germans', I hear a youngster say.[47]

Not that all the prisoners on that day were German. Capt. C.C. Craig, MP for South Antrim and brother of Col. James Craig (MP for East Down and motive force, along with Carson, behind the Northern resistance to Home Rule), was taken captive. He wrote to his wife from hospital in Gutersloh, Westphalia on 13 July 1916 to tell her that he had been hit by shrapnel in the back of the leg and had lain in a shell hole for six hours. He had been taken prisoner during a German counter-attack and escorted to a line of trenches 500 yards away from where he lay, by two Germans:

This was the worst experience I had, as my leg was stiff and painful. The space between the lines was being heavily shelled by our guns, and my two supporters were naturally anxious to get over the ground as quickly as possible, and did not give me much rest.

He spent the night in a German dug-out with a number of other prisoners and was moved the following day. His leg injury left him hobbling. To his great good fortune his condition was noticed by a sympathetic German artillery officer and he was given food and wine. More importantly an attempt was made to haul him on a makeshift sling/stretcher. 'This proved a failure; as I was so heavy, I nearly broke the men's shoulders. He then got a wheelbarrow, and in this I was wheeled a mile or more to the dressing station.'[48]

With the advance stalled and the Ulstermen beginning to melt back slowly there was a severe problem of lack of leadership in the German trenches still held by the 36th. 'It is now late afternoon. Most of my officers are dead and wounded', wrote Crozier. 'I send for twelve more who have been held in reserve, to swell the corpse roll. Other reinforcements arrive only to be thrown into the melting pot for a similar result.'[49] Rifleman James McRoberts of the 14th Rifles, a Queen's University science undergraduate and later Armagh Co. surveyor, found men of his own battalion who by the time they had reached their objective, the B line of German trenches, 'had lost nearly all their officers. There seemed to be nobody who had any authority and groups of men were sitting in clusters everywhere, doing nothing at about noon.' Thomas Johnstone uses this example (and there are many others) to make the point in his history of Irish involvement in the war, *Orange, Green and Khaki*, that:

> The decision to keep commanding officers at battalion headquarters was an error of judgement. It deprived the troops on the battlefield proper of direction, and brigade commanders of intelligent situation reports. Additional experienced officers on the spot could have saved the situation by galvanising the defence in more areas.[50]

When, at around noon, the second-in-command of the 9th Inniskillings, Major W.J. Peacocke, crossed to where a few small parties of men were holding out he managed to motivate them into taking aggressive action. At the Crucifix he gathered together a group of about 90 men (9th and 11th Inniskillings mostly) who, together, bombed six German dugouts and blew up a machine-gun.

But this band had no future in such an exposed position. Its numbers were few, its men were tired, dusty, parched and punch-drunk. And the guns of Thiepval were being trained on them whenever they attempted any concerted action. Lt.-Col. Ambrose Ricardo from Strabane, CO of the 9th Inniskillings (the Tyrone Volunteers), watched Peacocke's group. He had no-one left to send to their aid: 'There they were, a wedge driven into the German lines, only a few hundred yards wide ... even from behind they were not safe.' Peacocke sent a runner back looking for water and bombs

> but no one had any men in reserve, and no men were left to send across ... In the end at 10.30 p.m. (they had got to the third German line at 8.30 a.m.), the glorious band in front had to come back. They fought to the last and threw their last bomb, and were so exhausted that most of them could not speak.[51]

Peacocke's improvised company had been beaten back by fresh German troops brought up by train from Grandcourt nearby. (Peacocke survived the war only to be murdered in Cork by the IRA during the War of Independence.) 'By ten o'clock it did not appear that we had any troops in the German lines. That which had been won at a sacrifice so vast, had been lost for lack of support.'[52] In fact there were still some stragglers holding out in tight corners of the pock-marked battlefield. Attempts were made to reach them the following day at a cost of even more lives, but in essence, the fight was over for the 36th. They were relieved on the night of 2 July by the 49th Division, whom they would have been happier to see coming to their aid the previous day.

The Somme cost the Ulster Division more than 5500 casualties (nearly 2000 dead) out of the total British casualties of 56,000 (21,000 dead) on the first day; this represented the fourth highest losses of the divisions in the Fourth Army. Some battalions almost totally disappeared. The 9th Irish Fusiliers had no officers and only 80 men left uninjured after their attack north of the Ancre. Tommy Ervine's battalion, the 8th Rifles, was one of the luckier units; it had lost a 'mere' 20 officers and 426 men. The 9th and 10th Rifles had suffered horrendously. Davy Starret noted that only a handful of men returned to their reserve positions. 'Six hundred good men and true had gone west. Bernard, Gaffickin [*sic*]—why name any more? Each might have a book to himself. Killed in the glorious sunshine of a July day. Killed to make a world fit for other heroes to live in. And, failing in that, as they failed to retain their own lives.'[53]

Two days before Harry Bennet of the 10th Inniskillings had lost the lottery to decide which of the men of his battalion would take part in the attack. He had been left behind! His 'bad luck' was the most fortunate break of his young life. On the evening of 2 July his battalion, now four hundred fewer, paraded for a roll call. 'A name would be called and someone would answer, 'He's dead', then another name and the same answer ... I lost a lot of friends that day.'[54] William Montgomery, a young officer in Crozier's battalion, wrote to his father of the effects of the battle on the 9th Rifles.

> Mother would have cried and quite possibly you also when I called the remnant of my company to attention ... Not a few of the men cried and I cried. A hell of an hysterical exhibition it was. It is a very small company now. I took 115 other ranks and four officers (including myself) into action. I am the only officer and only 34 other ranks are with me now out of the 115.[55]

Some were conscious of the 'glory' which, through adversity, the 36th had won. William John Lynas, of the 15th Rifles, replied, stoically, to a letter written by his wife Mina back home in Tiger's Bay on the day of the battle. It reveals the important consolation many of the Ulstermen sought in their strong religious beliefs.

> They did not disgrace the name of Ulster or their forefathers. Little did you think as you sat writing that letter on the first day of July that our boys had mounted the top and made a name for Ulster that will never die in the annals of history. No doubt Belfast today and the rest of Ulster is in deep mourning for the dear ones that has given their life [*sic*] so manly. May the Lord comfort all of those who has lost a beloved husband, a brother & son. Lastly may the Lord watch over those dear orphans. As the Revd Cochrane used to repeat from the pulpit. 'Some are sick and some are sad. Some have lost the love they had.' Their [*sic*] is one great comfort to know that they fell doing their duty for King and country.'[56]

The men of the 36th had been recruited as 'Pals', served as 'Pals' and died as 'Pals'. The idea of forming a military unit around men with a common geographical background was born during the Great War. It too died a death at the Somme as entire villages in Tyrone and Yorkshire or streets in Belfast and Glasgow were denuded of their men. News of death would arrive for the families of the North of Ireland contained in small buff-coloured envelopes. In Derry, 'the women were out in the streets, screaming and crying. some homes had lost more than one man. It was ... just terrible on them.'[57] Often a local clergyman would bring the doleful news, and years later men and women who were children at the time would remember:

'My mother saw the minister up at the house and she called him down to where we were working. She just looked steady at him without blinking and said, Is it Ted [her brother] or Willie [my father]? ' He said, 'I'm sorry to say it's Willie.' She walked along the head-rig back to the house, her back as straight as that of a girl of nineteen ... it hit me that I'd never have my father around the place again. It broke my mother's heart but I never saw her crying except that first night.[58]

Eleven days after this calamity Ulster should have been staging its traditional Orange parades. There were none that year. On 12 July, from midday to five minutes past the hour a silence was observed to commemorate the dead of the battle. Orange lodges embroidered the now evocative names Thiepval, Ancre and Somme on their colourful banners. Newspapers, province-wide and local, carried long lists of the dead, letters from the wounded and poignant stories about families still waiting to hear from the missing. A miasma of gloom and mourning settled over Northern Ireland as it came to terms with the magnitude of its loss.

But gradually, as the events of 1 July became more distant and remote the Somme was to acquire a different resonance. The unionists of Ulster could have responded to the wholesale loss of life, as did many in Britain, as a form of class betrayal. The ruling elite, once again, proving their contempt for the 'lumpen' proletariat. After World War I the British ruling class would never again be able to despatch slum dwellers and peasant labourers to perdition *en masse*. But the unionist psyche chose to ignore that explotiation and betrayal and turn the sacrifice of the Somme into something much more positive. It became an affirmation of Ulster protestant loyalism. It is eminently possible to understand Irish republicanism without a knowledge of Suvla Bay or Guillemont and Ginchy: they are irrelevant to any discussion of the phenomenon. It is not possible to comprehend the nature of unionism without some awareness of the sacrifices of the Somme. It is stitched into unionist self-awareness as surely as the name 'Thiepval' is sewn into the banners of Orange lodges. Perhaps, like the Australian obsession with Gallipoli, it ignores the claims of others (such as Irish nationalists) to a share in the folk memory of the Somme offensive, but, despite its exclusivity, it has nurtured both the unionist sense of belonging and of betrayal up to the present day. It is easy to see fifty years of Stormont as an implicit reward for 2000 dead on 1 July. However, it is just as easy to resent the betrayal implicit in the callous despatch of so many men to their deaths.

And at the end of the day nothing substantial had been achieved. From 1 July until the offensive was formally ended when the first snows of winter began to fall on the plains of Picardy, as Martin Gilbert has put it, 'The Battle of the Somme became a daily struggle for small woods and even smaller villages.'[59] The British Army had lost more men in a single day than any other army in recorded military history. 'And yet ... to see the ground gained one needs a magnifying glass and a large-scale map.'[60] What had gone so badly wrong?

One contributory factor was undoubtedly the unimaginative and stylised tactics of the much-abused Field Marshal Sir Douglas Haig. There is nothing wrong with being predictable if you are also effective. Haig, in this, as in so many other instances, was not! He reposed too much faith in the sustained power of the preliminary bombardment. As we have seen, on the Somme, this did not achieve either the destruction of German defences or the demoralisation of its troops. As to the barrage which attended the attack itself, the policy of raining down ordnance on one trench line and then lifting the sights before passing onto the next set of trenches was akin to sending the Germans an uncoded message that it was safe to come out of their dug-outs.

When they did emerge it was to a bright sunlit day with total visibility. This was a function of the timing of the attack. Bob Grange from Ballyclare, no Sandhurst-trained military academic, cites the contibution of daylight to the disaster, pointing out that the French had asked Haig to postpone zero hour until 7.30 a.m. 'The result was that the men had to go over in broad daylight against the German machine-guns and artillery, whereas if there'd been a dawn attack they'd have been half across no man's land.'[61] In fact Haig was opposed to attacks conducted in darkness or even semi-darkness so he didn't take much convincing. Although they would hardly have known who to thank the German machine-gunners, highly efficient and courageous, owed him a debt of gratitude for the multiplicity of soft, clearly visible targets.

The Somme offensive didn't lack for preparatory homework, but there seems also to have been a dearth of worthwhile intelligence. The British side clearly did not know just how good the German defences were and that they were capable of withstanding far greater tonnages of high explosive than the British could throw at them. For a short while the Germans actually thought the attacks on 1 July, when they came, were merely a decoy for an offensive further north, where they were not so strongly dug in. There was an assumption that the British would never assault the better-prepared defences along the Somme.

The taking of the German trenches afforded an opportunity (however brief) to the Ulstermen to examine the impressive German defences. The British war correspondent Phillip Gibbs saw them for himself a few days later and considered them an affront to the lack of industry of the British Army: 'I went down flights of steps into German dug-outs astonished by their depth and strength. Our men did not build like this. This German industry was a rebuke to us ...'.[62] Pte. Anthony Brennan, of the 2nd Royal Irish Regiment, formed a similar opinion of the entrenchments near Mametz:

> It was in the nature of a revelation to us. The solidity and comfort of the dug-outs was a striking contrast to our own. Each one had been sunk to a depth of ten or fifteen feet; had two entrances, and was capable of accommodating twelve or sixteen men in comfortable wire netting bunks. I should imagine it would be shell-proof, except against the big stuff.[63]

The offensive also took place across too wide a front, without the benefit of surprise. The British artillery might have had a greater impact if it had been able to concentrate on blasting a smaller area. Some share of the blame must also be borne by the munitions factories which produced such a huge number of dud shells. Some estimates put this failure rate as high as 50 per cent in certain areas. In addition the manner of the attack was one guaranteed to send hundreds of men to utterly pointless deaths once the German machine-gunners had survived the artillery barrage and made it to their parapets before the first wave of advancing British soldiers swept into their trenches. Troops walking erect and upright, showing wonderful parade ground discipline, were easy targets for gunners, who hosed them with hundreds of thousands of machine-gun bullets. In such a situation attack was always going to be far more costly and far more risky than defence. So it proved in the casualty figures. The historian Martin Middlebrook has said that the Battle of the Somme was lost by a matter of seconds (the length of time by which the British lost the race to enemy parapets to the German machine-gunners). The fact that the Ulster Division saved a vital few seconds by massing in no man's land, may have contributed to their initial success, but that was soon dissipated as the German's counter-attacked the bulge left by the Ulster success.

The absence of senior officers also played a big part in the failure of the Somme offensive. Many of the troops used in the battle were going 'over the top' for the first time. Leaving them stranded in the middle of no man's land or in newly taken German trenches, without (in many cases) the two most experienced officers in each battalion, was not a very sensible approach to take with untested soldiers. It was also bad for longer term morale, smacking of an upper-crust military establishment which was prepared to sacrifice 'Tommy Atkins' but not members of its own immediate peer group.

It was that sort of blinkered military mentality, that rage of the inadequate, which caused his new company commander to reprimand Tommy Jordan after three days of gruelling labour with the Pioneers battalion (16th Rifles) during which he suffered burst eardrums. When Jordan presented himself in a tired and dishevelled state to this newly arrived martinet he was told 'How dare you? Look at those boots! How dare you come in before me dressed like that?' To which Jordan responded, 'Don't you know that I've been in a battle sir? I haven't had these boots off for weeks!' He lost a stripe for his insolence.[64] Jordan's deafness eventually forced him home. It was an abiding legacy of the Somme, which he carried with him to his grave, but one he made light of when he compared it to the permanent disabling injuries sustained by some of his friends: 'Bobby Mason had two hands off, bright lad, John Percy had two legs right off to there [above the knee] and still alive. Alfie, old Alfie lived down the road, he'd two feet off to there [just above the ankles] and an arm off, and he drove a motor car.'[65]

At the age of 90 Bob Grange could still recall the words of a French War correspondent who 'was sending despatches to his newspaper about the Ulster attack that day, and he described it, I think, very well indeed. He said that "the youth of Ulster entered the Battle of the Somme as enthusiastic young sportsmen and emerged from it as professional soldiers".' [66] That may well have been true of those who were left alive and not disabled by the battle, but the fact was that the nature of the Ulster division was radically altered after 1 July 1916. Recruitment in the north dwindled after the battle and, as with the 10th and 16th divisions, in the absence of conscription in Ireland, the numbers were made up by non-Irish troops, who lacked any sense of a mission to keep Ulster safe for the Union. The 36th, although still overwhelmingly unionist, was never again the covenanting army of loyalist 'Pals' which had gone into action on 1 July 1916 for its '... rendezvous with Death/ On some scarred slope or battered hill.'[67]

# 6   The 16th (Irish) Division at the Somme

GUILLEMONT

Today the rolling landscape of Picardy, dotted with small forests and abounding in wild poppies in summer, gives hardly the slightest indication of having once been a mud-soaked, bloody charnel house. You will look in vain at the oldest buildings in the small neat villages for signs of the conflict which overwhelmed them. Only the ever-present monuments, erected by the British, French, Canadian and other governments (though not the Irish), serve as a reminder that this is deceptive countryside. This is consecrated ground, the last resting place of hundreds of thousands of men who sacrificed their young lives to accomplish precisely nothing.

When you drive along the straight, open road between Peronne and Albert, with its relatively featureless panorama on either side, you pass by an unobtrusive signpost. This marks the limit of the gains made by the British forces during the infamous Battle of the Somme. A few short minutes later and you have reached the area where the catastrophic offensive began. It is a salutary lesson in the utter futility of war. The gains were eked out in yards and measured in lives. A short drive along pleasant, if circuitous, roads will bring you to the neighbouring villages of Guillemont and Ginchy. These are names which should loom large in the Irish psyche, not as prominently as does the name Thiepval in Ulster folk memory, but large nonetheless. That they do not is a function of the lack of acknowledgement that in 1916 most able-bodied young Irishmen were working on their family farms, in someone else's factory or business, or fighting for their lives against the Germans and the Bulgarians. They were not, even in September 1916, fighting against the forces of the British Crown in Ireland. Many who were in the trenches might have wished that they were, but instead they were engaged on His Majesty's behalf in France, Belgium and Salonika.

Most were a part of the 16th (Irish) Division the nationalist mirror image of the overwhelmingly unionist 36th. Unlike the relationship between the Ulster Division and the UVF, the 16th (largely due to the distrust of Kitchener, as well as irregular recruitment patterns) was not based directly on the units of the National Volunteers. These men had been encouraged by John Redmond at Woodenbridge in 1914 to make common cause with Britain in the confident expectation of self rule. As far as Redmond was concerned, Home Rule already existed and had merely been postponed by the war. Thus, he reasoned, Irishmen (by which he meant nationalists) who fought in the British Army were aiding allies, not abetting a colonising power. The Easter Rising of 1916 had, however, clouded that certainty.

The Somme offensive, which had been initiated with such high hopes of a breakthrough in July 1916, had quickly begun to peter out. The first day's gains, crucial to the success of the strategy for the battle, had failed to materialise, so much of the subsequent fighting has a desperate, piecemeal air about it. Guillemont and Ginchy were two small villages which happened to be in the way of the faltering British advance. There was nothing left of the original architecture by September, both hamlets had been ploughed back into the soil by tonnes of high explosive. Guillemont stood on high ground and was a well-protected strongpoint in the German lines. In front of it was an easily defensible wide-open plain, which had come to be known as 'Death Valley' by the troops who had attacked across it. The area around the two villages was dotted with reinforced concrete machine-gun positions.

One of the many failed efforts to take the town had involved the 24th Division, which included the 2nd Leinster Regiment. Before their attack on 18th August they were based near the desolate and notorious Trones Wood: '... Once, on a quiet morning, two officers of the Battalion wandered to the east of the wood, some way along the railway to Guillemont. The village itself on a slight eminence appeared harmless, and from the lips of each came the same words—"And that is Guillemont, seven times attacked".'[1] The 24th's effort was no more successful than any of the previous attempts despite an intensive preliminary barrage. As the attack floundered, the Leinsters, who had been expecting to move forward with one of the later waves of troops were, instead, ordered to stay in their trenches in case of a counter-attack. Waiting with his Company in the forward trenches was Capt. Frank Hitchcock:

> It had been a fine sight seeing the leading battalions advancing into action, but it was a most depressing one seeing them retiring. Streams of wounded, walking and on stretchers, were now beginning to drift by; men with smashed arms, limping, and with the worst of all to see— facial wounds. They all muttered of machine-guns in a sunken road, which enfiladed them and had broken up the attack.[2]

Despite being in reserve and not having had to go over the top, the 2nd Leinsters took heavy casualties from the German shells pummelling their lines. By the beginning of September, German troops still lurked in their hundreds in the village in intact dugouts and cellars.

The only salient difference between the Irish attack on Guillemont and that of all the previous efforts, was that the 7th Leinsters and 6th Connaughts of the 47th Brigade were successful in clearing the Germans out of the village. The 16th Division had been moved from the Loos area (where it had lost 1500 men) at the end of August to be fed into the Somme grinder. The 47th Brigade was taken from the 16th to make up the numbers for the 20th Division's attack on Guillemont. The 7th Leinsters and the 6th Connaughts would bear the brunt of the assault on the town itself.

The first obstacle to be overcome was basic geography. The movement of large numbers of troops to jumping off points usually took place in darkness, to avoid alerting the enemy. This made it difficult for troops unfamiliar with the terrain to find their starting positions. They were dependent on guides, many of whom were unreliable. What happened to the HQ staff of the 7th Leinsters was typical:

> Plodding on and passing through the northern part of Trones Wood the guide lost himself. Saying he would find out exactly where he was he climbed out of the trench and disappeared—true to the age long traditions of the Worshipful Company of Guides. He passed forever into the unknown ...[3]

The Leinsters (through blind luck in the above instance) got to their forward positions at around midnight on 2 September, and began scraping some cover for themselves with entrenching tools. According to William Adelbert Lyon, son of a Church of Ireland rector of Edgeworthstown, Co. Longford, who was a 24-year-old volunteer lieutenant with the Leinsters, the battalion was pounded by German shells for six hours before the assault. 'I have often wondered how the troops did it, why they did it, and why they didn't go in the opposite direction. For a six-hour plastering in such conditions is surely enough to sap the courage of the bravest.'[4]

Lt. J.F.B. O'Sullivan of the 6th Connaughts, writing to his mother after the fighting which finally took Guillemont, made a melancholy observation, recollected from watching his tired troops, already exhausted hours before going into battle. 'There we all lay, sprawled in a rough mass; snatching mouthfuls from the pieces of loaf and hunks of bully beef that had been in our packs all day, and trying to ease tired feet and shoulders. It was the last time that the old 6th Battalion would ever be compactly together ...'[5]. The ground over which his battalion would attack resembled a corpse-strewn moonscape:

> The area where we now found ourselves had been recently fought over—in fact it was very close to the limit gained by the original 1st

July push—and the ground had been churned into a lather of mud. The roadside was littered with discarded equipment; rifles, ammunition boxes, shell cases, grenades and reels of unused barbed wire. The stench from bloated horse carcasses overwhelmed one to the point of vomiting.[6]

O'Sullivan's guide who led the way to the front-line trenches was clearly of the same honourable fraternity as that of the 7th Leinsters. From the account of his performance it may even have been the same man:

We waded slowly through the cold sludge, tripping and tangling in the wire, and stumbled over a dead man. Lying on his back with arms and legs stretched out like an X. He was actually half afloat in the mud and nodded his head solemnly as each of us sloshed by. Shells were bursting dangerously close and one or two of the party began to get panicky at the thought of being trapped in such a dismal spot. The guide added the finishing touch when he announced that he was completely lost. So we turned about and retraced our path over the dead man and back to the edge of Trones.[7]

O'Sullivan's company finally stumbled on the Rangers HQ by accident. It was a an evil-smelling hole in the ground which masqueraded as a dugout. Ten steps led down from the main trench into a putrid cavern less than eight feet wide and not high enough for anyone other than the smallest to stand up. The officers whom the 6th Connaughts were relieving departed with alacrity as soon as Irish battalion arrived. Six officers, all with cold and wet feet, then squeezed onto benches and tried (with little success) to get a night's sleep. The following morning the battalion CO, Lt.-Col Lenox-Conyngham, briefed his officers on the plan of attack and issued the orders for the day: 'The session was barely over and the CO about to make a few extra comments when a blinding flash and shattering blast wrecked the doorway. Simultaneously a jet of wet dust spattered over us.' An orderly had been pulverised by the blast, 'I glanced at my notes and saw the 'wetness' to be nothing less than blood and bits of brain'.[8]

The British bombardment began at about 8.15 a.m. on 3 September. It was inaccurate and many shells fell woefully short. The 6th Connaughts took 200 casualties before they even went over the top and not all, by any means, were as a result of German shelling. (Nowadays the phenomenon is known, ironically, as 'friendly fire', then it was called 'unders'.) At noon, just before the troops were due to leave their trenches, the British shelling intensified. The 7th Leinsters were on the left of the 47th Brigade's assault force, occupying a system of shallow trenches known as 'The Gridiron'. These were 300

yards due north of the northern outskirts of Guillemont, near the railway
station. The Connaughts were to attack west to east. Released from the claustrophobic shell-racked trenches the two battalions let rip. One war correspondent wrote that 'the charge of the Irish troops through Guillemont was
one of the most astonishing feats of the war—almost too fast in its impetuos-
ity ... a wild and irrestistible assault.'[9] The regimental history of the Leinsters
records the ferocity of the Irish attack.

> The companies of the 7th Battalion went over in perfect lines through
> the enemy shelling and so eager were the men that they advanced into
> the zone of our own barrage. This impetuosity met with its well-
> deserved reward. The Germans were taken completely by surprise, and
> before they could leave their dug-outs or get their machine-guns into
> position the Leinsters were on top of them.[10]

It was at Guillemont that the 16th Division won its first Victoria Cross.
Lt. J.V. Holland, aged 27, one of eight children from Athy, Co. Kildare, led
the Leinster bombers, twenty-six in all. He had enlisted in the 2nd Life
Guards and as a result his nickname, according to Frank Hitchcock, was 'Tin
Belly'.[11] Taking a calculated gamble he led his men *ahead* of his own artillery's
barrage, thus ensuring that few Germans would have left the safety of their
well-protected dugouts. (The story goes that he had laid a five pound bet
with another officer that he would be first over the parapet when the whistle
blew.) As a result he caught many groups of enemy soldiers by surprise. His
VC citation read 'By this very gallant action he undoubtedly broke the spirit
of the enemy and thus saved us many casualties when the battalion made a
further advance'.[12] But the escapade was a costly one, only five members of
Holland's bombing platoon survived. One was shot, before Holland's eyes, by
a German officer who then raised his arms in surrender, a gesture which, to
his credit, Holland accepted. Some hours later, according to Holland himself,
he came across a wounded German who was probably a victim of one of his
bombs: 'I found this poor devil lying outside the place I bombed. He cried
out "You English, you English, don't leave me here to die." Along with a man
from the 6th Royal Irish Regiment, who had followed up the Leinsters and
Connaughts charge, he carried the wounded German to safety.'[13] Lt. Wallace
Lyon, was full of understandable admiration for Holland and his bombers but
harboured a jaundiced view of some of the 'gongs' handed out, ' ... the CO,
who during the whole period hadn't even stirred out of his dugout, got the
DSO'.[14] Lt. Holland lived through the war and saw service in World War II
before emigrating and settling in Tasmania.

The rest of the 7th Leinsters followed behind the barrage, among them
Wallace Lyon: 'We all charged across as fast as we could go and as soon as we

reached their lines the Boche got up and ran. It was one of the most exhilerating [*sic*] moments imaginable—just like pigsticking in Bihar.'[15] Both Lyon and another Leinster, L/Cpl. O'Shaughnessy were hit by the same bullet. Both were simple flesh wounds, Lyon's was in the thigh. His unpopular Company commander was shot in the jaw, 'But he was such a duffer that instead of passing the bandage under the chin and over the top of the head he tied it horizontally like a gag. It looked so funny we could not restrain our laughter. Perhaps it was a release of tension but in any case we never liked him ...'.[16] The Leinsters dug in to the east of the village along a sunken road but initially the main German reprisals were exacted upon their wounded who had to be evacuated across open fields to Trones Wood.

The Connaughts, to the south west of the Leinsters, had taken off a few minutes before zero hour because the battalion to their right did likewise. As O'Sullivan recalls

> They went over the top with a rush. A piper went with them blowing as if his cheeks would burst—though pathetically, nothing could be heard of the pipes above the screeching din ... Shouting was of course quite useless—I couldn't even hear myself—and, seeing Sinclair [his platoon Sergeant] looking up at me bewilderedly, in desperation gave the signal to charge. They came tumbling and doubling out and over the ridge and astounded me by a concerted yell and cheer that could be heard even above the bombardment. After the suspense and strain of the anxious waiting my own frame of mind had become somewhat apathetic and the unexpected battle yell touched me deeply. For me, the surrounding frenzy gave the illusion of taking place in the midst of a raging ocean tempest; and going over the top, like running shivering into ice-cold water.[17]

According to O'Sullivan, the German machine-gun fire was too high and missed most of the men. It was, however, deadly enough to kill the Connaught's CO Lieutenant-Colonel Lenox-Conyngham, who had gone into battle wielding his cane. He had been a popular CO, born of an Ulster protestant family although leading an Irish nationalist battalion. Soon, in the treacle-heavy going the charge slowed to a laboured trot and the wild cheering died down.

> The constant need to skirt the constellations of shell holes broke up our wave formation, which soon looked more like a post-match mob invading a football field. The bombardment crescendo reached its climax with the onset of an intense shrapnel umbrella ... here and there a man would suddenly huddle into a little bundle. Even as I watched, a

corporal close behind me pitched forward with arms stretched out and hands clutching frantically at the mud.[18]

The 16th Division's second VC was won in the assault on Guillemont by Pte. Thomas Hughes, the son of a farming family from Coravoo, Castleblaney, Co. Monaghan. His lack of physical stature can be gleaned from the fact that he had once been an apprentice jockey. Early on in the frenetic charge Hughes was wounded but instead of abandoning the attack, according to his citation 'he returned at once to the firing line after having his wound dressed. Later, seeing a hostile machine-gun he dashed out in front of his company, shot the gunner and single-handed captured the gun. Though again wounded he brought back three or four prisoners'.[19] He was still on crutches, a legacy of Guillemont, when he received his medal from the King. When he had completely recovered from his wounds he returned to the front with the rank of corporal. (He died in 1942 at the age of 57.) When another Ranger, who happened to be doing field punishment shortly after the battle, was told Hughes had been recommended for the VC he professed outrage, claiming to have been in Hughes' shadow throughout the engagement and demanding equal treatment.[20] We can choose to see this as yet another example of the essentially unjust distribution of military awards, or as another example of Irish begrudgery.

O'Sullivan's platoon found itself confronted by a concrete strongpoint, left unscathed by the British artillery barrage. Some of the men tried, unsuccessfully, to get close enough to lob grenades through the two narrow slits in its wall. O'Sullivan began probing for an entrance to the strongpoint and as he did so he 'suddenly felt a terrific thump and a streak of burning pain across the shoulders; stumbled on for a few paces, tripped over some wire and fell flat on my face and realised that a bullet had got me'. He had been hit in the upper body. To his consternation, his fall had been interepreted by the men of his platoon as the Lieutenant taking a breather, so naturally, they did likewise:

> In a frenzy I got up and shrieked myself hoarse but to no purpose. To signal with my arms was painful and slow, but by dragging the rifle by its muzzle and going forward at least indicated that the advance should go on. Moments later they were all up and going again. The unrehearsed breather was a lucky chance, because once on their feet the men recovered the wild abandon of the charge just at the moment when Germans began to emerge from shell holes and wrecked trenches. Behind the strong point a scuffle and scramble developed as a group put up a hectic resistance that was overwhelmed by the bayonet stabbing onslaught; a vortex of shrieking; of yells and brutish grunting— then rushing ahead leaving the crumpled bodies in a stink of blood and high explosive.[21]

An exploding phosphorous bomb temporarily choked and blinded O'Sullivan and by the time he had staggered out of the smoke and his eyes had cleared the 'tide of men had swept on and was already into the heart of Guillemont'.

After seven failures the village had finally been taken, and by relatively untested troops.

> Had this feat of arms occurred in the Peninsula or Marlborough's days there would for all time have been stirring pictures of the wearied victors resting by the breach or embrasure, with the battered but still existing walls of the village forming an admirable background. Alas, modern war had *change tout cela*. Guillemont, except as a name or a tactical position, had long ceased to be, and on all sides one heard the muttered query 'Where is the ------- village?[22]

Despite the razing of the village, it was still possible to distinguish the outline of what had once been the neat streets of Guillemont. What astonished the wounded O'Sullivan was the hundreds of dead Germans whose corpses littered the landscape: 'They lay in every imaginable attitude and in all directions. To go ahead it was now not a matter of walking round the bodies but of having to step over them. One huge officer in my path was lying across his own "stick" grenade and I heaved on the stick to see if he had any spark of life, but he just rolled over like a sack.'[23]

The pain and weakness induced by his wound now got the better of O'Sullivan. Spotting two stretcher-bearers he got treatment for his injury. After they had dressed his shoulder he followed them further into the wreckage of the town, but, overcome by nausea he decided to turn back.

> The slow dragging return over the contorted bodies seemed never ending—and unspeakably depressing. Shortly before reaching our old front-line the sight of a negro Highlander lying in one of the shell holes made me doubt my own sanity, till I remembered previous British raids in this sector and realised that the Scotsman's skin had been weathered and darkened by long exposure.[24]

He returned to Battalion Headquarters to be told of the death of the CO and to hear a long list of other casualties. The second-in-command, Major Campbell, was wounded and dying, and the battalion now had less than 400 men.

O'Sullivan's wounds meant he played no part in defending the hard-won gains against German counter-attacks. But for Wallace Lyon of the 7th Leinsters that period was every bit as harrowing as the taking of the village:

We had no food but our iron rations, and what we could scrounge from the dead. No water but what we carried in our water bottles, and what rain we could catch in ground sheets and no contact with anyone but the enemy who seemed to appear on every side. On the third night a captain of the third Battalion of the Grenadier Guards came along with his troops and told me his battalion was taking over the position from what was left of our Brigade. By that time I could have kissed him. I wasn't even certain of the best way back, but he told me not to wait on formalities but go. I limped off with about 40 odd men, many of them wounded, all that was left of the 150 that had started out.[25]

On their way back to the 'sanctuary' of the nearby Carnoy area the 7th showed the effects of their sojourn in Guillemont. Lt. Charles Weld noted in his diary, 'we were all so tired I thought we would never reach the place, having had no rest or sleep since the night before the attack. Quite a number of men dropped from sheer exhaustion and lack of sleep ... Many familiar faces are absent.'[26] All told the Leinsters had lost 12 officers and 219 men.

The attack on Guillemont had been a notable victory, but a notably costly one as well. The 47th Brigade had put a total of 2400 men into the field of whom 1147 were killed or wounded. Even the two battalions who had passed through the Leinsters and Connaughts after their initial successs had suffered heavily. The 6th Royal Irish lost 314 men, the 8th Munsters 265. And there was to be no rest for the 47th Brigade. In just a few days they would be reunited with the 16th Division, this time for an attack on the neighbouring village of Ginchy.


### GINCHY


John Breen, a career army man who had first joined up in 1911 and had served with the 2nd Royal Irish Regiment, found himself with the 16th Division in Picardy. He fought at Guillemont and Ginchy and has no doubts about which battle he would choose to forget first, if he could: 'Guillemont was easy enough and that was the first battle that we fought there. But Ginchy was tough, there was no doubt about it.'[27] Emmet d'Alton, then a young 18-year-old lieutenant with the 9th Dublins, later a major figure in the War of Independence remembered Ginchy as 'Sad ... a glorious victory with terrific losses.'[28]

As was the case with Guillemont, the 16th Division was not the first unit to be let loose on the town. On the same day as the former battle in which the 47th Brigade took Guillemont, the 7th Division had failed to capture the prize of the neighbouring Ginchy (a subsequent attack on 6 September also failed). One of the Regular Army battalions with the 7th was the 2nd Royal Irish Regiment. It had sustained such huge losses that fresh drafts of troops had totally diluted the Irish element in its ranks. A group of Channel Islanders, many French speaking, was among the ranks. (They had been spread around a number of Irish regiments and acquired a reputation for being resourceful fighters with the added luxury of culpably failing to understand orders—in English—when it suited them.) A Sgt. de Margry has left his recollections of that attack behind. He was a platoon sergeant with A Company and a healthy scepticism towards authority peppers his memoir. For a start he was not impressed by the gung-ho briefing on the forthcoming attack given by the battalion's officers, he'd heard it all before:

> As usual we were briefed in a few words about this action, stress being laid on the weakness of the enemy opposition and the strength of the support we would receive from flanking and rear units close by, not to mention aerial co-operation by the RFC. This briefing seemed to us a minor echo of the one we received prior to our attack on Mametz Wood where we had been badly beaten back on failing to overcome a whole German Division.[29]

One of the officers responsible for the overly upbeat briefing was soon mortally wounded.

> No sooner were we exposed to view than we came under murderous enemy fire. The air about us was literally buzzing with the peculiar whine of flying bullets from rifle and machine-gun fire, and one of the very first to fall was our company captain (Capt. H.J. O' Reilly) and as I hurriedly helped his batman (Pte. Tatam) to carry him to a nearby shell-hole we soon realised that he had been shot right through the chest, from side to side. When I asked him if I could be of any further help he murmured 'No, thank you—my batman will attend to me— you're more badly needed with the others'. Obeying a sudden impulse I gave his batman my field dressing to help staunch the double flow of blood from his wounds and I then re-joined the fight in earnest.[30]

In that fight de Margry himself survived shell concussion and being buried alive but the attack itself was a fiasco.

Notwithstanding their conspicuous lack of success, the philosophy that drove Field Marshall Haig and his General Staff was a simple one, 'If at first you don't succeed, keep despatching men to pointless oblivion until you do'. Haig visited Fourth Army HQ and announced the taking of Ginchy was imperative if the Somme offensive was to have any hope of success. He still refused to accept that it had already failed, on 1 July. Another ill-fated attack near the village, on 5 September, by the 7th Royal Irish Fusiliers resulted in that battalion being caught on concealed barbed wire in a shoulder-high cornfield and being picked to pieces by German machine-guns and snipers.

All of that was mere prologue!

Today the village of Ginchy dominates all approaches but the countryside around is dotted with small wooded areas and criss-crossed by rural hedgerows of the kind we are used to in Ireland, thus obscuring views of it from certain angles. In September 1916 such was not the case. Most of the vegetation surrounding the village had been obliterated. In military 'real estate' terms it 'offered a desirable panoramic field of fire' for determined defenders. Long since cleared of its inhabitants it was in the hands of a Bavarian division. Leading up to the first real concerted assault by the 16th Division, the troops commanded by General Hickie had been taken from him piecemeal, much as had Mahon's at Suvla. The 47th Brigade at Guillemont had been under the aegis of the 20th Division. Hickie had also lost units, albeit temporarily, to the similarly depleted 5th Division. He should have been commanding fresh troops in adequate numbers. Instead, where some of his battalions were concerned, he was leading exhausted, shellshocked wraiths greatly depleted in numbers. Human wastage had ensured that even subalterns (2nd Lieutenants) in the 16th division were leading companies (they should only have been in charge of platoons) and many platoons were led by sergeants. Two battalions, the 7th Inniskillings and the 9th Dublins, were led into action by captains. The 47th Brigade was, numerically, a battalion rather than a full brigade. This was the state of the force at the disposal of Maj.-Gen. Hickie on 9 September.

The 6th Connaught Rangers were a case in point. They had suffered heavily at Guillemont and, in an ideal world, would not have been asked to undertake an even tougher assignment just a few days later. But General Staff knew nothing about ideal worlds (and, it appeared, showed little empathy for a demoralised unit licking its wounds). The Rangers were fortunate in that the man sent to replace Lt.-Col. Lenox-Conyngham was not some old-school martinet with the sensitivity of a General Staff officer, but a former Coldstream Guard who had been through it all himself. Lt.-Col. Rowland Feilding (who earned the affectionate nickname 'Snowball' from his troops because his hair was prematurely white) was an outstanding leader whose thoughts on the war, and on the Irish soldiers under his command, were well expressed in letters sent home from the front. These were subsequently collected and published in one of the best of such volumes to emerge from the post-war glut of recollections, *War Letters to a Wife*. On the day he assumed temporary command of the 6th Connaughts (now reduced in number to 365 other ranks after Guillemont) he confided to his wife, 'one would not expect a battalion straight out of one exhausting attack, and so punished as was this one, to be ordered back, without rest, into another. Yet such is the case.'[31]

In the general assault which began on 9 September 1916, the 16th Division was aimed at Ginchy itself. Hickie chose the 48th Brigade to take the village, its brigadier (Ramsay) was promised that, given the weakened state of his brigade, it would be relieved as soon as that task was accomplished. The 47th Brigade, backed up by two battalions of the 49th (as was the 48th) was to cover the right flank of the 48th and attack a defensive stronghold called the Quadrilateral, 500 yards to the east of Ginchy. The assault would be led by the 8th Munsters and 6th Royal Irish. An unusual feature of the battle plan was the timing of the attack, it would take place at 4.45 p.m. (after an artillery bombardment beginning at 7 a.m.). The lateness of the hour was designed to catch the Germans by surprise and to discourage a night-time counter-attack.

As the 6th Connaught Rangers moved up to the assembly trenches around Ginchy they passed the ruins of Guillemont. Lt.-Col. Feilding leading a 'battalion' of 250 men and who had not been involved in that attack, was astonished at the extent of the destruction of the small town.

> ... not a brick or stone is to be seen, except it has been churned up by a bursting shell. Not a tree stands. Not a square foot of surface has escaped mutilation. There is nothing but the mud and the gaping shell-holes—a chaotic wilderness of shell-holes, rim overlapping rim— and, in the bottom of many, the bodies of the dead.[32]

True to form, the guide bringing the 6th Connaughts to their start-off positions lost his bearings. As the battalion filed forward, in pitch darkness, led by Feilding, a man who had barely met the officers under his charge, it was constantly shelled. The guide was hit but, gamely, carried on and the Rangers finally reached their assembly position at the junction of the Guillemont-Combles road and a sunken road leading to Ginchy. The troops settled into their trenches, which were little more than glorified shell holes. Two men couldn't pass without climbing around each other and exposing themselves to German machine-gunners or snipers. Then they waited almost two days for zero hour!

The British barrage began, as scheduled, in the early hours of the morning of 9 September. It was to be the most intense artillery preparation for a battle up to that point in the war. But, despite the substantial distance between the 47th Brigade and the enemy trenches, many of the shells fell short, while many of those which did land on the German trenches failed to explode (once again up to 50 per cent according to some observers). Watching, from a hill above the town, was one of the 16th Division's famous chaplains, the Jesuit,

Father Willie Doyle. Amid the smoke, cordite and splashing mud he managed to spot some examples of Irish insouciance (or plain foolhardiness):

> one Paddy was seen sitting calmly in a shell hole, smoking his pipe and sewing a button on his trousers, regardless of the fact that bullets and shells were falling like hail all round him! Another lad was half way through a tin of bully beef, when the order came to 'go over the top' and take the town. As he charged up the slope of that awful inferno— I saw it and even now cannot understand how anyone got through alive—he wired into that beef till the last scrap was gone, then flung away the tin, unslung his rifle and bayonet and made for Berlin in track of the fleeing Germans.[33]

To allow for a final massive bombardment of the German lines immediately in front of the attackers the assault was held up for two minutes. But the 48th Brigade either did not get or chose to ignore the order to wait until 4.47 p.m. and went ahead at the originally scheduled zero hour. This may have worked to their advantage but it was of no assistance to the 47th Brigade who were still in their trenches as the German artillery retaliated. Father Doyle:

> ... was just in time to see our men leap from their trenches and dart up the slope, only to be met by a storm of bullets from concealed machine-guns. It was my first real view of a battle at close quarters, an experience not easily forgotten. Almost simultaneously all our guns, big and little, opened a terrific barrage behind the village, to prevent the enemy bringing up reinforcements, and in half a minute the scene was hidden by the smoke of thousands of bursting shells, British and German.[34]

The 47th Brigade the 6th Royal Irish Regiment and the 8th Munsters advanced in four waves, each 50 paces apart. The 6th Connaughts and a company of the 7th Leinsters emerged from the trenches to form two more waves. As luck would have it (German luck) the trench in front of the 47th had emerged almost unscathed from the British barrage because it was not seen as a threat (which is why it had been allotted to the badly-scarred 47th). Naturally the Germans had gravitated towards it in large numbers so it was no longer as innocuous as it had been before the bombardment began. 'Such are the surprises of war!' observed Feilding, rather laconically, to his wife, describing the trench as a 'hornet's nest':

> While the battle was in progress one of our aeroplanes, after flying overhead, dropped a map reporting the enemy in force there, but the

news came too late to be of value. To the left of the Brigade, where
heavy opposition had been expected and provided for, comparatively
little was encountered. The artillery had done its work well and the
infantry was able to push forward and enter Ginchy.[35]

Alongside the Rangers the Leinsters were taking a similar pasting.

No sooner did the attacking waves leave their trenches than they were
swept back by a torrent of machine-gun fire ... practically at the same
moment down came the German barrage and it was impossible to
move an inch. Meanwhile the Leinsters, according to orders, left their
position and in a couple of minutes arrived into this hurricane of steel
and lead. The front-line, hardly big enough to hold the original occupants, now had to accommodate more, as the only thing to do was to
drop into the trench and get any cover possible.[36]

Within a few minutes all but two of the battalion's few remaining officers had
become casualties.

'The trenches were, by this, a perfect shambles ... full of dead and wounded
with the parapet and parados covered with dismembered corpses.'[37] The experience confirmed for Feilding what he had concluded when taking command of the Rangers. 'It was more than ever apparent that, apart altogether
from the effects of the ordeal through which they had passed and were still
passing (since the enemy artillery was still pounding furiously, while the
machine-guns were raking up the parapets of our shallow trench), they were
in no condition for battle of this strenuous order ...'. Total casualties for the
47th Brigade, which had begun the day with a complement of just over a
thousand, were 448. Eleven of the brigade's officers had been killed and
another 28 were wounded or missing.

Among the injured a young, cheerful and obliging company commander
named Steuart was one of the most serious cases

I had known him only two days, but had formed the very highest
opinion of his character, and, since our first meeting, had counted
much on his help during the trying times that were before us. He was
full of life and spirits and daring—the acme of the perfect soldier. But
such men are rare: they often die young; and this, I fear, is to be his
fate. The bullet that hit him penetrated his hip, and, glancing upwards,
is reported to have touched a vital part. He lay some hours in the
trench, till his turn came, and the firing had quieted down sufficiently
to send him away, never once by word or gesture betraying the pain he
must have been enduring.

Steuart, as Feilding half expected, died of his wounds on 16 September. The Rangers lost 92 more men at Ginchy out of the 16 officers and 250 other ranks who had begun the battle. Total casualties for the battalion arising out of nationalist Ireland's brush with Nemesis at the Somme was 23 officers and 407 other ranks.

The 48th Brigade, directed at the supposedly tougher target of Ginchy itself, was more fortunate than the 47th. Because of the distance between the most advanced British positions and the village, the 48th had been forced to entrench in makeshift shelters closer to their objective. Not that anybody bothered to inform the artillery that there were friendly troops waiting in what had been no man's land. Shells fell short regularly. Many men died as a result of these 'unders' as they prepared for the assault. Little wonder that they didn't delay their departure from the trenches beyond the originally scheduled time. As they raced pell-mell into their own side's barrage, a young subaltern, in action for the first time, took in the scene.

> As you look half right, obliquely down along no man's land, you behold a great host of yellow-coated men rise out of the earth and surge forward and upward in a torrent—not in extended order, as you might expect, but in one mass. There seems to be no end to them. Just when you think the flood is subsiding, another wave comes surging up the bend towards Guinchy.[38]

Leading off the attack on the right flank were the 1st Munsters, transferred from the 29th Division to the 16th and with a handful of the veterans of V Beach among the 700 or so members of the battalion who had begun the Somme campaign on 4 September. By 9 September there were just over 400 of them left. Their progress was nil and their losses severe, each of the company commanders became a casualty.

The 7th Royal Irish Rifles, reinforced by the 7th Royal Irish Fusiliers, led the attack from the left, among them was a 2nd Lieutenant Young. He described watching a shell land in the middle of a bunch of men about seventy yards away from him:

> I have a most vivid recollection of seeing a tremendous burst of clay and earth go shooting up into the air—yes, and even parts of human bodies—and that when the smoke cleared away there was nothing left. I shall never forget that horrifying spectacle as long as I live, but I shall remember it as a sight only, for I can associate no sound with it ... I remember men lying in shell holes holding out their arms and beseeching water. I remember men crawling about and coughing up blood, as

they searched around for some place in which they could shelter until help could reach them.[39]

The Rifles and the Fusiliers swept into Ginchy, and, having secured their objective waited for the two battalions of the Royal Dublin Fusiliers, the 8th and 9th, to carry the attack forward. This they did, well beyond the village, until they were forced back into Ginchy. According to Fr Willie Doyle ' ... The wild rush of our Irish lads swept the Germans away like chaff. The first line went clean through the village and out the other side, and were it not for the officers, acting under order, would certainly be in Berlin by this time.'[40] Their progress was obstructed by the sheer weight of the debris which was all that was left of the village. As one officer wrote, 'We had to clamber over all manner of obstacle—fallen trees, beams, great mounds of brick and rubble— in fact, over the ruins of Ginchy. It seems like a nightmare to me now.'[41] The Irishmen charged a German trench occupied by about 200 Bavarian soldiers who had clearly had enough. 'Some of them had their hands up. Others were kneeling and holding their arms out to us. Still others were running up and down the trench, distracted, as if they didn't know which way to go, but as we got closer they went down on their knees too.'[42] (According to Willie Redmond the Bavarians were not unhappy to have been captured by a Roman Catholic brigade and enthusiastically surrounded the Division's chaplains when they were brought back to the reserve area.)

Leading his company of the 9th R.D.F. Tom Kettle, poet, barrister and former nationalist MP was killed. In the following group was young Emmet d'Alton who ran forward to help when he saw Kettle fall, but the politician/ poet was already dead. Kettle could easily have avoided Ginchy, he was offered the chance of a staff job or of being invalided out of the service due to ill health. Instead, despite his growing ambivalence towards the cause for which he fought, he had chosen to stay, and die, with the men he called 'my beloved Dublin Fusiliers'. His body was removed from the field by the Welsh Guards who came to relieve the Dublins on 10 September. d'Alton, who was to take the course of militant nationalism after the war, won the Military Cross that day. Michael McDonagh in his book *The Irish on the Somme* calls him the 'boy hero of Guinchy [sic]' The 18-year-old subalterns citation read:

> When, owing to the loss of officers, the men of two companies were left without leaders, he took command and led these companies to their final objective ... After dark whilst going about supervising the consolidation of the position he, with only one sergeant escorting, found himself confronted by a party of the enemy, consisting of one officer and twenty men. By his prompt determination the party were overawed and, after a few shots, threw up their arms and surrendered.[43]

Among those to win the DSO, a more exalted honour than the Military Cross (which had been established to reduce the number of DSO's and 'save' its prestige) was Captain (later Major) John Patrick ('Jack') Hunt of the 8th Dublin Fusiliers. Hunt had been, according to Frank Laird who joined the 8th Dublins as an officer shortly afterwards, 'a drill instructor in a Dublin school before the war'[44] (St Andrews). Like d'Alton, he would eventually throw in his lot with the IRA in the War of Independence, using his talents as a military instructor to good effect.[45] Hunt won his DSO for a ten-hour rearguard action in which he and his company had frustrated the efforts of the Germans to turn the flank of the 16th's attack. Somewhere among the ranks of the fighting men of the Division were three mess servants whose job it was to cater to the needs of the officers of one of the Division's battalions. They had not been allowed into the assault on Guillemont and were not prepared to accept an order to miss out on Ginchy as well, so they deserted their posts and ventured *into* the fight, leaving a note which read, 'If all right back tomorrow. Very sorry.'[46]

Major Willie Redmond, MP, brother of the Nationalist Party leader, was on the staff of the 16th Division. Shortly after Ginchy was taken he went to see what was left of the village for himself.

> I met a Munster Fusilier who in the confusion of the battle had got separated from his battalion. He was resting by the road waiting to find some one who could direct him to his headquarters. He was covered with mud, but full of genuine enthusiasm. I asked if his battalion had made many prisoners. He replied 'Yes'; but added that once or twice the Germans had tried treacherous tricks. One party advanced as if to surrender, shouting 'Kamerad! Kamerad!' and when about twenty yards off opened fire. I asked the Munster man what then took place, and he replied, 'We knocked them over till further orders.'[47]

The German prisoners seen by Redmond were hungry, bedraggled and woebegone. The British artillery barrage had been so heavy in the hours and days preceeding the assault that the Bavarians had had no rations for three days. Almost invariably the first request of every prisoner was for water. Father Willie Doyle had spent his day dispensing water, and words of comfort, to the wounded and the dying at Ginchy. Doyle was not a rear-echelon chaplain and was never far behind the lead troops in any assault. By his own account this first experience of the effects of a pulverising bombardment and close combat on men of mere flesh and blood, was an agonising and distressing one. Allied to this was his very natural fear that, at any moment, he would be blown into eternity like the dead and dying to whom he ministered. For his personal courage he was one of many in the 16th Division to be awarded a Military Cross. (The 16th gained over 300 such military battle honours as a result of Guillemont and Ginchy.)

The 48th Brigade's casualty list was long. Over 1400 dead or wounded (nearly 200 of whom had been killed). The toll of officers, as always, was particularly high (21 dead, 62 wounded). And the day was not over, the stark terror of the assault, dissipated by adrenalin, turned into a defensive nightmare as the Germans got ready to hammer the salient which the 48th had created by their success and the failure of the units on either flank (the 47th Brigade and 55th Division) to make any progress. The 8th Royal Irish Fusiliers were sent up to reinforce the Dublins. Second Lieutenant Young remembers passing a miserable night in which he was, at one and the same time, cold and thirsty. 'We got them—Irish Fusiliers, Inniskillings and Dublins—to dig in by linking up the shell craters, and though the men were tired ... they worked with a will, and before long we had got a pretty decent trench outlined.'[48] According to Feilding, the German shelling was so intense that night that it was impossible for a brigade of Guards to relieve the 47th and 48th at 9 p.m., as promised. They were not able to do so until 4.40 a.m. on the morning of 10 September.

The achievement of the 48th Brigade in taking Ginchy was, like that of the 47th at Guillemont, a considerable one. Willie Redmond quotes an enemy officer as saying that the Germans had considered Ginchy well-nigh impregnable. 'But,' he added, 'you attacked us with devils, not men—no one could withstand them.'[49] On their way back to a brief period of rest at Carnoy few of the men of the 16th Division were disposed to celebrate. After three sleepless nights and horrendous losses they were shelled for most of the journey back to where the offensive had begun in that sector of the line on 1 July. Feilding walked behind the stretchered corpse of Lt.-Col. Curzon, CO of the 6th Royal Irish Regiment. 'The scene was very weird as we picked our way back this morning, through the waste of shell-holes with their mournful contents.'[50] Capt. J.H. Staniforth, who served at different times with both the 6th Connaughts and the 7th Leinsters, had no time, writing home from the front, for any talk of victory or honour. 'Fresh battle honours for the colours, "Heroes of Guillemont" and all the rest. But that doesn't make up for empty chairs, shreds of companies, scraps of platoons.'[51] It is reported that some of the members of the 16th, as they filed back from Ginchy, spotted a peculiar-looking armoured machine hidden away in a wooded area. They did not know that they were looking at prototype tanks, and, in their particular mood, would probably not have greatly cared.

Within the first ten days of its introduction to the Somme the 16th Division had lost almost half of its 11,000 officers and men. It suffered a 10 per cent death rate. The divisional commander, Maj.-Gen. Hickie, now considered his men 'a force to be reckoned with'. Unlikely! They may have proved themselves on the Somme, but at half strength to describe them as a 'force' and especially one 'to be reckoned with' sounds like a feeble attempt at irony. The capture of Guillemont and Ginchy did not alter the course of the war; it didn't even change the course of the battle of the Somme, which was already unwinnable long before the 16th Divison had even arrived in that sector. It merely changed the course of the lives of over 1000 Irishmen, by ending those lives peremptorily and prematurely, and did likewise to the lives of 4000 others by inflicting wounds upon them, some of a horrendous nature. What the Irish had achieved was a demonstration of their sheer physical courage and tenacity (which had already been established on the Somme by the 36th Division.) What they had accomplished for the generals who sent them to their deaths was a few more notches in the numbers game that would eventually wear down the adult male population of Germany to a point where it could no longer sustain the loss of life caused by maintaining a war on so many different fronts.

The losses led to a reorganisation of the Division. Ghost battalions were disbanded or amalgamated. Following on the insertion of a regular battalion (the 1st Munsters) into the Division the practice was repeated when Hickie's volunteer force was joined by the 2nd Royal Irish Regiment and the 2nd Royal Dublin Fusiliers of the Old Contemptibles (not that there were too many of *them* left by that stage; by then regular army units were overwhelmingly composed of new conscripts or volunteers). Their arrival made up for the disbanding of the virtually non-existent 8th Munsters and the amalgamation of the 7th and 8th Royal Irish Fusiliers of the 49th Brigade. But like the 36th Division before it, a link to the Volunteer force, from which it had sprung, had been weakened by such attrition.

Before finishing with the Somme it is worth mentioning one other battle site of Irish interest. On the same day as the service battalions of the Ulster Division were throwing themselves at the well defended Schwaben Redoubt nearby, two Irish battalions of the 29th Division, who had already suffered horrendously at the hands of the Turks at V Beach, were offered up to the Germans at that other Somme site of ill-repute for many an Irish soldier, Beaumont-Hamel. The attempts to take the village provide two neat bookends to the Irish involvement in the Somme offensive. On the opening day of the First Somme the 1st Dublins failed to make it to the German trenches before being mown down as they were ensnared by the unbreached barbed wire. The Inniskillings succeeded in getting beyond the first German trench line but lost more than half their battalion strength in so doing.

Therefore it was appropriate that the final shots in the Somme offensive were fired, in a withering snowstorm, at the same fortress village. Taking part in that assault were the 10th Royal Dublin Fusiliers. Jimmy O'Brien, a young

Dubliner, had joined the battalion in December 1915 at the age of 18. Beaumont Hamel was his first experience of warfare.

> The village of Beaumont Hamel was a few bricks, it had been shelled to pieces. Zero hour was 6.30 in the morning. At that time in the morning 7000 guns opened fire on the German trenches and the whole earth shook with the terrific explosions from these guns. We went over the top to take the German trenches. It was the first time that I saw tanks, they were coming behind us. We didn't know what they were, we'd never heard of them. They were huge cumbersome things and they went over the land and over the trenches and of course a lot of our men had been killed and wounded. They were lying on the ground and the tanks went over them because they couldn't see them.[52]

In fact the tanks were of precious little use (there were only two of them) and they got bogged down in the wet and heavy chalk soil, described by Charles Cecil Miller of the Inniskilling Fusiliers as 'a gigantic plate of porridge'.[53] Jimmy O'Brien lost many friends and comrades there. 'The battle of Beaumont Hamel lasted about three days. We went into action with a thousand fighting men and we lost seven hundred in that action.'[54]

However, Beaumont Hamel hadn't finished with the Irish just because the 1916 offensive was over. The next spring the 2nd Inniskilling Fusiliers would find themselves there, defending a sunken road, the only visible landmark in a wasted, pockmarked landscape.

> 'That sunken road at Beaumont Hamel is my worst war recollection in the way of futile waste of good lives,' Charles Cecil Miller recalled a decade later. 'We were there to withstand a counter attack but the German had no intention of launching a counter attack; he knew exactly where we were and he preferred to kill us at long range ... I should have thought it would have been obvious to anyone of even medium intelligence that the one position not to occupy was that infernal deathtrap of a road, but the great ones ordered us to hold it, and then I think must have forgotten that we were there at all, as we were there for eleven days and nights on end. When we went in I had in my company three subalterns and about seventy men. I left with no subalterns and twelve men.[55]

By then the First Battle of the Somme had long since ended, on 18 November, 1916, or as Pte. Anthony Brennan of the 2nd Royal Irish Regiment put it, 'the battle of the Somme petered out in seas of mud and futile attempts to pretend to the troops that we had won a glorious victory.'[56] Total

British casualties amounted to a staggering 420,000 (though far less staggering when compared with Russian and German losses on the Eastern Front).
Those British losses alone would account for almost half the population of
greater Dublin today. The offensive had succeeded in gaining a few square
miles of Picardy much of which was used to bury the dead.

When you go to visit those dead today, in the neat, well-kept Common-
wealth Graves Commission cemeteries which leap out of the landscape in all
sorts of places (at the side of roads, in the middle of cornfields) you can see
who else has been there before you by looking in the visitors' books for their
signatures. Few come and go without leaving at least their names. If you visit,
for example, the Lonsdale Cemetery near Aveluy, not far from places with
more evocative names like Thiepval, Guillemont or Ginchy, where 19927
Rifleman J.P. O'Reilly of the 2nd Battalion, Royal Irish Rifles, a grand-uncle
of the author, lies buried, you will see the thick, black-leather visitors' book.
Should you go there after 1 July of any year you will notice the names of
many visitors from the north of Ireland. But despite the fact that many of the
men who lie in that cemetery do not come from Northern Ireland, but from
the Republic of Ireland you will search the book in vain for southern names
and addresses. Understandably perhaps, 1916, 'The Year of Killing' (John
Terraine) has altogether different resonances for the people of Northern Ireland than for those of the Republic. Tom Kettle has been borne out in his
resigned acceptance that the deaths of a relatively small number of committed
and determined men in Dublin at Easter would, ultimately for nationalist
Ireland, count for more than the deaths of thousands of Irishmen in the Great
War.

THE BATTLE MESSINES

Every now and again the generals got it right, thus proving that it was·
possible and throwing the more egregious and far more numerous failures
into starker relief. Nineteen-seventeen gave them a victory based on imagination, thoroughness and sheer hard work, spiced with just the right proportion
of dash (at Messines) as well as an evil and futile maelstrom of mud, ghastly
death and thoroughgoing ineptitude at Third Ypres. Or to give it its far more
evocative title, Passchendaele.

The irony of Messines is that it further highlights the incompetence of
most of the ranking commanders of the British Army on the Western Front.
It is like a glittering diamond in a paste tiara. It was the first entirely successful single operation on the British front since the outbreak of the war,[1] and it
took until 1917 before it happened. Its success owes much to one of the more
human and humane generals of the Great War, Field Marshal Herbert Charles
Plumer. Ironically this popular and efficient general, with his round red face
and thick white moustache, became the physical template for David Low's
cartoon character Colonel Blimp, the die-hard reactionary who epitomised the
ignorant and elitist attitudes of many of that generation of senior officers.
Plumer, possibly the best British general of the war, spared the lives of his
men by not sparing himself or his staff. While divisional generals or brigadiers
were safely tucked away in their HQ's, Plumer was more likely to be out
inspecting the trenches and defences of his Second Army. He was more
familiar to the ordinary 'Tommies' than many of the senior officers with more
direct authority over them. His willingness to spend time in the front lines
gave him an understanding of the realities of trench warfare which far ex-
ceeded that of his peers. Above all he was trusted by the men whose lives he
was putting at risk. He, along with the likes of Allenby, was one of the few
commanders on the left side of the British military brain in the Great War.

Messines was a triumph won by good staff work. Mindful of Wellington's
famous phrase about Waterloo, that it had been won on the playing fields of
Eton, Rowland Feilding, CO of the 6th Connaughts, wrote to his wife pro-
posing to substitute the 'offices of the Empire' where the Messines success
was concerned.

From the offices have been introduced business methods which are essential to the complicated operations of nowadays. The staff work yesterday was perfect ... We were inundated with paper beforehand on this occasion, so much so that it became a saying: 'If ink will win this war, then we shall certainly win it.'[2]

After the blood-fever of the Somme both the 16th and 36th Divisions were fortunate to find themselves in Plumer's Second Army, stationed near Ypres, facing a salient in the German lines near the villages of Wytschaete and Messines an area of southern Belgium dotted with small woodlands. Confronting the two Irish divisions was a ridge running between the two villages, on a north/south axis, atop which sat the German trenches. (The Messines Ridge never rose to a height of more than 200 ft.) As was so often the case (Thiepval, Guillemont and Ginchy), the Germans dominated the high ground. According to W.A. Lyon of the 7th Leinsters, 'Always the enemy had higher and dryer positions than ourselves.'[3] Not that either division had too much to complain about. The Germans who held the area around Messines didn't seem terribly enthusiastic about war and tended to try and keep to themselves. Their artillery was fitfully active, but the infantry had not been infected with the 'raiding' (or 'hate') bug. (As the offensive approached the British would become far more aggressive in their raiding.) Light casualties in the winter of 1916–17 were some compensation for badly built and maintained trenches and Arctic weather conditions experienced by the Irish. Low temperatures were exacerbated by a chill wind which blew across the rolling Flanders plains, uninterrupted by the small woods which had been denuded of trees.

Long-term preparation began in January for another Somme-type offensive, to be launched around Ypres towards the end of the summer. But Haig decided that, to enhance the prospects of this huge push, a more limited offensive in early June would be required to clear the Germans out of the bulge around Messines. Organisation was left to the Second Army, while Haig got on with planning the blood and mudbath which would become the Third Battle of Ypres. The two Irish divisions benefitted from the former's meticulous expertise, but unfortunately did not escape the latter.

Frank Laird, fully recovered from a Turkish bullet at Suvla, was one of the D Company, 7th R.D.F. members who had opted for a Commission. The build-up to the Messines offensive found him in the 8th Dublin Fusiliers, mainly supervising the digging of six-foot-deep trenches for telephone wire. This stretched all the way up to the front-line, and would go well beyond that when the 'push' began. It was tedious and tiring work, not appreciated by the men with the shovels hefting large sods of Flanders mud. But it testified to a level of preparedness never before seen on any Great War front. And there was much more. Staff service in Plumer's Second Army cultivated planners whose imaginations went beyond a five day bombardment and the despatching of warm bodies over the top to stop bullets until there were none left to stop. 'The preparations for June 7th included a water supply laid on in pipes to the front-line, a tunnel, with large dugouts, which ran from the entrance to the communications trenches to the front-line also, and various new roads cut out from the back areas to the line ...'.[4]

Working on the assumption that troops' time might be better occupied in exercises designed to save their lives than with endless, often meaningless fatigues, Plumer's staff had trenches dug which were an exact facsimile of those his Army would be assaulting. Mock attacks were organised, rehearsals for the real thing, with flag-waving soldiers replacing the creeping barrage. Wallace Lyon of the 7th Leinsters was impressed, and it was heinously difficult to dazzle front-line soldiers with staff work

> ... we were moved right back into the countryside behind the reserve positions where we had weeks of reconditioning and training, ending up with an assault practice which simulated what we expected to carry out in the near future. Then we were issued with appropriate maps with objectives marked on them.[5]

The Second Army staff also built a replica of the German defences soon to be attacked. Officers, in particular, were encouraged to go and examine it. Like some grim and solemn miniature 'theme' park (less than an acre in area) it had been designed by an engineer near Locre, a few miles behind British lines. Its existence was such a novelty that it raised questions in the mind of Frank Laird:

> This ... was an exact model of the hill and all the systems of trenches with their respective names. It was altered as new trenches were spotted by the aeroplanes or old ones smashed up by our fire. A high wooden platform ran round it from which a bird's eye view could be obtained. This open advertisement of our intentions struck a good many officers with surprise.

No attempt was made to disguise the model; civilians could, and did, view it. 'Some held the opinion that the whole thing was a blind for the spies, and that we were not going to attack there at all, but the event proved wrong.'[6] Consideration was also given to the inevitable casualties, and the main Advanced Dressing Station was built close to the main road, in such a way that the wounded would enter from the North, receive attention, and be evacuated through an exit to the West. A semi-circular road was constructed outside so that ambulances didn't even have to turn to get back onto the main road.

Such painstaking preparation spoke volumes to the ordinary Tommies. Here was a general who wanted success and survival, not futile sacrifice. The Second Army did not function with the governors in the penthouse and the governed in the ghetto. Neither was it a complex tapestry of autonomous kingdoms ruled over by hypersensitive potentates. Kingdom spoke unto kingdom; Plumer saw that they did. He once said that he never ticked off anyone below the rank of general, but he could, when necessary, tear strips off anyone who behaved like an aristocratic 'prima donna'. What this meant was that, for example, Artillery commanders actually communicated with the infantry about potential targets and about the results of their bombardments. It must have been oddly liberating and encouraging for front-line units that 'A trench or concrete work which did not appear to have been sufficently shelled was noted, and request made that it should receive further attention next day. *Such requests were invariably met.*'[7] (My italics.)

The process by which the Germans were softened up began and ended with a 'bombardment without equal in history'[8] and was punctuated by a series of raids on German trenches which produced hundreds of prisoners and a lot of valuable intelligence. To Frank Laird it was as if the huge artillery pieces had begun to breed and proliferate.

> During these months of preparation the British shell fire was unceasing, and grew in volume week by week as more guns were mounted. At last they became so plentiful that all idea of hiding them was abandoned, and we saw the unusual spectacle of guns lying wheel by wheel in the open.[9]

The preliminary bombardment at Messines employed more than 2000 guns. They fired off more than 3,000,000 shells. In a single week the 16th Division's artillery loosed off almost 180,000 shells of its own. General Alexander Godley, commander of the 2nd ANZACs, called it 'the heaviest there has ever been in the history of the world.'[10] Writing home to his father, the 16th's famous chaplain, Fr Willie Doyle, told him that,

> I think I am accurate in saying that not for ten minutes at any time during these sixteen days did the roar of our guns cease. At times one or two batteries would keep the ball rolling, and then with a majestic crash every gun, from the rasping field piece up to the giant fifteen-inch howitzer, would answer to the call of battle, till not only the walls of the ruined houses shook and swayed but the very ground quivered.[11]

But the massive, breathtaking bombardment was only the knock on the front door, a clear announcement of intentions. An approach was also being made via the back door, or, to put it more aptly, through the basement. Since the Spring of 1915 miners had been digging underground towards the German positions. The intention was to pack the mines with high explosive. It was foul, backbreaking work through waterlogged sub-strata of land. The Germans, although occasionally suspicious and undertaking minor efforts of their own, never seriously believed the British would expend so much energy on a vast subterranean system of mines. Just as the British had paid dearly for underestimating German construction work at the Somme the Germans would suffer for their complacency. They were, however, aware that something was going on and did their best to ascertain the scale of it. 'Sometimes we could hear the enemy sapping', according to W.A. Lyon. 'It was touch and go whether they succeeded in intercepting and blowing us up before we were ready to blow them sky high.'[12]

There were 19 mines in all. One spacious underground gallery was 720 yards long and they were dug at depths, in some cases, of over 100 ft. They stretched for over eight miles along the German front-line and were packed with nearly one million pounds of high explosive. The explosive, ammonal, was concentrated under known German strongpoints which it was feared would not be destroyed by the aerial bombardment. When triggered the mines would unleash the 'greatest artificial eruption which ever shattered the earth's crust'.[13]

The 16th and 36th Divisions were in IX Corps on the morning of 7 June, side-by-side with the Ulster division on the right of the attack and the nationalists in the centre. In the preceding days officers had been inundated with paper from Second Army Staff as final intricate details were ironed out and transmitted to the infantry. A series of well-planned and clinically executed raids in the run up to the 'push' itself had brought improved intelligence-gathering. Overhead the Royal Flying Corps was, as it had been for weeks past, monitoring events. It was perhaps the best prepared and supported British army to go into action until the minor miracle of 'D-Day' itself, twenty-seven years later. Such groundwork deserved and got a measure of luck. The day was perfect, bright and cloudless, ideal for observation of the battle that was about to take place. The Irish units' objectives were all around the village of Wytschaete. The 7th of June was to be, as Sir Frank Fox has put it, 'distinguishable in the current account as an "Irish Day" '.[14]

Three ten a.m. had been chosen as zero hour. It would still be almost pitch dark but it was reckoned that, at that hour, men would be able to see for a distance of 100 yards. No more attacks across exposed ground at 7.30 a.m! In the hours before midnight soldiers were moved up to the front trenches; smoking or naked lights were forbidden. Just after 2.30 a.m. the British guns fell silent to give the gunners a breather before the final tumultuous barrage would begin.

In Fr Willie Doyle's account of what happened next he begins,

> Punctually to the second at 3.10 a.m. there was a deep muffled roar; the ground in front of where I stood rose up, as if some giant had wakened from his sleep and was bursting his way through the earth's crust ... I never before realized what an earthquake was like, for not only did the ground quiver and shake, but actually rocked backwards and forwards, so that I kept on my feet with difficulty.[15]

To the right of the 16th, Cyril Falls, historian of the 36th Division and an Inniskilling Fusiliers officer, recorded how,

> the great semi-circle of mines exploded, spewing up, as it seemed, the solid earth, of which fragments fell half a mile away, and sending to the skies great towers of crimson flame, that hung a moment ere they were choked by the clouds of dense black smoke which followed them from their caverns.[16]

One of the mines, in the 36th's sector, failed to explode for fifteen seconds and the Ulstermen dutifully obeyed instructions and didn't wait for it to go off. Many of the men of the Division had scaled the ladders and were on their way across no man's land when it spat up the earth in front of them. The leading wave, from the 14th Rifles, had men thrown completely off their feet but suffered no casualties.

A few days later an Irish officer walked among the craters scooped out of the earth by the massive charge. Afterwards he wrote:

> It was said that the officer responsible for the mines was so relieved when all of them successfully blew up that he was not fit for duty for the rest of the day. That may be a slander but if it is true he had done his work well and was fully entitled to relieve his feelings. Those mines must have had a most demoralising effect on the Germans. They were tunnelled under swampy ground and I doubt if the Hun suspected their existence.[17]

Thomas Gibson, of the 10th Inniskillings, waited for the massive explosion in pensive silence (some of the Irish soldiers are said to have got down on their knees in the trenches and prayed for the hundreds of Germans they knew were about to be atomised): 'As soon as the mines went up we went over the top ... the whole place was devastated.'[18] Bob Grange from Ballyclare, promoted to Sergeant since the Somme, had to claw at the sides of the trench to keep himself upright, so close were the 12th Irish Rifles to the massive Spanbroekmoelen mine. Later that day when a German-speaking officer of his battalion questioned some prisoners, he was told that a huge party of 300 men had been assembled directly over the mine for a raid at 6 a.m.

> They were all packed into Spanbroekmoelen, getting ready for the raid, and unfortunately for them we started ours at 3.10 a.m., so they all went up in the air. I never saw carnage like it in such a short space. There wasn't a human body [intact] lying around that place ... just bits and pieces, arms, heads, feet, legs. Terrible mess.[19]

So devastating was the sheer power of the mines that the IX Corps race to the first German line (the 19th Division was, by the way, the third unit in the Corps) was virtually unopposed. In front of them went their 'creeping' barrage, lifting and moving forward precisely as planned. The 7th Inniskillings took only twenty minutes to reach their first objectives but were unsure that they'd actually reached them because they could find no trace of the German trenches. One of the few problems encountered was from the near-volcanic craters wrenched out of the earth by the highly efficient ammonal. Companies had to divide as they circumvented them and would have been in danger of losing their bearings but for the thoughtful issuing by Second Army of compasses to platoon commanders.

As the 8th Dublins made ready to go over the top, Frank Laird, who had been ballotted out of the action the previous night along with two other officers, watched as those officers who would be leading their platoons switched into the uniforms of the 'Tommy' to make themselves less conspicuous. He saw the CO take Father Willie Doyle aside, the courageous and much-revered 16th Division chaplain, for a final, private word before the battalion moved off. (Possibly to point out to him that, yet again, he wasn't wearing his steel hat or gas respirator: Doyle normally couldn't be bothered with them.) Then, with the pockmarked Flanders countryside still shrouded in gloom, the first mine went off; Laird was a safe distance away

> ... but the hill on which we stood shook under our feet like a mass of jelly. The debris thrown upwards by the mines still hung in the air when our tremendous barrage opened. Terrifying as the mines appeared, the barrage looked worse. The whole line was enveloped in clouds of smoke and dust and flashing flame.[20]

The barrage was, however, not an entirely one-sided affair. As Laird watched, entranced, some miles behind the front lines, his colleagues sheltering behind a sandbag parapet known as the 'Chinese Wall' were taking a hammering from the German artillery. One shell scored a direct hit, blowing three men fifty yards into no man's land and burying five more alive. Fr Doyle, as was his custom, scurried out to the dying men to give them absolution. Turning to the living he saw that no one was doing much to assist them, bar one sergeant whose profanities tore through the June twilight ('[his] language was worthy of the occasion and rose to a noble height of sublimity'[21] was Doyle's own tongue-in-cheek observation) as his hands tore through the sacking and sand. Doyle galvanised the men around him by racing to assist the scatological NCO. They managed to dig out three of the men alive, the other two had been killed outright. Doyle ensured that the sergeant got the Distinguished Conduct Medal—'The poor chap is very proud of his medal, which I told him he won by his eloquent language.'[22]

The 2nd Royal Irish Regiment had joined the 16th Division at the end of 1916. Anthony Brennan from Kilkenny, who had fought with the 7th Division at the Somme, was now ready to go into action with an Irish division. Just before dawn Brennan, second-in-command of a Lewis machine-gun unit, wrote another 'final' letter home and entrusted it to one of the stretcher-bearers, Tom Rowe, from Callan in Co. Kilkenny, who would not taking part in the action that day. Immediately prior to the attack 'there were the usual lavish tots of rum. I was not nervous or frightened, but exhilarated and eager to start the adventure—a feeling which as far as one could see was common to all my comrades.'[23] In charge of Brennan's machine-gun section was a former Dublin Fusilier, L/Cpl. O'Brien. O'Brien had been at Gallipoli but Messines would be his first battle on the Western Front. 'Dead on time the mine went up. We were a few hundred yards to the rear of it and it was a magnificent sight. There was very little concussion or blast ...'.[24]

Heavy shelling accompanied the Royal Irish over the top; the British artillery was fastening on the German rear trenches while the German shells, as usual, were churning up no man's land and the British front-lines. Amid the awesome cacophany Brennan and O'Brien failed to notice immediately that they had been deserted by the other four members of their section. (All later turned up in hospital; 'as far as we could make out none was seriously wounded', Brennan observed drily.) The mine had done it's work well and the first German trenches were taken with relative ease. As the battalion advanced on the next German line, the two men, along with the Company Lewis Gun Sergeant were, ordered forward by the Battalion Lewis Gun Sergeant to give covering fire. O'Brien was reluctant but was encouraged to move by threats from the Battalion Sergeant to shoot him if he didn't! Brennan had to carry several panniers of ammunition which would normally have been hefted by the four missing men, he being the only 'Indian' among the 'Non-Comm Chiefs'.

Brennan concluded early in proceedings that 'our gallant Battalion Sergeant was evidently after a medal because he insisted on penetrating still deeper towards the German lines.' Eventually, without having seen a single enemy soldier or used the Lewis gun once, they ran into a German barrage and had to duck into a shell hole for cover. Taking advantage of a chance remark about the paucity of ammunition, O'Brien offered, with considerable enthusiasm, to go and get some. As Brennan suspected, that was the last they saw of him outside of the safety of their reserve billets that day ('I fancy he behaved with discretion if not with valour'). Unable to move with the gun and unwilling to abandon it, the Sergeant and Brennan stayed in their shell hole, made tea and ate their emergency rations until the shelling abated sufficently to allow them to withdraw.

> On the return journey I carried back the Lewis gun, the spare parts and about four panniers of ammunition. The two Sergeants got Divisional honours for their exploits [a green diamond embroidered on the left sleeve]. I got nothing, being a mere private, and later in the day was amused to hear the Platoon Commander—whose first appearance it was on any fighting front and whom incidentally I had not seen during the battle—ask O'Brien of all people how Brennan had carried himself in the battle! I might have told him had I been asked that I had not only carried myself but the whole section as well.

The casualties of the 2nd Royal Irish were relatively light, less than a hundred, though Brennan's platoon lost one—Charley Kavanagh, a member of the dwindling band which had survived Mons.

Lt. Wallace Lyon, of the 7th Leinsters, was given first choice of objective from among the battalion's officers. He chose carefully and opted to go with the first wave which would be expected to take the advance German trenches. On the Somme he would probably have been signing his own death warrant, but at Messines there were clear advantages. 'The distance was shorter, there was a much greater element of surprise than for the following leap-frogging waves and finally an earlier relief after completion of the operation.' There was, however, a rather large debit factor niggling at Lyon, a doubt which made his flesh creep. That was 'the possibility that we might be blown sky high in the event of any delay of the mine explosion ... the orders were to go on the first shot of the artillery barrage whether the mine went up or not.'[25]

Since the bloodbath of the Somme only two officers per company led their troops into action, so Lyon was accompanied by a young subaltern named Hamilton, who lost no time in getting 'over the top' at zero hour. 'But soon we were confronted by a vast crater full of smoke and gas which extended the complete length of our front, so without loss of time I took half the Company

round one side, and Hamilton the remainder round the other flank.' The
opposition was token and easily mopped up, and Lyon and his Company had
no dificulty reaching the German trenches. 'We found them with few exceptions well shaken with the explosion and we bombed all the dugouts beyond
the crater. Although we must have collected and sent back between two and
three hundred prisoners, the whole operation as far as I was concerned was a
cakewalk.'[26] Lyon's gamble paid off. The subsequent waves which moved
beyond the German front-line experienced more difficulties and correspond-
ingly greater casualties. By midday his unit was back in the rear 'celebrating
with mugs of Black Velvet'. Lyon himself, because of his fluency in Hindustani
was transferred to the Indian Army Corps. His move was fortunate, 'for
shortly afterwards was that ghastly mud and blood bath at Paschendale [*sic*],
which I was to miss.'[27]

The 6th Connaughts, under Rowland Feilding, were broken up and par-
celled out among other units for the attack. They 'mopped up' and they
fetched and carried all day, allowing Feilding the opportunity to observe the
proceedings dispassionately, all the more so as,

> Our men advanced almost without a check. The enemy—such of them
> as were not killed—were paralysed and surrendered. In Wytschaete
> Village they rushed forward with their hands up, waving handkerchiefs
> and things. And no one can blame them. The ordeal through which
> they have been passing the last fortnight must have surprassed the
> torments of hell itself.[28]

Some of his men claimed to have found a dead German machine-gunner
chained to his gun: somebody, probably the man himself, had decided he was
not going to abandon his post and surrender.

At the Somme, with the 36th Division, Capt. Henry Gallaugher of the
11th Inniskillings, from Manorcunningham, Co. Donegal, had won the Distinguished Service Order. He had been recommended for promotion to the
rank of Major and for the French Legion d'Honneur. Frightening casualties
among officers had led to a reluctance to send too many of them 'over the top'
at any one time. Gallaugher outlined in one of his letters home how he had
had to plead with his commanding officer to allow him to lead his company
into action.

> I had a long talk with the Colonel today and I must say he does listen
> to reason and he has decided to let me go along with the coy [*sic*] when
> going over the top and I trust it is for the best. You see all the officers
> I have are very young and inexperienced and it would hardly be play-
> ing the game to leave them, not saying that I could do much more than

they could, but I have a little more experience & I know the men a little better, besides they have stood by me pretty well.[29]

It was to be his final letter home.

Shortly after the 36th went into action his right arm was shattered by a shell fragment. Had he chosen to he could have returned to the Regimental Aid Post. Instead he threw his rifle away and continued forward with his revolver in his left hand shouting, in Donegal vernacular, 'This will do me rightly'. Once his company had reached its objective common sense prevailed and he decided to have the arm seen to. On his way back to the British front-lines, however, a German shell ended his life. He was buried in what had, up to that morning, been no man's land. In a letter devoid of much of the ritualistic cant of such doleful missives, Gallaugher's CO, Lt.-Col. A.C. Pratt, wrote to the Donegal man's father: 'His loss is most keenly felt by us, he was universally beloved and was one of the finest characters I have ever met, he was a true soldier, and a great leader and organiser.'[30]

White-haired Willie Redmond, MP, brother of the Nationalist Party leader, a man, like his friend and colleague Tom Kettle, too old (at 56) and too physically unfit for front-line duty, wanted one last turn of the wheel before he accepted the inevitable inroads of *anno domini* and took a permanent staff job. He had been attached, temporarily, to the Divisional staff and had been repeatedly refused permission by Hickie to return to the 6th Royal Irish so that he could join his battalion on the morning of 7 June. Redmond had also been kept out of the action at Guillemont and Ginchy and was receiving anonymous letters from Ireland 'accusing him of staying behind because he was afraid'.[31] He felt a definite sense of duty to the soldiers of his unit, men who had been encouraged to join up by the blandishments and speeches of his brother. He may also have felt lucky, or confident that the ground had, on this occasion as never before, been well prepared. Additionally he would have been intrigued at the prospect of accompanying the 36th Ulster Division into battle. Redmond, as his final speeches indicate, was one of those optimists who believed that solidarity between Orange and Green in Flanders and Picardy was eroding domestic antagonisms. His persistent entreaties finally prevailed and he was released, on condition that he return to the rear once the first objective was taken. Obviously his return to the ranks was a tonic of some sort because the troops cheered him when he rejoined them, like some popular management figure who decides to throw in his lot with the workers in a strike. His batman, who possessed the unfortunate surname Organ, was not impressed. 'Sir', he said disapprovingly, 'this cheering is not good for you.'[32]

Anecdotal evidence, possibly fanciful, has Redmond going over the top, first of the Royal Irish, within seconds of the mines ripping up the ground under the Germans, 'before the burning earth had time to fall.' As he picked his way around the shell holes and the massive craters, which must have looked like the after-effects of a meteorite shower, Redmond faced, 'what to us looked something like an overflow of hell itself. You can form no true idea of the diabolic beauty and fury of the whole scene—the flashes and thunder of a thousand guns, the smell of poisonous gas, the morning light stifled at its birth by the smoke of battle.'[33] Redmond was hit twice, in the leg and the wrist. He was found, ironically, by stretcher-bearers of the Ulster Division and brought to their Aid Post. He died in the Field Ambulance which was taking him back to hospital. John Breen, who had joined the 2nd Royal Irish in 1911, had been posted to the 6th and was a member of Redmond's old company: 'Before we went over the top that morning he was with us; all he said was, "Come on, the Royal Irish." I don't know where he was killed. I didn't see him after we got over the top, because, I needn't tell you, we were looking out for ourselves.'[34] Redmond was buried in the grounds of a convent in the village of Locre. His wounds would hardly have been life-threatening in a younger man. (The 16th also had amongst the ranks a 52-year-old subaltern! He was 2nd Lt. Maloney of the 1st Munsters, who led a group of men through Oostaverne Wood and brought back a parcel of prisoners.)

Sadness at Redmond's death was universal and transcended Irish political barriers. One staunch unionist, who didn't know Redmond personally, attended his funeral at Locre Convent and felt 'He was far too old for soldiering but we all respected him, political enemy though he was.'[35] The Chaplains of the 16th and 36th Divisions both officiated at his funeral; troops from both divisons fired a salute over his grave. Redmond's hope that proximity in the firing line and increased mutual familiarity were creating an understanding between unionist and nationalist, may not have been entirely ephemeral. Rowland Feilding, CO of the 6th Connaughts, was a 'Tory' brought up to regard the likes of Redmond as 'anathema'. (Redmond was buried in the corner of the convent grounds that Feilding had chosen for himself.) It was not mere sentimentality at the latter's death that caused him to write to his wife, 'How one's ideas change! And how war makes one loathe the party politics that condone and even approve when his opponents revile such a man as this!' Feilding, however, then goes on to ask the apposite question, 'What effect will his death have in Ireland? I wonder. Will he be a saint or a traitor?[36]

He would, of course, be reviled yet again, this time by many of his erstwhile supporters, before being consigned to the historical scrapheap adjoining the gibbet erected for his brother. Gen. Sir Alexander Godley, the CO of the 2nd Anzac Corps which had taken its place at Messines, remarked that 'We are all very sorry about Willie Redmond having been killed. He was a very charming personality, and I only hope that it may at any rate help to compose the Irish differences.'[37] Redmond's final *apologia* was discovered after his death in a sealed message left behind in Ireland; it read: 'I should like all my friends to know that in joining the Irish Brigade and going to France, I sincerely believed, as all Irish soldiers do, that I was doing my best for the welfare of Ireland in every way.'[38]

While Redmond lay dying, the initial 'cakewalk' phase of the offensive had ended and greater casualties were being taken in attacks against German rear trench positions and from, in some areas, German counter-attacks. But these were never serious enough to jeopardise the success of the mission. Inevitably there were casualties; both the 16th and 36th lost men, in Redmond and Gallaugher, who were, for very different reasons, iconic figures. The acting CO of the 7th Leinsters, Major Stannus, a barrister in civilian life, was killed by a shell which also wiped out his adjutant. Feilding described him as 'one of the wittiest raconteurs I have ever met'. When he found the Major's body someone had thrown a sandbag over his face. Feilding lifted it. The young lawyer's face 'was discoloured by the explosion of the shell that had killed him but was otherwise quite untouched, and it wore the same slight smile that in life used to precede and follow his wonderful sallies.'[39] In addition to Gallaugher the men of the 36th mourned the death of Lt. Brian Boyd of the Young Citizen Volunteers from Belfast (14th Rifles). Another senior officer, Major McKee, lost a leg and won a DSO. His military career thus abruptly ended he went on to become Secretary to the Headmaster at the famous Campbell College in Belfast. But the Irish casualties were pastel pink to the bright red of the Germans. The 16th lost 748 men killed and wounded; the 36th lost 700. The Germans admitted to 23,000 casualties and the British and Anzac forces captured another 144 German officers, 7210 other ranks, 48 guns, 218 machine-guns and 60 trench mortars.[40]

The 'limited offensive' at Messines had gained ground (more than three miles—a massive advance in the context of the Western Front) but in doing so it had captured only mythical 'towns'. All around the landscape bore witness to the destructive power of artillery ordnance and expertise, both built up over the preceding three years. Near the forward slopes of Messines Ridge was the aptly named Bois d'Enfer, literally, the Wood of Hell, 'which had remained a considerable copse through years of shell-fire [and] was now but an indeterminate collection of stumps.' A stream which had run through the wood could no longer be described as such. 'Its path was marked by mud thicker than elsewhere, and where its bed had been the shell-holes were full of water. There were a number of dead Germans in the valley, with their faces turned towards the hill. They had run back before the dreadful moving wall of the British barrage, and had been caught by it in the marshy ground. Some lay on their faces, arms outstretched.'[41]

Fr Willie Doyle had spent the day scurrying around the battlefield, offering comfort to wounded men:

There was not a yard of ground on which a shell had not pitched, which made getting about very laborious, sliding down one crater and climbing up the next, and also increased the difficulty of finding the wounded ... The things I remember best of that day of twenty four hours work are: the sweltering heat, a devouring thirst which comes from the excitement of battle, physical weakness from want of food, and a weariness and footsoreness which I trust will pay a little at least of St Peter's heavy score against me.[42]

The 'footsoreness' came from 'blood blisters' which Doyle had developed from having to wear his boots for too long. Two days after the battle it was the stench in Wytschaete which disturbed the soldiers. It was a sensory memory which many carried away from the battlefield. 'The smell in Wytschete [*sic*] was terrible. A cemetery had been disturbed by our shelling. Dead Germans still lay about although burial parties had been busy ... After I had returned to my tent between Drainoutre and Locre the mere lighting of a cigarette would recall the stench of Wytschaete.'[43]

Veterans of Messines, writing about the battle then or later, were unanimous in attributing due credit for its success to Second Army and his staff. The avuncular Plumer managed, unlike most of his peers on the Western front, to cross the no-man's-land which separated the hierarchical, public school, priveliged culture of the generals from that of the men they led. From that empathy and understanding, that sense of duty and obligation stretching both ways, all else flowed. Attention was paid to minute details because the time thus spent might save one or two lives. Lives, the loss of which other Generals would accept as 'inevitable casualties'. But as the 16th was to discover, the British Army possessed few generals like Plumer. Many were arrogant, insensitive prigs of vapid intellect like the 'Irish' Fifth Army commander Gen. Sir Hubert Gough (the man who had led the Curragh mutiny in 1914) whose slapdash staff work and overbearing manner were legendary through the Army, but whose dismissal would have appalled the Old Boys network which protected so many men of limited efficiency in prominent roles in the Great War armies. Fate dealt the 16th and 36th Divisions an ugly blow when it decreed that Gough should seek, and obtain, the services of both Divisions, for the Third Battle of Ypres.

## THE IRISH DIVISIONS AT THE THIRD BATTLE OF YPRES

Messines was a cracking overture to a turgid and tragic opera. The line had been straightened, and now Haig's master plan to push forward from Ypres and drive the enemy from their submarine bases at Ostend and Zeebrugge could go ahead. Between the concept and the delivery of the plan, however, a major political reality intervened. Thousands of French soldiers had mutinied. Executions 'pour encourager les autres' had taken place after a number of courts martial. The situation had been brought under control, but French troops had made it plain that they were not going to take part in any major offensive action in the near future. Third Ypres became, in part at least, a mechanism for keeping the Germans occupied and well away from the French. The main offensive was entrusted to the talentless and uninspired Gough, whose Fifth Army staff reflected his own nature as surely as did the Second Army reflect that of Plumer.

Among the Tommies Ypres (or 'Wipers' as it became known to tongues unused to such a succession of consonants) was an ugly and ill-famed name. It was a place where you didn't want to go, and if you'd been there you didn't want to go back to. Jack Christie, a 36th Division medical orderly, had begun hearing about its reputation for sudden death shortly after his arrival in France:

> In the cafes you would have met the old soldiers, those who would have been out with the regular army at the start of the war and when we would be talking about our exploits, and they would say, 'Have you been to Ypres' and then they nodded. It was like a very exclusive club, to have been to Ypres, and it meant, 'Don't talk, you know nothing about war till you get to Ypres.'[44]

And when you got there!

> There was a smell of bodies in it. And I don't mean metaphorically, I mean literally. You smelled that this was the place where you shouldn't be, get out of it ... It was a swamp and they couldn't build trenches, as fast as you dug them the earth fell in again. And this was August, there had been the Lamis (mid-summer) floods which coincided with our being there.[45]

Christie's 36th Divison was, once again, side by side with the 16th. Anthony Brennan, of the 2nd Royal Irish, was just as intimidated by the reputation and reality of the town: 'I remember trailing across the much-shelled square of Ypres and looking at the ruins of the Cloth Hall, about which we had heard so much. Although we had only been a few days in the Ypres salient we had already seen enough to realise that we were in a hot spot.'[46]

John Breen, once a colleague of Brennan's in the 2nd Royal Irish, had, by 1917, moved to Willie Redmond's old battalion, the 6th Royal Irish. He remembers that the Germans in the Ypres Salient owned the high ground. 'Passchendaele was a place where nobody could attack but the Germans were up on top of a ridge. They were fair enough, they were out of the mud anyway ...'.[47]

German command of the heights overlooking the British and French lines at Ypres in a semi-circle which snaked from east to north meant that British preparations for the offensive were done in full view of the German observers. German artillery proved crucial during the different phases of the campaign, hampering British efforts to improve communications, which had played such an important part in the Messines battle. According to Ned Byrne, who served with the Royal Artillery, the gunners 'got the worst of it at Passchendaele. The German artillery blew the British artillery to bits in it ... The British guns were so close that the Germans couldn't miss. There were gunners, drivers, officers lying all over and guns blown back.'[48] Byrne, despite having men killed and injured around him, escaped death half a dozen times at Third Ypres before finally being wounded and invalided home.

The British guns, despite expending millions of tons of high explosive, never gained mastery of the artillery exchanges to the extent that they had done at Messines. They failed to knock out the German artillery and they signally failed to deal with the new defensive system recently inaugurated by the Germans, the pill-box. The Germans 'had by now realized that continuous trenches afforded poor protection against the terrific bombardments of the allies, unless abundant underground cover could be provided, for which the waterlogged terrain of Flanders was unsuited.' So they introduced ' ... small concrete blockhouses with walls of great thickness each garrisoned by about twenty men with two or three machine-guns.'[49] Part of the difficulty in dealing with this new phenomenon, according to Jack Christie, was the heavy ground around Ypres. 'As long as you had machine-gunners in it, at the slit, they could keep a regiment at bay in ground like that. There was no running in that mud, you had to fight your way through every inch of it ...'.[50]

The 'pill-boxes' would face their first test at Ypres and come through with flying colours, largely because the British troops attacking them had no experience to call upon in dealing with them. They had been introduced by the German 4th Army commander General von Armin, and although the 16th and 36th Divisions had come across some at Messines that did not constitute a proper military introduction. Gough's Fifth Army seemed to adhere to the philosophy of letting the rabid dog bite first before shooting it. Therefore no formal training took place in how to cope with this new defensive threat. Capt. Frank Hitchcock of the 2nd Leinsters points out in *Stand To* that, 'Our troops quickly adapted themselves to Pill Box fighting, but at first, mainly owing to their surprise element, we were baffled, and suffered heavy losses.'[51]

The Ypres Salient, into which the men of the 16th and 36th Divisions were thrust a few short weeks after Messines, managed, in contravention of the best scientific principles, to combine the elements of fire and water very effectively. It was Hell-fire with mud. Shortly after the arrival of the two divisions, to prepare for the Battle of Langemarck in the middle of August (one of the battles lumped together under the title Third Ypres—of which the infamous Passchendaele was the paludal climax) it began to rain. A summer shower, the experts predicted, it was, after all, the end of July. It was anything but a summer shower though and soon the land over which Gough proposed to send his troops to take the German pill-boxes perched on the German-held heights, was a quagmire, a swamp which immobilised mind and body.

Thomas Gibson of the 10th Inniskillings, seventy years after the event, retained memories of a countryside 'full of great, big shell holes, and they were full of water, and if you were passing along and fell into one of them you had a chance of being drowned before anyone could get you out'.[52] For Jack Christie the featureless landscape reflected the unforgiving and hostile nature of the environment:

> There wasn't a tree left in it, they were all gone. Unbelievable, no trees higher than that [indicates knee high], all cut up by shells and men had to live in that. You were up to here [indicates thigh] in mud, and if you went down in that, and if you had been wounded and went down, that was the end of you, that was you finished.[53]

A friend of Harry Bennet in the 10th Inniskillings, with typical mordant wit, put it more succinctly: 'Harry, this is a terrible place they've took us,' Herbie Andrews told Bennet; 'if you stand up you're shot and if you stoop down you're drowned.'[54]

As at Messines there was preparation. Attacking units had the opportunity to co-ordinate their assaults with full-dress rehearsals. Units were taken out of the line for three weeks to ready themselves. But whatever advantage was thus gained was later thoroughly and egregiously dissipated. Fr Willie Doyle, the perrenial professional optimist, was skeptical of official assurances. He had heard them all at the Somme. ' "Success is certain", our Generals tell us, but I cannot help wondering what are the plans of the Great Leader, and what the result will be when He has issued His orders.'[55] His remarks could be seen as intimations of his own mortality.

The two Irish divisions went into action in support of an assault on 31 July, the 6th Connaught Rangers and the 2nd Dublins being praised for their work as stretcher-bearers at Pilckem Ridge on 1 August. Both divisions were then included in a planned attack on 4 August, but 'the rain started at about 8.00 that morning and it got heavier and heavier until there was stairrods coming down. And it rained like that for six days and six nights without a break.'[56] Fr Willie Doyle saw that men were 'soaked to the skin and beyond it ... standing up to their knees in a river of mud and water.'[57] G.A.C. Walker, a signals officer with the 7th Inniskillings, noted that this 'was all in favour of the enemy. Within a few hours the forward zone was little better than a quagmire of water logged shell holes, a sea of mud and water in a land of absolute desolation.'[58]

The assault was postponed until 14 August. In Plumer's Second Army it was policy to give assaulting battalions as much rest as possible before an attack. Such niceties were foreign to the culture of Fifth Army; both the 16th and the 36th were left in the front-lines for the next two weeks, the 16th in the Frezenberg sector, the 36th, to their left, near Wieltje. The troops existed

> in conditions of misery which beggar description. In every battalion hundreds were killed, wounded, gassed or overcome with trench fever and swollen feet. Units were relieved and rotated. But often the hardship of the journey out of and into the line outweighed the value of a few hour's rest.[59]

Some of the troops in the 16th had recently returned from Salonika where they had been invalided out with malaria. The experience brought on many relapses.

The dug-outs of the 36th Division (in which General Nugent tried as best he could to give his assaulting battalions as much rest as possible) were execrable underground hell-holes:

> Wieltje dug-outs. Who that saw it will forget that abominable mine with ... its thirteen entrances, the water that flowed down its main passages and poured down its walls, its electric light gleaming dully through steam-coated lamps, its sickly atmosphere, its smells, its huge population of men—and of rats? From behind the sack-curtained door-ways the coughing and groaning of men in uneasy slumber mingled with the click of type-writers.[60]

But at least the occupants were safe. The 7th Leinsters HQ at the Frezenberg Redoubt was an old German Regimental Command Post, on which the enemy gunners had drawn a bead.

> In an interior eight feet across the battalion HQ tried to function whilst providing a home for 12 officers and men. The Germans knew the exact location of their old post to the inch, and their shelling was chillingly accurate. Any movement in the open was foolhardy, and an old tin can in the room had to be used as a lavatory.[61]

Capt. J.H Staniforth considered it to be 'worse than the Somme' and wrote of how he had witnessed a Scottish officer, driven crazy by the pain from an intestinal wound, put a gun to his own head and blow his brains out.[62]

The highly regarded 16th Division officer, Brigadier General Pereira, noted in a report on the failed offensive which was to come that,

> Without the glory and excitement of going over the top as you did at Guillemont and Wytschaete, you have had the far harder task and drudgery of holding the line under heavy bombardments, lying in shell holes full of water ... You came in for the worst of the weather ... and up to your first relief in the early hours of August 6th you have had to stand or lie in the open without overhead protection, with everything soaked and sore feet, whilst the continuous bombardment banished all chance of sleep for four days.[63]

Not that the Ulsters were in any less precarious a position. Cross-country tracks had been constructed for resupply purposes as the German gunners knew where the roads were. But it didn't take them long to locate these temporary paths either.

> No one who used them but had at some point to lie crouched on his belly, watching huge columns of earth and water spout up with the burst of the big shells. Horrors were not new, nor did the sight of dead bodies affect men overmuch, but there was one vision upon one of these tracks, the mangled remains of a complete party of artillery carriers, six men and twelve horses, which burnt itself upon the brains of those that saw it.[64]

During that long destructive sojourn in the front-lines, Anthony Brennan sheltered in what he describes as an old mine shaft. Despite heavy shelling on the first night in the forward trenches he managed to get some sleep. He was woken by his comrade, O'Brien, who warned him that the bombardment was geting heavier and to advised him to move. Brennan was reluctant, but,

> The next shell settled the question. It was high explosive and burst just above us. I saw my trouser knees suddenly go red and could tell from their calling for stretcher-bearers that my comrades had also been wounded ... As far as the war was concerned this was the end of the road for me. Of my three comrades who had been wounded at the same time I heard later that O'Brien died of his wounds, Sullivan had both legs broken and MacCarthy was only slightly wounded.[65]

Brennan spent a year in hospital in St Albans and then in Dublin. He was discharged from the Army in September 1918.

In making such an early exit from the Ypres campaign, Brennan may have avoided death less than a fortnight later. Both the 16th and 36th Divisions, having lost in the region of 2000 men each in the lead up to the Battle of Langemarck on 16 August, were, incredibly, ordered to attack well-defended positions across open sodden ground. The two divisions made significant gains but, debilitated and exhausted, were beaten back and lost as many men again. Bob Grange, of the 12th Rifles, watched as the Belfast Young Citizen Volunteers, the 14th Rifles, waded ankle deep through mud to get to the German lines. As Thomas Gibson of the 10th Inniskillings waited for the off the British preliminary barrage lifted, the sign to go over the top.

> These parapets were pretty high and slimy and I was only a young fellow at that time and I was struggling to get up and put my rifle on top ... and this big Colonel, he just got me by the seat of the trousers and the back of the coat and he just shoved me onto the parapet and he said, 'Away you go, sonny.'[66]

Among the targets of the Ulster Division that day were farms codenamed, ominously, Somme and Gallipoli. On the borderline between the operations of the 16th and the 36th was 'Gallipoli Copse'. The facsimiles proved no more auspicious for the Irishmen than had the originals. They went into battle understrength and ill prepared to combat the German pill-box formations. Casualties among officers and NCO's meant they were also lacking in men with leadership experience. Initial gains were made by both divisions but raking German machine-gun fire from various strong points and from two low hills (35 and 37) soon stalled the advance.

> All the ground below two knolls of earth called Hill 35 and Hill 37, which were defended by German pill-boxes ... became an Irish shambles. In spite of their dreadful losses the survivors in the Irish battalions went forward to the assault with desperate valour ... [67]

The need to take the pill-box strongpoints, rather than leave them to the 'moppers up' delayed the advance on both fronts and meant that the troops got too far behind the creeping barrage. This had a deadly domino effect, the more they delayed the better prepared were the next line of German defences to check their progress.

The 16th Division's third Victoria Cross was won by L/Cpl. Room of the 2nd Royal Irish, a stretcher-bearer who spent that entire day exposed to enemy fire, ferrying wounded men to the Regimental Aid Post. The RAP's were on the sheltered side of the Frezenberg Ridge, but in order to get there, the bearers, like Room, had to crest the ridge and present themselves as a target for the German gunners. Room performed this feat unflaggingly through-out the day. Wounded had to be carried back more than 2000 yards. Condi-tions were so glutinous it often took up to eight men to carry a single stretcher. One of the men brought to safety in this manner, through the ankle deep mud was John Breen of the Royal Irish Regiment, who had carried his heavy pack through hundreds of yards of the sponge-like wasteland before being hit. 'They had to cut the clothes off me in the dressing station. They couldn't get them off me. They were stuck together with mud and water and filth.'[68]

The German counter-attack, when it came, did so without warning. Com-munications across the wasteland were a virtual impossibility. Runners were used, and if they died in the attempt to get a message through the vital information which needed to be conveyed, more often than not, died with them. Those who had advanced now found themselves outflanked, overrun or surrounded. Exhausted men, who should never have been thrown into battle in the first place, now fought desperate rearguard actions just to make their way back to their own lines. The 16th and the 36th were forced to withdraw to their starting positions. Hickie and Nugent were ordered to press the attacks forward again but informed XIX Corps that their ranks were too depleted and their men too exhausted to have any chance of success. Nugent wrote to his wife that for his 36th Division: 'It has been a truly terrible day. Worse than 1 July I am afraid. The whole division had been driven back with terrible losses.'[69] Hickie, commander of the 16th, anticipating failure, had tried to have the 16 August assault cancelled. He had been warned by a junior Divisional staff officer, Major Noel Holmes of the Royal Irish Regiment, that the task, in the swamp which existed all around them, was beyond the physi-cal capabilities of tired men. Holmes, himself a noted athlete, had been physi-cally drained by the act of merely walking from 16th Division HQ to the front-line. Afterwards he wrote that, 'I said to General Hickie that I don't think the men could do it. To which Hickie replied, "I'm not going to mention your name or else they'll say what does that young pup know". He telephoned somebody else who telephoned somebody else. I suppose it went to the top, but nothing was done.'[70]

By the end of July 1917 Fr Wille Doyle had found himself ministering to all four battalions of the 48th Brigade. Fr Francis Browne, a fellow Jesuit, had been transferred to the Irish Guards and a clerical error had resulted in his being replaced by the wrong man. This priest, when he discovered the mis-take, refused point blank to go to Ypres. All the while Doyle's fame was spreading. Unlike many chaplains, he seemed to spend most of his time in the front line. He was revered by the men of the 16th, and, despite his religious beliefs, greatly respected and admired by the overwhelmingly protestant 36th

Division. Although a natural optimist, occasionally black despair showed through in his diaries. Just a few days before the Battle of Langemarck he wrote about some of the men of his Brigade whom he had seen die:

> My poor brave boys! They are lying now out on the battle-field; some in a little grave dug and blessed by their chaplain, who loves them all as if they were his own children; others stiff and stark with staring eyes, hidden in a shell-hole where they had crept to die ... Do you wonder ... that many a time the tears gather in my eyes, as I think of those who are gone?[71]

On the night of 6 August his life was spared by a typically unselfish decision to help out at a Dressing Station. A shell burst at the entrance to a block-house he'd been occupying and set off several boxes of Very lights which caused horrendous burns to the occupants. His diaries are of full of stories of similar fortunate escapes. His very mobility providing some sort of guarantee of safety.

As the German shells found their marks during the extended front-line spell of the 16th much of his time was spent ministering to the wounded and burying the dead. He wrote on 7 August of reaching a group of smashed and bleeding bodies after one shell had done its work.

> The first thing I saw almost unnerved me; a young soldier lying on his back, his hands and face a mass of blue phosphorous flame, smoking horribly in the darkness. He was the first victim I had seen of the new gas the Germans are using, a fresh horror in this awful war ... The poor lad recognized me, I anointed him on a little spot of unburnt flesh, not a little nervously as the place was reeking with gas, gave him a drink, which he begged for so earnestly and then hastened to the others.[72]

Later that night two more men were hit, Doyle cradled one of them in the darkness as he died, until a flash of gunfire revealed that the young dying soldier was his own servant. Doyle's empathy with the men in the line is clear from his writing, he suffered for them and he suffered with them. His inability to harden himself and set aside his own natural feelings of sympathy for the plight of others must have made his own torment even more intense.

One of Doyle's last diary entries, a note to his father written on 14 August, is hauntingly ironic. His numerous brushes with death seem to have convinced him that he was being preserved for a higher purpose. He wrote, 'I have told you all my escapes, dearest father, because I think what I have written will give you the same confidence which I feel, that my old armchair

up in heaven is not ready yet, and I do not want you to be uneasy about me.'
Before the letter reached home he was dead. He had used up his own and one
or two other shares of good fortune, his desire to be with the troops as they
went forward, was his inevitable undoing. The disastrous attack on 16 August
had already broken down when the Germans counter-attacked. Doyle was
ordered to the rear. He reluctantly agreed to go but didn't stay there for long.
Within a couple of hours he was forward again looking for the wounded and
the dying to offer what physical or spiritual help he could.

The specific details of Doyle's death are still shrouded in some mystery,
and, such was his fame, many were anxious to become retrospective 'wit-
nesses' to his death. His orderly, Pte. McInespie, has most claim to being a
credible witness. According to his account Doyle was having a discussion
with three other officers on the morning of 17 August when a shell burst
amongst them. Corroborating evidence establishes that McInespie did indeed
stagger into the Regimental Aid Post declaring 'Fr Doyle has been killed'.
However, his body was never found, although one group of Dublin Fusiliers
insist that they came across it and buried him under severe shellfire. Jimmy
O'Brien, another Dublin Fusilier, 20 years old at the time of Third Ypres, 76
when interviewed about his war experiences insists that, 'I was with Father
Willie Doyle, the Jesuit, he was shot down beside me and I was wounded in
the shoulder. [Then] I lay in a shell hole up to my neck in water.'[73]

The 16th Division was devastated by Doyle's death. His courage, apparent
invulnerability, his energy and his compassion had been an inspiration for all
of the many thousands who encountered him. Capt. Healy of the 8th Dublins,
who remembered Doyle arriving regularly with sweets and cigarettes for the
men, wrote, 'If I had gone through the thousandth part of what Fr Doyle did,
or if I had run a hundredth part of the risks he ran, I would have been dead
long ago.'[74] Sergeant T. Flynn wrote to the *Irish News*:

> He did not know what fear was and everybody in the battalion, Catho-
> lic and Protestant alike, idolised him ... Everybody says that he has
> earned the VC many times over, and I can vouch for it myself from
> what I have seen him do many a time.'

In fact Doyle was recommended for the VC but it was not granted, an
omission which reflected no credit whatever on those responsible for the
decision.

One of the most moving tributes came in a letter to the *Glasgow Weekly
News* from a Belfast Presbyterian soldier who wrote that:

> Father Doyle was a good deal among us. We couldn't possibly agree
> with his religious opinions, but we simply worshipped him for other

things. He didn't know the meaning of fear and he didn't know what bigotry was. He was as ready to risk his life to take a drop of water to a wounded Ulsterman as to assist men of his own faith and regiment. If he risked his life in looking after Ulster Protestant soldiers once he did it a hundred times in the last few days ... The Ulstermen felt his loss more keenly than anybody ...

The elation after Messines had been short-lived. Casualties in both the 16th and 36th Divisions had been heavy, even before the assault of 16 August. Given the weather, the ground conditions, the intact German defences and the battering the troops had endured, a wiser Army Commander would have postponed the attack. But the self-regarding Gough, who badly needed a feather in his cap, would hear of no postponement. Later he tried to blame the 16th Division for the failure of the Battle of Langemarck when Haig visited his HQ on 17 August. His subsequent self-justification included the contention that 'I was aware that the division was not of the highest standard'.[75] This hardly squares with Gen. Hickie's claim that 'The 16th Division ... was specially applied for by the Commander of the Fifth Army in view of the impending Third Battle of Ypres'.[76] Later Gough would attempt to rewrite history and disputed the evaluation of the battle by an official historian G.C. Wynne who said the attacks at Pilckem Ridge and Langemarck had been 'thoroughly bad in their planning ... [Gough] should have been sacked for them without a pension'.[77]

Among the Irish dead, in addition to Fr Willie Doyle, was the poet Francis Ledwidge, killed when he was hit by a shell while in reserve on the 31 July. A much later fatality was Lt.-Col. A.D. Murphy, of the 2nd Leinsters, Frank Hitchcock's CO. The Leinster's were with the 24th Division and had gone into the 31 July attack with only 400 men. They returned with 150. Murphy survived that but died towards the end of Third Ypres, at the Passchendaele battle. He was only 27 years of age when he died and on the verge of promotion to brigadier. In 1914 he had been a subaltern and transport officer. His rapid rise through the ranks was only due in part to 'natural wastage'.

Sixty-six thousand British soldiers died during the Third Ypres offensive, amongst a total casualty list of almost a quarter of a million. As John North wrote in *The Fading Vision*:

> Never before have Englishmen been slain at such a rate on such a scale. No High Command in the whole history of war—where success is 'almost in mathematical ratio' to the degree of surprise—can have contributed less in manoeuvre, or demanded more in slaughter; its appetite for men to fling into the cauldron of its offensives knew no appeasement: 'I want *Men*', wrote the Commander-in-Chief at Passchendaele.[78]

For the Irish the battle was another disaster, on a par with the Somme and not to be approached again until the massive German offensive of March/April 1918.

Between 2 and 18 August the 36th lost 144 officers and 3441 men (casualties) and continued to be diluted by the introduction of British conscripts (a number of the Royal Irish Rifle battalions had to be amalgamated). As Philip Orr puts it graphically: 'The quagmire of shell-churned earth swallowed up men who had survived the bullets of Thiepval, and pillboxes and strong wire helped keep the German line immoveable'.[79] The 16th Division lost 221 officers and 4064 men. More than 2000 of those casualties occuring in a two-day-period around the Langemarck battle. Less than 300 of the bodies of the 16th Division's 1000 dead were ever recovered. The rest had been atomised or drowned.

All for five miles of ground!

Charles Miller of the 2nd Inniskillings, soon to join the 36th and Gough's Fifth Army, is scathing in his writings of the choice of Ypres for the push:

> If they had had the power to dry up miles and miles of waist deep mud there would have been some sense in it. As it was the Ypres battlefield just represented one gigantic slough of despond into which floundered battalions brigades and divisions of infantry without end, to be shot to pieces or drowned, until at last and with immeasurable slaughter we had gained a few miles of liquid mud which were of no use to anyone.[80]

Lt.-Col Rowland Feilding, whose 6th Connaughts were as badly cut up as any of the other units in the 16th Division, missed the mire of Third Ypres when he was injured in a riding accident and despatched back to England. But he heard enough from his Acting CO Capt. Brett and others to write to his wife that 'after four or five days waiting in the trenches, the men were so exhausted with the shelling, and their feet so sore and swollen from the wet, that when the time came to attack they were so weak that they could scarcely have blown out a candle.'[81] War Correspondent Phillip Gibbs wrote that the story of the two Irish Divisions:

> ... is black in tragedy. They were left in the line for sixteen days before the battle, and were shelled and gassed incessantly as they crouchd in wet ditches. Every day groups of men were blown to bits, until the ditches were bloody, and the living lay by the corpses of their comrades.[82]

Much of the blame can be laid at the door of Gough and his staff. Even Cyril Falls in his history of the 36th-Division points the finger in the Fifth

Army's direction, and his natural inclination might well have been to defend the man who would have mutinied rather than bring his troops north to tackle the UVF in 1914. He contrasted the leadership of Plumer and Gough, to the detriment of the latter:

> The private soldier knew the [Second] Army Commander and his eyeglass as he knew no Corps Commander under whom he fought. The difficulties at Ypres were infinitely greater than at Messines; that everyone recognised. But in the former case they did not appear to be met with quite the precision, care and forethought of the latter. The private soldier felt a difference. He may have been unfair in is estimate, but that estimate was none the less of importance. For what the private soldier felt had a marked effect upon what the private soldier, the only ultimate winner of battles, accomplished.[83]

Phillip Gibbs, who was able to write little enough at the time about the ineptitude of the High Command (he was once threatened with execution by the generals),[84] in his book *The Realities of War* wrote of the churlish manner in which the 16th and 36th Divisions were treated by the braided neanderthals of the Fifth Army:

> The two Irish Divisions were broken to bits, and their Brigadiers called it murder. They were violent in their denunciation of the 5th Army for having put their men into the attack after those thirteen days of heavy shelling, and, after the battle, they complained that they were cast aside like old shoes, no care being taken for the comfort of the men who survived. No motor lorries were sent to meet them and bring them down, but they had to tramp back, exhausted and dazed. The remnants of the 16th Division, the poor despairing remnants, were sent, without rest or baths, straight into the line again, down south.[85]

Although Plumer's Second Army staff was reckoned to have an intimate knowledge of every shellhole in the Ypres Salient, perhaps they might not have been any more successful in the campaign. They would have had no massive mines to soften up the defenders and they would have been attacking from a salient, rather than marching towards an unnatural bulge in the enemy lines. But they would surely have known when to stop beating their soldier's brains against German blockhouses or filling their lungs with viscous, mottled, muddy water. Gough did not know when to stop. Gough could not afford to stop. He needed a success and because he was Haig's man, blindly pursuing 'Haig-think' (the prosecution of war by means of the accumulation of corpses) he had to be defended by the military establishment. (Only generals like Allenby, who questioned or opposed, were 'without the walls' of that establishment.) Haig recognised that divisional commanders (or at least those who had any regard for their troops) wanted nothing to do with the Fifth Army. But still he stood down Plumer and placed Gough in charge of Third Ypres. Ironically, his retention in a position of authority meant he was around to use as a convenient scapegoat for the losses suffered during the final German offensive of March 1918.

Both the 16th and 36th Divisions had managed, despite frightening losses, to preserve some of their national character and integrity. But after Third Ypres the 16th was no longer the khaki manifestation of the National Volunteers while the 36th was merely the skeleton of the old Ulster Volunteer Force. And, as Tom Johnstone eloquently puts it:

> There was another, longer lasting, consequence to Langemarck. Gen. Plumer, that most 'blimpish' looking and beloved of English generals, had at Messines used an Irish assault corps with resounding success. Irishman Hubert Gough destroyed that concept. With its destruction ended the hope that between Orange and Green factions, the friendship and esteem engendered by successful collaboration in France would endure after the war. That for Ireland was the real tragedy of Third Ypres.[86]

The dream of Willie Redmond had died with him just a few short weeks after its most credible and emphatic expression.

The dubious honour of membership of Gough's Fifth Army had obliterated memories of Messines and left a bad taste in the mouths of the two Irish Divisions. As winter turned to spring and, for very different reasons, the supply of Irishmen, north and south, dwindled to a trickle, the young conscripts of England, Scotland and Wales, began to swell the ranks of those uniquely Irish divisions and reduce their claim to Irishness. The following Spring would see them mangled and pulverised into virtual oblivion.

# 8    1918: From Calamity to Triumph

The Entente military and political hierarchy found it difficult to focus its aggression on the Germans in 1918, so busy were its constituent parts in the much more convivial task of fighting and bickering amongst themselves. Lloyd George and Haig entertained wholly different notions of how to prosecute the war while the French and the British armies were at loggerheads over the extent of the line held by the British. The French wanted their allies to take responsibility for a far greater portion of the Entente trenches and they won the argument.

In 1918 Gough's Fifth Army, which still included the two Irish divisions (the 36th in Gen. Maxse's XVIII Corps and the 16th in Gen. Congreve's VII Corps), found itself defending a front covering 42 miles, with each division responsible for 5–6000 yards of saturated entrenchments which were being constantly reclaimed by the earth from which they had been cut. Troop numbers were patently inadequate for the task, even against a German army which had suffered numinous manpower losses of its own. But the Fifth Army was facing a revitalised enemy. The Germans were no longer fighting a war on two fronts. In 1917 they had accepted the surrender of Russia and had already begun moving battle-hardened divisions from east to west to prepare for a spring offensive designed to end the war before the recent entry of the USA into the conflict could tip the balance in favour of the Entente.

As a consequence of egregious losses, unable to sustain the traditional structure of the Army, Haig had agreed to a radical reformation which resulted in divisions being reduced in size from twelve battalions to nine and brigades from four to three. Surplus troops were gathered together into what were known as Entrenching Battalions. This led to the merging and disbandment of many of the Volunteer units of Kitchener's Army (the old war-horse himself had gone down with the HMS *Hampshire* en route to Russia in 1916). They now became subsumed into the regular Army battalions most of which had been part of the old BEF in 1914. It was a cultural change which had many detractors:

> The brigade of four battalions was the traditional British formation, just as the regiment of three was the continental. It was the formation which British commanders had handled in training and practice, upon

which their conceptions of infantry in war were based. The moral loss was no less great, particularly in divisions and brigades with strong territorial associations and sentiment.'[1]

This was especially true of the 36th Ulster Division, whose fervent loyalist ethos became even further diluted and whose UVF origins were but a dim memory. Five of its nine battalions were regular Army units: ' ... the characteristics of the Ulster Division were entirely changed. Its infantry, formed originally from the UVF, had now Ulster-Scot and Celt intermingled, and received English recruits as well'.[2] Such was the radical change in the composition of the division that on St Patrick's Day, 1918, Roman Catholic Mass was celebrated and shamrock was distributed!

The 16th had already gone the same way, with its nationalist mien dissipated by the introduction of drafts of non-Irish troops. Frank Hitchcock of the 2nd Leinsters noted in his diary that, 'The failure of recruiting in Ireland had rendered it impossible to maintain all the Irish battalions'. (This was just as true of Ulster as it was of the rest of the country.) The 2nd Leinsters absorbed the 7th Leinsters. 'This had the outstanding merit of preserving nationality and regimental *esprit de corps* ... It was most unfortunate that the new organisation had hardly been completed before the enemy launched his colossal attack in March'.[3] Kipling refers in his history of the Irish Guards (not a 16th Division battalion) to the fact that, as usual on St Patrick's Day, 1918, shamrock was distributed. 'This ... was almost superfluous as a large proportion of the Battalion had ceased to be Irish.'[4] This dilution was occuring across all Irish units even while drafts of Irishmen were being sent to British regiments, prompting a suspicion that this was being done as a matter of policy. Of even greater consequence for the 16th Division was the loss of its CO, Gen. Hickie. He went home sick and was replaced by a highly respected Englishman Maj.-Gen. Sir Amyatt Hull.

But no matter what structural changes were imposed on the fabric of the British Army, it was still a rotting, crumbling fabric. Troop numbers were not adequate for the tasks the soldiers were expected to perform. Divisions had consisted of roughly 12,000 men. After the reorganisation they should have numbered 9000. In fact they rarely went above 6000. As a consequence a radical rethink of defensive systems began. This led to little more than the mere plagiarising of techniques devised and used successfully (particularly at Third Ypres) by the Germans. It was described as 'defence in depth' and was an invention spawned by the inability to defend in breadth. The line was divided into three sectors, Forward, Battle and Rear. The former consisted of the existing front-line and reserve trenches, the Battle zone (which came into play if the Forward zone was breached) was immediately behind this area and stretched for about 2000 to 3000 yards. Rear was further back (and usually

where the generals were to be found). In addition a decision was taken because there were simply not enough bayonets in the front trenches, to resort
to the use of 'strongpoints' in the line. These were (in theory) well constructed dug-outs, capable of withstanding German shells and disgorging the
troops they sheltered when the enemy barrage lifted.

The theory, expectation, or more likely, the hope, was that the troops in
the Forward zone would fall back to the Battle zone after slowing down the
enemy and that they would there be reinforced by fresh troops. But in practice it proved more fantasy than theory. 'The implementation of the system
required tactical sophistication of a high order from the defenders. Such
battle-craft was lacking in the British army, not least the under-trained 16th
Division.'[5]

The excellent *theoretical* base of the new system was appreciated by Capt.
Charles Miller of the 2nd Inniskillings:

> The Higher Command for once in its life planned something unortho-
> dox. Our actual strength for holding the line amounted to about one
> bayonet for fifteen yards of trench, and they reached the obvious con-
> clusion that however heroic the man behind the bayonet might be, the
> odds were probably a bit greater than he could tackle. They therefore
> propounded the simple and excellent plan of not holding the trench
> line as a line at all ... the attacking troops would have little or no
> difficulty in piercing the line, but having done so would find them-
> selves in a maze of tiny fortresses from which the defending troops
> would be shooting them down ... Everyone knew by then that in all
> probability we were in for a very bad time, but at least this much more
> elastic type of defence did give us a better chance of holding on and
> fighting back. After three and a half years of war Thomas Atkins was
> becoming tired of being treated purely as cannon fodder and ordered
> to throw away his life on a point of prestige.[6]

In early 1918 the very birds in the few trees left on the Picardy battle-
front knew that the Germans were going to launch a major attack as soon as
the weather would allow. The British daily newspapers openly speculated
about it. Intelligence indicated that the assault would take place at the end of
March 1918. There was a body of opinion which anticipated an attack to the
north, followed by a concerted German move on the Channel ports. Capt.
Guy Nightingale, of the 1st Munsters, was confident that wherever the hammer fell, it wouldn't be on Fifth Army on the Somme, 'There are only three
places it will be worth his while to push and this is not one of them'. Nightingale believed the Germans were bluffing and were actually reorganising
their forces while awaiting the arrival of the new threat, from the Americans.

Others in Fifth Army looked at the size of the area they were being asked to defend and put themselves in the shoes of a German High Command looking for a quick victory to drive a wedge between the French and British armies. So when the 36th Division took up its new stretch of the line, near St Quentin, Charles Miller was not overly consoled by the lack of activity, ' ... it was obvious to any soldier that we had a desperately long line to hold for the forces at our disposal. It was also widely believed and, as was subsequently proved, truly believed that the Germans were planning a crashing onslaught on the very weak Fifth Army.'[7] A Divisional Claims Officer for the 36th in the build-up to the offensive, dealing with claims by French civilians for damage caused directly by the British Army was due to attend an Inquiry on 21 March but, 'I wondered what would happen as I knew before that this was the day on which the great German offensive was expected'.[8] In anticipation all leave had been cancelled on 20 March.

In borrowing generously from German defensive tactics the High Command had omitted one vital element—that of time. German dispositions had been assembled over a period of months, even years. The Fifth Army, which took over trenches left in an appalling state by the French, had only days and weeks to prepare for an unparalleled German onslaught.

> ... The strategic question of the actual location of the strong points seemed to me of minor importance. What was vitally necessary was that we should have time to make them as strong as possible, and also time to accustom the men by practice on the spot, so that when the time came everyone should know the ropes and the strong points should be occupied with the minimum of delay.[9]

What actually happened was that, in the race against time to construct properly built and positioned strongpoints troops were driven to the brink of exhaustion. Already, because of falling numbers, battalions were being left in the front-lines for longer periods. Now when they were, theoretically, in reserve, they were being used in a frantic building programme. When the German attack finally came the 2nd Dublins had just spent forty consecutive days in the line, the 1st Munsters, forty-three![10] Rowland Feilding, CO of the 6th Connaughts, wrote to his wife on 5 March that:

> The battalion wants a rest. It had been up for forty-two days when, last night, it was relieved, and even now I doubt if the rest is in sight, since an order has just come in to go up tomorrow for the day, to dig. I leave you to imagine the state of the men's bodies and clothing after so long a time in the line, almost without a wash.[11]

Training for troops was a virtual impossibility. The enemy would send well-prepared and well-rested troops into the fray. The German units holding the line up to 21 March were not the men who would undertake the initial assault. Capt. Guy Nightingale of the 1st Munsters, after a successful raid in mid-March told his mother in a letter home that 'The Boshe prisoners were an awful lot of women, the most miserable crowd ...'.[12] The troops who would carry the weight of the offensive were elsewhere!

Initially, in the construction of strongpoints some reference was made to battalion commanders in the line. Their advice was sought on the positioning of these enlarged and reinforced dugouts. But this new found flexibilty on the part of the General Staff wasn't to last. The result was the worst, and the last example of bungling Charles Miller experienced at the hands of the Army:

> We had already started to dig the strong points in the sites selected by the Colonels when the Brigadier chose to inspect them, and of course decided to alter the positions. We started all over again but there were lots of other brass hats who had to have their say in the matter, and time and time again the position of the strong points was changed. The result was chaotic. In the first place the men were tired to death, in the second place since the position of the strong points was constantly being changed it was impossible to organise a regular drill by which every man knew his strong point and got there in the quickest possible time when ordered to do so; lastly, instead of being deeply dug and strongly revetted and wired it was quite obvious that when the moment came to use them the strong points would hardly be strong enough to keep out a well-aimed snowball. The appalling and crass stupidity of it all.[13]

One night, having supervised yet another of the interminable fatigue details Miller mounted his horse to lead his company from the 'construction site'. He fell asleep on his horse and woke up the following morning in a ditch. None of his men had bothered to waken him up and not even the fall had roused him.

> It really is inconceivable when one thinks of it. The brass hats knew that almost certainly in a very short time we should be engaged in one of the most crucial battles in British history, and yet because of their silly little whims and fancies they were driving the men who were going to fight that battle almost to breaking strain by unnecessary labour.[14]

With orders flying about in a frenetic fashion without the personnel to ensure that they were actually being carried out, staff fantasies became official realities. In the 2nd Leinsters area fictional defensive lines (colour-coded Green, Yellow, etc.) appeared on maps without any excavations having even begun to turn these imagined fortifications into genuine defensive positions.

> On one occasion the Battalion received orders to hold the front with one company and to withdraw the remainder to [the] Yellow line. The commanding officer pointed out that this line did not exist: 'this caused alarm and despondency up above, and a staff officer came to see for himself'.[15]

March was a season of false alarms, tense expectation and occasional German raids as the enemy attempted to build up a picture of the defensive line facing them, or possibly double check that it was as frail a construction as their Intelligence told them it was. Guy Nightingale wrote home, still agnostic or at least sceptical on the subject of the impending German push, about periodic 'hurricanes' or 'cyclones', aggressive episodes on either side. On 16 March he wrote 'there was another hurricane this morning—in fact quite a cyclone caused by some Boshe [*sic*] prisoners the 2nd Bn got, saying that the offensive was to come off this morning. We stood-to again most of the night till 8 a.m, and it *was* cold.'[16] But mostly it was a case of waiting. Digging and waiting. And hoping. Hoping your battalion would not be in the Forward zone when the German push began. 'Uncanny work it was awaiting, in the silence of quietest of quiet lines, a mighty attack of which for very long there was scarce an indication'.[17]

Then, on 21 March, 71 German divisions, across three armies (2nd, 17th and 18th) struck what German High Command hoped would be the decisive blow which would end the war. For the next two weeks a dazed Fifth Army would sink (backwards) into the lowest level of Hell. It was a journey from which the 16th Irish Division would never return.

Rowland Feilding, commanding the 6th Connaughts, recorded his impressions of the beginning of the end of his association with the battalion:

> After several days of uncanny silence the enemy's artillery opened at about half past four on the morning of the 21st with a violence which certainly equalled, if it did not surpass, anything of the kind which has been seen before in the war, both as regards the concentrated character of the shooting and the extent over which the bombardment was spread.[18]

The front-line trenches were doused with poison gas, and, to ensure that it was impossible to reinforce, the thinly defended vanguard areas a strip five miles wide behind the trenches was comprehensively shelled. To make matters worse for the defenders the Germans had a great piece of good fortune. An early morning fog blanketed the Somme region. The mist and gas (which required the defenders to don respirators) made it impossible for the front-line British troops to even see the Germans until they were right on top of them.

The overwhelming impression one gets from reading first-hand accounts of the fighting is of multilayered confusion, verging on and often spilling over into utter mayhem. As the historian of the Leinsters puts it, 'The man who can write a coherent, intelligible, and readable narrative of those first hours of the Somme, 1918, has yet to be born'.[19] Men lived by their instincts, if their intuition was right they survived, if it let them down then they perished or were marched off to German POW camps. More often than not they didn't know why they did what they did to survive.

> We was *all* defensive flank and front-line at one and the same time. But if any one tells you that any one knew what was done, or why 'twas done, in these days, ye will have strong reason to doubt them. We was anywhere and Jerry was everywhere, and our own guns was as big a nuisance as Jerry. When we had done all we could we fell back. We did not walk away by platoons.[20]

The German troops were like men with a mission, men who had been reined in for weeks and were now being unleashed. As a company of the 12th Royal Irish Rifles attempted to withdraw from the danger zone, a single German soldier is reported to have undertaken a one-man bayonet charge against (the remnants of) the entire company. Like the proverbial wolf attacking a fold of sheep, the Germans had quickly quietened the British machine-guns which had been expected to offer supporting fire to the troops in the strongpoints. 'The Germans swept on them, as it were, out of nothingness. Few can have had opportunity to fire a shot ere they were rushed.'[21] Within hours the battalions defending the Forward zones had been annihilated and Gough was having no luck impressing the seriousness of his position on GHQ. In one conversation he was assured that the Germans would be content with their gains on the first day and would 'not come on again the next day ... I disagreed emphatically but failed to make much impression'.[22] Gough, who would become the scapegoat for the entire fiasco, was finding himself 'at the receiving end of the same obtuseness which his own corps and divisional commanders had experienced [from him] at Passchendaele'.[23]

A young subaltern with the Leinsters, who lost almost their entire complement of officers and men, was experiencing his first taste of war. His name was Morrison. Five hours after the affair began he was in command of the battalion, the only officer left alive in the field, leading men who were surrounded and cut off by the ferocity, rapidity and efficiency of the German assault:

> Towards evening I met a full lieutenant named Kirkpatrick and promptly informed him that I had a Battalion to present to him. His first day in action too ... He and I did our best for the lads ... and led them safely from one position to another until we finally got them safely, or comparatively so, out of it on the third day. Fritz gave us no rest at all during the day, but at night we managed to do a bit extra and thus gained on him.[24]

The Kirkpatrick referred to is Lt. Frank Kirkpatrick, mentioned in despatches and subsequently decorated for bravery for jointly operating a Lewis gun along with a Leinster private (Pte. Drinkwater) and fending off a German attack for hours.

On the 36th Division's front events took a similar course. The battalions in the forward zones were quickly eaten up by the onrushing Germans. One unit, C Company, of the 12th Rifles, was bypassed in the mist and almost forgotten about by the Germans. Until, that was, the mist cleared and it trained its Lewis guns on a line of German transport vehicles, 300 yards long. The guns brought the column juddering to halt but drew the fire of the German infantry and artillery. On the orders of Company commander, Capt. L.J. Johnson, C Company, though under fire on both flanks, managed to pull back (it was during this manoeuvre that it was attacked by the one-man bayonet charge). However, in its new defensive position it was quickly surrounded and Johnston (later decorated) surrendered with 100 of his men. Similar losses were recorded by the 1st Inniskillings, ordered to cover the retreat of the rest of the 36th. Almost 100 men died in beating back a dozen attacks by an entire German division.

The night before the attack Capt. Charles Miller of the 2nd Inniskillings was distributing the platoons of his company around the strongpoints in the line held by the 36th Ulster division. He was unhappy with what had been prepared for one platoon in particular 'I hated the look of it, couple of dugouts hastily made and inadequately wired and I wished that I had disobeyed orders, and put them into one of the previously discarded strong points'.[25] His own group, he felt, was more secure in a dugout 'capable of holding us all and protecting us from the effects of shell fire, but a death trap if the enemy infantry got in before we could get out of it'.[26] He positioned his men close to the main entrance to the strongpoint, ready to rush out as soon as there was any evidence that the barrage had been lifted. When it did the air around the strongpoint was thick with fog and the smell of cordite. Suddenly shadows began to appear in the mist, it was a group of German soldiers working their way around the barbed wire in front of the trench. One by one they were picked off but they kept coming on and began to flood into the trenches:

> I remember vaguely that I had two men coming at me with their bayonets one of whom I think I shot with my revolver, whilst a sergeant of mine standing just behind me shot the other at point blank range with his rifle barrel over my shoulder, but almost at the same second a German stick bomb came whistling into the trench from the parapet right into the bunch of us and killed or wounded practically the whole lot of us, English and German alike.

Before slipping into unconsciousness Miller gave the order to surrender ' ... and hope I succeeded thereby in saving a few lives. We had done our best'.[27] Miller was taken prisoner. When he woke up he had lost his sight but, fortunately, regained this fully within a few days. He spent the rest of the war in various German POW camps.

The German attack on 16th Division line, situated near Ronssoy, was systematic and thorough. The preliminary barrage, with shells whistling in through the mist, completely cut telephone cables from company to battalion to brigade and on up the line. 'Command and control along the front became deaf and dumb as well as blind.'[28]

Gas shells ensured further reduction in visibility because of the necessity to wear respirators. Guy Nightingale got a rude awakening on the morning of 21 March as he lay in a dugout with his battalion CO Lt.-Col. Kane:

> At about 4.30 I was woken up by my door being blown in and as cloud of phosgene gas coming in Kane and I dressed as best we could. There was a tremendous bombardment and our mess next door went sky high so we thought it was time to quit. We stumbled along in the dark with our gas masks on and the devil of a bombardment and got up into our battle positions. We had 6 hours intense bombardment with phosgene, chlorine and mustard gas included. We all got a bit gassed and I was as sick as a cat ... [29]

One by one units of the 16th were surrounded and cut off. Because the Corps commander, Gen. Congreve, had insisted on placing five of the division's nine battalion's in the Forward zone (and only one in the back-up Battle zone—he was supported in this by Gough) the early casualties were unbearable. The two remaining battalions of the Royal Irish (the 2nd and 7th) and the merged 7th/8th Inniskillings, all of the 49th Brigade, effectively ceased to exist within hours of the 4.30 a.m. preliminary German barrage.

In the sort of futile gesture which is dreamt up in the rear echelons and carried out by the front-line infantry, a tactical genius on board the Brigade staff of the 49th, under whose command the 6th Connaughts 'most unfortunately' came, ordered Feilding's battalion, and the 1st Munsters, to *counterattack* near St Emilie. It was the only such action undertaken, or even contemplated in Fifth Army on 21 March, and was like asking a fox to turn and attack a pack of rampaging hounds. Wiser counsel prevailed at Divisional staff and the order was countermanded, the 1st Munsters turned back but in the chaos of that day no-one was able to get to the 6th Connaughts to call them off.

Lt. Desmond McWeeney, a young officer attached to Battalion HQ couldn't fathom the order to attack. 'Under the conditions then prevailing anything more futile and suicidal could hardly be conceived. To be brief the whole front in the divisional area had obviously been overwhelmed and destroyed.' The battalion was ordered to advance to one of the lines of defence, the Brown line. It was, in fact, hardly a line at all, but a partially dug trench:

> no more than a line of outposts which had been completely obliterated by ten hours of intense and accurate bombardment. Such rigidity of mind was worthy of the Crimean War and this, combined with an inability to see that the situation was long past a local solution, ensured the destruction of the Battalion.[30]

Two companies (A & D) were used in the attack at 3.30 p.m. A Company was led by Tommy Crofton, heir to one of the oldest baronetcys in Connaught. With him was Maurice Moore, of Moore Hall, a descendant of the one and only 'President of the Republic of Connacht' established during the 'Year of the French', in 1798. Both were killed within the first few minutes, leaving A Company without officers. D Company, advancing on the right lost three officers. 'This left 2nd Lt. Hall, who, with the few men who survived the rushes across the open ground, was cut off, and all were shortly surrounded and captured.'[31] The support companies were, similarly, cut to ribbons by German troops who must have scratched their heads at the sheer wasteful folly of it all.

Rowland Feilding, who had, reluctantly, said goodbye to the company commanders before sending out his already depleted battalion wrote, mournfully to his wife, 'The battalion was now reduced to the Headquarters Company and thirty-four stragglers'.[32] Feilding himself, for the fourth time in his career, had been reported killed. On 30 March he wrote to his wife that, 'We have crammed years of life into a week, during which my usual Providence protected me, though the Battalion—indeed the whole Division—is practically gone'.[33] Feilding's Brigade, the 47th, at the end of that day, numbered only 240 men, out of a theoretical retinue of 3000. Out of about 5000 men which the 16th could put into the field nearly 750 were killed on 21–2 March with more than 2000 wounded and/or taken prisoner.

The confusion which reigned during the first hours of the massive German attack was followed, not by the restoration of calm as Gough's powers of leadership reasserted themselves, but by a further descent into anarchy as the Fifth Army headed for the west bank of the Somme. What followed was a retreat comparable to that from Mons in 1914. This withdrawal, however, took place at varying speeds. One Corps, that of Gen. Maxse (XVIII), which included the 36th Division, made it across the Somme on 22 March. Other (much smaller) units never made it at all. Communications difficulties are a traumatic occupational hazard for a retreating army. Here they were further complicated by the fact that adjacent French troops were also in full retreat and the backward paths of these two armies were tending to diverge. Language differences turned this headache into a nightmare. Gaps opened up between the British and the French, and between separate units within the two armies. Gaps which the jubilant Germans were quick to exploit.

Days of fatigue, disorientation and terror followed for ordinary Irish soldiers. Bill McMahon was responsible for horse transport with what remained of the Royal Irish Regiment:

> It was real hell that first couple of days. We'd move back a few miles every day ... as soon as darkness came we had to go back up again, bring up wire, bring up ammunition. We could only lead the horses, we couldn't use the wagons. I had a mule at the time. You'd lead them up and get the stuff in as quick as you could and you wouldn't be right out of it till you had to go back up again with another bloody lot.[34]

Peter McBride of the 7th/8th Inniskillings was hit in the arm and trudged without sleep or medical assistance for three days and nights before being allowed some rest in old entrenchments. Despite his personal pain and discomfort he had no trouble sleeping. By the fourth night the battalion had covered about thirty miles, only then did he get any treatment for his arm,

> A young French soldier brought me down to this cellar. They got an ambulance round the next day and we were driven a long distance away. I remember there was a wounded German cavalryman in the same ambulance ... the driver had somebody beside him and he was telling him how he'd been captured the previous night by the Germans and recaptured by the French.

His arm wasn't finally seen to for another 36 hours. By then it was too late to save it. He was brought to a makeshift field hospital and left out of doors, 'just lying there on the stretcher looking up at the sky. I was brought in then to a tent. I remember there were three candles and my arm was taken off by candlelight'.[35]

Some of the remnants of battalions which had managed to survive the initial 'blitzkrieg' disappeared altogether in the chaos of the retreat. On 24 March the 2nd Rifles, of the 36th Division, down to 7 officers and about 200 men, were defending positions on the outskirts of a town called Cugny. A German attack was beaten off at 10 p.m. but the 2nd Rifles found themselves almost entirely devoid of ammunition. Essentially they became entrenched snipers, ordered to pick off clear and obvious targets only, when the Germans attacked again. The battalion, having lost its more senior officers, was commanded by a junior Captain, J.C. Bryans. Orders for the battalion to withdraw were sent up but all the runners who bore the messages were killed as they made their way across the open ground to the woefully exposed and dwindling group of men.

Bryans decided that across the open ground a dignified and orderly retreat would quickly turn into a rout. He saw no option but to stay and take his chances. At 2 p.m. the Germans attacked again, in overwhelming numbers, supported by artillery fire and the machine-gun bullets of low-flying aircraft. The 2nd Rifles had nothing left to fire at them. Captain Bryans wrote afterwards that 'Many had only their bayonets left. Rather than wait for the end, they jumped from the entrenchments and met it gallantly. It was an unforgettable sight. We were overwhelmed, but not disgraced.'[36] The Germans mopped up what was left of the 2nd Rifles and moved on. Of the 150 men who had been left standing to face the final German attack over 100 were killed or wounded.

The race across the Somme, to provide even a temporary respite, had to be accompanied by the blowing up of all bridges in the path of the Germans. This was the responsibility of the Royal Engineers. Two officers of the 36th Division's 150th Field Company had the task, between them, of destroying twelve bridges on the night of 21 March. One, at Tugny, the responsibility of Lt. C.L. Knox, almost fell into the hands of the Germans before it could be blown: ' ... the Germans were advancing on the main steel-girder bridges when the time-fuse failed. The night dew or mist had spoiled it. As Lt. Knox rushed forward the foremost of the enemy were on the bridge, a long one. He tore away the useless time-fuse, clambered under the framework of the bridge, and lit the instantaneous fuse. The bridge was destroyed, and, by some miracle, Lt. Knox was uninjured. He received the Victoria Cross.'[37]

As they retreated troops became overwhelmed with tiredness. They moved, as had their predecessors in 1914, like automatons. They were allowed a brief respite every hour but many company commanders abandoned this as they found it impossible to get their men going again after they had stopped moving. Most, but not all, were completely oblivious of their surroundings. Some, however, unfamiliar with anything other than the gloom and morbidity of the trenches (and stimulated, no doubt, by lack of sleep) experienced a strange exaltation from the chase and from their new ever-changing surroundings: 'We were encamped in a field of daisies ... it seems so curious to have the war in this peaceful countryside, without any of the curious accessories of approaches to the trenches, shelled areas behind the lines and so on. I wonder if they felt like that in 1914'.[38]

Frank Laird was attached to a 16th Division Entrenching Battalion a safe 20 miles behind the lines 'engaged in laying light railway lines for the use of the Boche, as it proved'.[39] On the morning of 21 March he could hear the rumbling of artillery a safe distance away, or so he thought. The first inkling Laird got that things were going badly was the arrival of an artillery officer 'more or less in rags'. He told Laird how the British gunners had been shelled with gas for eight hours 'and no one who has not worn a gas mask for half an hour or so can understand what that means'. He described how the Germans had broken through behind the guns in the mist and opened up on the British gunners from the rear. He and a couple of privates had been the only men from his unit to escape.

Laird and his military navvies then watched for the next two days as a steady stream of lorries and cars passed them heading west. As is so often the case they were starved of information and almost left behind themselves. 'The Somme bridges at Peronne were being blown up as we left, and shells were dropping on the opposite river bank as we passed along parallel to it. One general was seen later swimmng back across the Somme'[40] (Brig.-Gen. Ramsay of the 48th Brigade—later promoted to Maj.-Gen.). Laird was soon in the line assisting the remnants of the 1st and 2nd Dublins. outside the village of Morcourt. He was hit in an ill-advised and futile counter-attack but was saved by one of those great clichés of war literature: 'The whistle in my breast pocket turned the bullet and changed what would have been a serious wound into a comparitively light one'. He expected his life to flash before him, as per the same literature, but was disappointed:

> As well as I remember, I felt rather disgusted at finding myself in such an unpleasant predicament, and wondered how long I should take to go off. My experience has been that you never do feel the proper sentiments as described by the magazine story and the novel dealing with warfare.[41]

Unable to move Laird was taken prisoner by the German unit whose advance he had sought to stymie. He finished off the war in Germany. In the 1920s

Laird began writing about his experiences and was at work on the unfinished book (which was eventually published incomplete) when, according to his wife 'as a result of his war service, he developed a fatal illness'. He died on 6 January 1925.

The 2nd Dublin Fusiliers, a Regular Army battalion which had seen many changes to its composition and circumstances was in the 16th Division, in Gough's hapless Fifth Army when the German hammer blow fell. Those few members of the battalion who had been in France in August 1914 must have experienced something of a sense of *déjà vu*, the terrain might have altered but there was nothing different about the frantic and exhausting retreat which they were carrying out, losing more ground in a day than they had lost for most of the three-and-a-half years since the conflict had degenerated into one between largely static armies.

The battalion commander, Major Wheeler, came perilously close to re-peating the experience of the unfortunate Major Shewan when the war was in its savage infancy. He had been instructed to dig in near the town of Morcourt on 27 March and to hold out to the last man in an effort to delay the advance of the enemy and allow the retreat to continue in some sort of good order. Flanking him were the remnants of 1st and 2nd Munsters. His own battalion had taken a heavy battering as well. Wheeler held his ground at Morcourt until he was virtually surrounded, then, sensibly, he decided to pull out, along with the Munsters. The heavily depleted battalions headed for a bridge cross-ing near the town of Ecluse. It was dark by the time they reached their objective, which they found to be already in the hands of the Germans. They retraced their steps, bypassing Morcourt and marched towards another bridge at Cerisy. This too, they found to be held by the Germans. They were now isolated and effectively surrounded. They decided, rather than concede de-feat, to rush the bridge and take their chances once they got across.

Wheeler's servant, Pte. Byrne, was singled out by his CO for special duties. He was the divisional heavyweight boxing champion. 'I called him up,' Wheeler recalled later, 'and had him placed in the leading section of fours *without his rifle!* He knew without being told what he was likely to have to do.' They managed to get within fifteen yards of the bridge without being spotted. Once detected, 'we immediately rushed forward, Fusilier Byrne knock-ing out two Boches with a right and a left'. The rest of the guards took flight and Wheeler was able to get his men, 250 in total, across safely. Byrne won the DCM for his display of pugilisim, probably one of a very few men to get such an award for his skill with his fists! But the March retreat had been costly for the 2nd Dublins, by the time the line stabilised they were left with only 3 officers and 44 other ranks. They had lost 18 killed, 169 wounded, 730 missing and 38 gassed.

One can get into all sorts of semantic arguments about the fate of the two Irish divisions post-Somme, 1918, but, essentially, the 16th and the 36th had been obliterated. Capt. John Staniforth of the Leinsters summed up the plight of the 16th succinctly as he chided himself for not having been with his men. 'The Division has ceased to exist. Wiped off the map ... they took the Boche attack full smack, the first day they were in the trenches. They died fighting, while I was hanging round a base depot.'[42] The 16th was disbanded and its battalions, now mostly old Regular Army units anyway, were scattered amongst the other divisions of the Army. The 36th was, if language can be stretched that far, more fortunate, but only insofar as it retained its status as a division. Its distinctive character as a corps of covenanting loyalists, already eroded, was shattered by the March offensive. Its historian Cyril Falls, of the Inniskillings, noted lugubriously when the division left the line in April that it had required a fleet of trains to transport them to the Somme but only one was needed to take them away. The Divisional commander, Gen. Nugent wrote that 'I doubt if the whole Division could produce more than the equivalent of a full battalion. It has been the worst battle of the war, as far as we are concerned.'

The casualty figures are infinitely more telling than any commentary. Total official casualties (which in the confusion were difficult to estimate) for the 16th Division came to just over 7000. The 36th's figure was just over 6000. In both cases, between 60 per cent and 70 per cent. The figure for 'missing' was exceptionally high in both cases (5176 for the 16th, 4458 for the 36th) The category 'mising' applies both to 'missing presumed dead' and 'prisoners'. These figures subsequently led to the allegation that the 16th Division in particular had preferred to surrender in huge numbers rather than fight. In fact, according to a closer study of the figures by Tom Johnstone, only about 2000 of the 16th 'missing' were prisoners, and half of those had been wounded when captured.

The myth of the collapse of the 16th (part and parcel of the insidious stereotype of the Irishman as courageous and aggressive in attack but feeble and undisciplined in defence) was perpetuated by an entry for 22 March in Haig's War Diary. 'Our 16th (Irish) Division which was on the right of 7th Corps and lost Ronssoy, is said not to be so full of fight as the others. In fact certain Irish units did very badly and gave way immediately the enemy showed.'[43] That Haig was clearly on top of the situation on 22 March and completely in touch with realities on the ground can be gleaned from the opening entry in his diary that day which reads cheerily, 'All reports show our men in great spirits. All speak of the wonderful targets they had to fire at yesterday.' The Corps commander Congreve (whose policy of putting too many men in the exposed Forward zone had contributed to the disaster) observed sniffily, 'The real truth is that their [the 16th's] reserve brigade did not fight at all and their right brigade very indifferently, but there are excuses to be made for them in the length of time they had been in the line and in the late reorganisation of units.'[44] Congreve, in his comment on the reserve battalion, ilustrates how well informed *he* was. The 6th Connaughts, who had been overwhelmed in the senseless 'counter-attack' at St Emilie, were one of the battalions in the reserve brigade. The general, incidentally, had covered himself well in advance, in the event of failure, by writing to Gough (from whom he would have assumed a certain sympathy might be forthcoming) 'expressing his anxiety at the reliability of the division and saying that its morale was being undermined by political propaganda'.

Despite statements in the House of Commons exonerating the 16th, the Division was forced to endure taunts of 'There go the Sinn Feiners'. It was a galling experience for Englishman Guy Nightingale who had served with the 1st Munsters since before the war began. He resented the slur on the Irish troops although he was glad to see the back of the 16th Division Staff. 'It was a rotten staff & it was entirely due to the bad staff work that Haig didn't mention the Div more in his communiques. however we were the only British division which was mentioned by the Boshe as putting up a stubborn defence on the first day.'[45] In fact the 16th were unfortunate enough to have been right in the path of a determined German push, hampered by an unequalled barrage, chronic fatigue, fog, respirators, badly positioned and constructed defences, bad staff work and a host of other disadvantages.

To some extent the myth that the 16th Division had capitulated to the Germans on the first day of the offensive, without putting up a fight, emanated from the suspicion with which the Irish regiments were viewed by this time. Guy Nightingale in another of his lengthy and entertaining epistles to his mother tells of an English officer who, under the misapprehension that he was talking to officers of the Leicester Regiment asserted with total confidence that:

> the Irishmen were holding the front-line when the offensive began, and as soon as the Boshe attacked the whole division, every officer and man put down their arms and walked over to the Boshe and have been fighting D——D well for him since, against us, and only the staff of the Division are left and they're all Englishmen.[46]

Nightingale blames this sort of rumour-mongering on 'the Sinn Fein trouble. An Irish Div. or Irish regiment is mud out here or anywhere, however fine it did ... goodness knows we lost enough fine officers & men & killed as many Boshe as any division in Gough's Army & it's only because we can get no recruits that we had to be broken up like this'. Irish regiments began to be taunted by bigots in other units. The magazine *John Bull* on the basis of the desertion of two *English* officers in an Irish battalion (the 10th Dublins) wrote 'Between Russia and the 16th Division it's no wonder we can't win the war'. Rumours of Irish 'treachery' began to spread so fast the Army threatened to court martial anyone discovered fomenting them. The stories incensed the very English Guy Nightingale to the point where he wrote to his family:

> I'm glad I'm an Englishman in an Irish regiment, as I can go unpreju-
> diced to those outside fellows and tell them straight that though I'm
> not an Irishman I would sooner be in an Irish regiment with Irish
> soldiers behind me in a scrap than any English or Scotch troops they
> would like to produce.[47]

On the credit side of the account was the sacking of Gough. A head was required, Haig's was the obvious choice and his cause was indeed a deserving one but his departure would have been inconvenient at the time. As Gough's Army was in total disarray anyway and as he had shown little enough ability in its management even in better times, he became a suitable case for dis-missal. Within a week of the start of the March offensive he was gone, sacked ironically, at the behest of the men (Sir Henry Wilson and Lord Milner) whose puppet he had been at the time of the Curragh Mutiny.

> Within two weeks Lloyd George made much in the House of Com-
> mons of Gough's failure and that of his army. The public were satisfied
> at the thought of an incompetent general and poor troops being the
> cause of so deep a retreat. The nature of the German onslaught and the
> ferocity of the British response, and the lack of manpower at the front,
> were overlooked.[48]

Ironically, as Martin Gilbert hints, Gough's sacking on this specific issue was probably unjustified, but on the basis of previous form was long overdue. As Gen. Nugent of the 36th wrote bitterly: 'if it had only been six months earlier'.[49]

Rowland Feilding, recovering from a dislocated elbow in hospital in Lon-don dwelt on the reverse of 21 March:

> The necessity of rest for fighting troops is well appreciated by the
> Germans, but seems often to be disregarded by our Higher Staff ... the
> attentuated front-line of the 5th Army was not in a fit condition to
> meet the overwhelming hordes that fell upon it on March 21, when
> forty divisions, which for two months had been training like gladiators
> behind the German lines, reinforced by eight or ten more divisions on

March 22 and 23, were thrust against fourteen Divisions of tired, overstrained, under-trained trench diggers and cable-buriers!'[50]

Luck too played a large part in the offensive. Fortune favoured the Germans on 21 March. Dry ground allowed them to move their guns with ease while the fog masked their troops as they crossed no man's land. It favoured the British, however, on 27 March when the Germans had Amiens at their mercy and failed to press home. (Rumour had it that the Germans found liquor in the BEF stores and got drunk instead.)

After forty days the German offensive foundered thanks to the stubborn rearguard resistance of the BEF. The great German General Ludendorff moved on to the French in May, having failed to drive the British out of the war. He failed there as well, though a French retreat of twelve miles in a single day gave them an inkling of what the British had been forced to bear at the Somme in March. Therafter the French and British operated more in concert under the unified leadership of the French General Foch. The two failed German offensives and the growing influence of American troops (despite the reluctance of the US Commander Pershing to involve his raw forces prematurely) had neutralised the Germans and it was the Entente powers, who, from the summer of 1918, now began to regain ground lost in March and, slowly, to retake towns and villages which had been in German hands since 1914.

This six-month build-up to the final German capitulation was achieved without the assistance of any nationalist Irish Division, even though the recall of the 10th Division from Palestine and the existence of intact Irish battalions in other divisions could, with a will for reorganisation, have made this possible. Instead it appears that advantage was taken of the March debacle to split the potentially disloyal Irish units up and 'insulate' them by adding them to already existing divisions. The rise of Sinn Fein and the conscription crisis in Ireland in 1918 brought out all the latent prejudices towards Irish nationalists of the likes of Sir Henry Wilson, Chief of the Imperial General Staff. Various excuses were offered for the complete rupture of the old 16th (even though enough Irish 'New Army' battalions existed to reconstitute it). The old Army tradition of mixing the various 'British' nationalities was cited even though the continued existence of the 36th and of separate Australian and Canadian Corps contradicted this explanation. The widespread presence of malaria among members of the 10th Division supposedly made it unwise to keep that unit together, so its battalions too, were distributed amongst other divisions.

The 6th Dublins (assigned to the 66th Division) were to end the war where so many battalions from the 16th (Irish) Division had begun theirs, on the Somme. Unaccustomed to the sights, smells and sounds of the Western

Front, Capt. N.E. Drury, marching over ground that had already witnessed the deaths of thousands, was shocked by what he saw:

> As we climbed the bare scarp of the ridge on which runs the main Route Nationale from Amiens to Vermand and Peronne, we could see on our left hand the remains of some woods which had been so smashed by shell fire that at first glance one would not know what they were. The tree trunks were just masses of big splinters sticking up about 5 or 6 feet out of a dense mass of rotting vegetation and worse. It looks as if nobody had lived in the district for years and I am sure nobody will for years to come.[51]

Drury was intrigued to find himself in places familiar to him by name, places where friends of his had fought and died.

With the Germans on the run warfare had reverted to the rapid movement of early 1914, where large areas of ground were covered in short periods of time. Land which had been disputed, and had changed hands regularly over a three-year period, was now overrun in a matter of hours or days. With no trenches prepared in the event of a wholesale retreat the Germans were unable to revert to the static warfare of attrition. However fast the progress was it was insufficiently so for Drury. 'This most leisurely battle would not have suited Allenby if he were here' he wrote of 'The Bull'. 'The Bosch are given plenty of time to clear off and take all their gear with them.'[52]

Guy Nightingale, now with the 1st Munsters in the 57th Division, kept up his campaign to right what he saw as some of the injustices being done to Irish battalions, such as his own. He defied the authorities in so doing but also displayed considerable *naïveté* in his assessment of sentiments 'back home'. He wrote to his mother in September 1918, incensed after reading in the *Times* about the role played by Canadian, English and Scottish regiments in the taking of four villages.

> Not a word about the Irish, though we and the Royal Irish took Bullecourt & Queant & Rincourt & Coquecourt & I am at this minute sitting in Bn HQ in the Hindenburg Line just by Inchy! I don't care twopence if this is opened by a Censor & wish it was taken up to GHQ ... The Govt. are fools not to let people know the few Irish Bns are still fighting & doing well, as it would mean a thousand recruits a day to us.[53]

The same letter, and subsequent ones, conveys something of the disarray being experienced by the German Army in the Autumn of 1918 as the final Allied offensive built success upon success.

> The Boche is evidently very worried and doesn't know where he is. He is shelling very unmethodically & mostly with big guns further back than usual ... Jerry is gassing us at present, but so wildly & vaguely that it can do no harm. His dugouts, which we've now got, are wonderful, endless tunnels and underground passages.

The main difficulty he found with occupying positions in what had been German trenches was that enemy gunners knew the exact co-ordinates of the HQ dugouts and made life difficult for Battalion staff. But he was consoled by the crumbling morale of the German forces. On 13 September the 1st Munsters took a number of extremely co-operative German prisoners. 'The Boche prisoners we took this morning, said they were flogged on to the attack last night & ended by shooting their officer!'[54] Three weeks later Nightingale was forced to take command of the 1st Munsters after its CO Lt.-Col. Kane was killed. He was left in charge of a glorified company, the battalion's complement having been reduced to 7 officers and 261 men.

The autumn offensive brought Capt. Frank Hitchcock and the 2nd Leinsters —now incorporating their 7th (Service) Battalion—back to Ypres, but this time with the 29th Division: 'I was unable to recognise any old features or landmarks, so completely was the place altered. To return to the Salient after three years absence like this gave one a good idea of what modern shell-fire can do.' The town itself had been virtually razed into the ground. 'With the exception of a large husk of masonry which towered above the tortured city from the vicinty of the Cloth Hall, nothing was left. There was no shelling going on, and the deathly silence palled on one. Ypres had a stillness of its own which had a depressing effect.'[55] Passing through Hooge on 28 September at the head of an attacking column the story was much the same. 'Nothing was left of Hooge; only the colour of the ground was slightly red from the bricks. Not one of the old landmarks was left, and the Salient from this ridge looked as featureless as the Sahara.'[56]

Gradually the prizes were falling to the advancing Allies. Accounts by Irish soldiers tell, in vague and specific terms, of excesses and abuses by the retreating Germans, retribution exacted on the local French and Belgian populations for their own failures. In mid-October the 57th Division was on the outskirts of Lille. Nightingale wrote 'I think Jerry is burning Lille just the same as every other place. We are not allowed to go into it. He is a swine'.[57] Frank Hitchcock had watched, horrified and revolted, near the village of Luinghe, at

> half a dozen bare-footed women tearing off flesh from a mule, which had been killed some days previously in the advance. They had pulled the skin off the quarters, and with knives and forks were cutting off

> chunks, and putting them into handkerchiefs. They were ravenous
> with hunger.[58]

What food was still to be had in the area had gone to the retreating Germans.
'The inhabitants were poor and hungry looking, and the children were delighted with pieces of biscuit given them by the men, "Good-bye, Tommy"
and similar farewells were now to be found on farmhouse doors—the last
pleasantry of the retiring Hun.'[59] On 13 September French troops retook the
town of St Mihiel. 'Among those liberated was an Irish girl, Aline Henry,
who had been trapped there for four years, having gone to learn French in the
town in June 1914.'[60]

Small wonder in such circumstances and after four years of German occu-
pation that wherever they went the British troops were greeted as Liberators:

> This morning we walked into a city with 125,000 civilians still there,
> mostly women & all in a high state of excitement! I laughed till I nearly
> fell off my horse. It was a bit early in the morning and they were not
> expecting to see any troops, but were brought from their beds by the
> sound of our band playing *O'Brien Bourru* & the *Marseillaise*! They
> were laughing & screaming & crying & flinging themselves round the
> necks of the men & I was very glad I was on my horse & even then I
> was nearly pulled off several times. I never knew before what a large
> crowd of excited French people could do ... They have awful tales of
> the Boche & it all came as a surprise to them as they didn't know we
> were winning.[61]

For an army which had, in the main, either stayed put for four years,
wasted its strength on ill-conceived and futile offensives or, latterly, been
driven back with huge losses, the last months of the Great War were a
dizzying period of unaccustomed movement and untrammelled success. There
was much talk of 'Giving Jerry a bit of his own back' and the like. So the
Armistice came as something of an anti-climax, almost a disappointment. It
seems distinctly bizarre that after putting up with such a deplorable and
hazardous existence for such a lengthy period soldiers should wish to see that
agony prolonged. But diaries, letters, memoirs or subsequent interviews reveal men who felt greatly relieved, only tentatively trusting that it was all for
real, and somewhat cheated as well. The Armistice '... was celebrated by the
troops in France without that wild hilarity, wild almost to hysteria, that
greeted it in London. Perhaps the man who had been trudging forward, week
by week, facing the machine-guns, if in front, sniffing for gas, and, by night,
listening anxiously for the purr [of shells] hardly realised that it was all
over.'[62]

The reaction of the 2nd Leinsters was typical. At 9 a.m. on the morning of 11 November the battalion's four companies got orders to rendezvous at Arc-ainieres.

> Here we found a grandiloquent notice in German and French to the effect that the gallant soldiers of the Fatherland, after holding and defeating the world for four and a half years, were now to carry out a strategic retirement—and much comforting flapdoodle in this strain.[63]

> While on the march the Brigadier had galloped up and yelled out: 'The War is over! The Kaiser has abdicated!' We were typically Irish, and never cheered except under adverse conditions, such as shell-fire and rain. Somewhat crestfallen the Brigadier rode slowly off to communicate his glad tidings to an English battalion, who, no doubt took the news in a different way.[64]

Amongst the Leinsters there was a general air of incredulity and mistrust, mixed with emotions of bitter nostalgia:

> Many discussed the situation, some arguing that the Germans were bluffing. But optimism and pessimism centred more on the question whether or no a sequence of four rumless days would be broken. Every now and then officers and signallers would furtively glance at their watches. At last the hands pointed to the hour. The words 'eleven o'clock' were passed down the column. The news was taken in silence ... Shortly afterwards a thin rain began to fall. The Battalion moved onward in silence and soon even the sound of its footsteps died away.[65]

But as 'the eleventh hour of the eleventh day of the eleventh month' drew closer men had waited in anticipation, not wanting to betray either anxiety or delight. 'Every now and then officers and signallers would furtively glance at their watches. At last the hands pointed to the hour, and I called out to the Company the words: "Eleven o'clock!". Thus the most dramatic moment passed as we marched on in silence'.[66] Ironically the Leinsters were less than eight miles from the famous battlefield at Fontenoy where the Irish Brigade under Marshal de Saxe helped beat back the English army of the Duke of Cumberland.

Corporal David Starret, Brigadier Percy Crozier's batman, long since separated from his pals in the 36th Division was going about his Brigadier's business on the night of the 10th November when he was approached by a Sergeant of Signals who had a message for battalion staff. The Sergeant asked Starret,

'What about a tot?' I asked him what he'd done to deserve it, and he answered 'Because I've got here for the old man a message to say the war is over!' The message read. 'Hostilities will cease tomorrow, 11th November, at 11 a.m.' So the pontoon that night was merrier than ever it had been and I lost money gladly for once. I took the message into the mess, and the general passed it round his staff, saying rather regretfully, 'And we've got them on the run and nearly home'. All thought we should now go right on to Berlin, and rejoiced in the thought that somehow we might still knock hell out of the Kaiser and his advisers, but we had a rude shock about that. The Kaiser was not to be hanged. He'd saved his neck by running away ... if the armistice had sounded when we were in the mud at Bray-sur-Somme or Bourlon Wood we should have welcomed it. But now?[67]

Guy Nightingale, veteran of V Beach, Suvla and the German March offensive, was one of the few members of the original 1st Munsters who had come ashore at Gallipoli still alive to greet the Armistice. A week later he wrote to his mother. There is a palpable sense of disillusionment, of 'Now what?' about the terse maner in which he dismisses the end of the affair:

I expect you had a great time when the Armistice was signed. We had a very quiet time. We were in Lille & heard about it about 9 a.m. nothing happened. We had parades till 12.30 as usual ... there was no excitement in the place we were in. I believe they rang the bells at some of the big churches in Lille, but that was all. Since then we've been training harder than ever and had several inspections by Generals.[68]

More than four years previously Terence Poulter had stood in Landsdowne Road with the other men of the D Company, 7th Dublin Fusiliers, and pledged loyalty to a unique corps of athletic 'Pals'. On 11 November 1918, having come through Suvla and seen the last of some of those good friends, he was no longer with an Irish unit but was an officer with the 23rd Royal Fusiliers. He appreciated the irony of his location when the guns fell silent:

When the armistice came we were at Le Cateau, that's near Mons where it all started. As a company commander you got a chit to say 'Hostilities will cease at 11.00 am on 11th day of the 11th month. After that time all firing will cease'. This was joyous news. Approaching eleven o'clock in our sector you could have heard a pin drop. When eleven o'clock came there were loud cheers. The war was over as far as we were concerned.

At the time the nearest Germans were a mile away in full retreat. Poulter's sympathy was with the local population who had put up with a lot during the last days of the war:

> We came across some shocking state of affairs with the French in the area that the Germans had been occupying. The civilians were in a deplorable condition. They were in the houses you see when we were advancing in the last month of the war. The Germans were billeted with them. They were starved you know.[69]

Capt. Noel Drury whose lengthy diaries chronicled the course of the 'forgotten' campaigns, in Salonika and Palestine (as well as the unforgettable Suvla) was present to see the whole tragic enterprise laid to rest. His company was working on a road, filling in a mine crater to make the route serviceable when the new Battalion CO Col. Little approached. '[He] casually remarked "Well, we stop to-day" '. Drury misinterpreted this as referring to the work on the road until Little told him that an armistice had been signed and that the war was over. Drury was unsure how to react,

> it's like when one heard of the death of a friend—a sort of forlorn feeling. I went along and read the order to the men, but they just stared at me and showed no enthusiasm at all. One or two just muttered 'We were just getting a bit of our own back'. They all had the look of hounds whipped off just as they were about to kill.[70]

Later in the evening, however, their spirits rose and a recently acquired firework store was raided for a spectacular display. All night requests came from other units for supplies of flares so that the light show (Drury calls it a 'Brick's Benefit') could be repeated elsewhere along the line.

Capt. E.H. de Stacpoole, Military Cross winner, whose back had been peppered with shrapnel in service with the 2nd Leinsters in June 1915, was closer to the enemy when the moment came to put the guns aside. So stretched had lines of supply and communication become in the last great strides of the BEF, that he had been ordered to stop pursuing the Germans. Only the cavalry were to be allowed follow them if they pulled further back:

> About five in the morning our telephone went and I was told that the armistice would start at eleven and that I was to assemble the Brigade bugles and blow 'Stand Fast' and 'Ceasefire'. You couldn't assemble brigade bugles, that was nonsense, but each battalion sounded a bugle and the Germans stood up, took off their hats, bowed to us and walked

away ... we had taken eleven prisoners that morning in a pub and we had to let them go.[71]

In England, after the prolonged dominance of the seas around the coast by the Germans civilians were not in the best condition either. Tommy Cusack, from Waterford, who had joined the Royal Navy at the outbreak of hostilities was in Devonport at the time of the Armistice. 'Though we didn't have much to celebrate on at the time, very little, but we did our best.'[72] Denis Kelly from Dysart, Co. Roscommon, an Irish Guard who had joined the regiment while living in England was also at home recovering from a wound received in 1917. 'All I'm sorry for is that I wasn't there when the Germans put up the white flag for peace, that I wasn't there to win the war.'[73]

But even in its final moments the Great War was capable of dispensing destruction and further tragedy. The three Geoghegan brothers, who had served in separate units during the war met up, by coincidence, near the shifting front with the Germans on the night of 10 November 1918. Somehow they contrived to spend the night together, celebrating the imminent ceasefire. Early on the morning of the 11th they were in a tent behind the lines, one of the three was shaving, when a German shell burst over them killing all three.[74]

Just as the Great War was a senseless and brutal conflict which resolved nothing in terms of European power politics the effect of nationalist and unionist units fighting side by side had no lasting significance for this country either. The prospect of something positive emerging from wartime collaboration proved illusory. Within the nationalist divisions themselves there was little succour for those advocates of 'England's difficulty, Ireland's difficulty' who wanted to make common cause with Britain.. The 1916 executions and the ill-judged attempt by Lloyd George's government to introduce conscription to Ireland in 1918 had helped create a new Irish *Zeitgeist*, one which excluded the men who had fought for Britain through three and four years of debilitating war. The government for whom they fought, already assuming their disloyalty as virtually axiomatic, had dispersed the remnants of the 16th Division throughout the Army.

> When the guns fell silent on 11 November 1918 on the western front no Irishmen would be wearing the shamrock badge of the 16th (Irish) Division. Its veterans returned to an Ireland little prepared to give them a hero's welcome.[75]

Later, during the War of Independence, many ex-servicemen would be shot as spies by the IRA. As the assumption grew that adherence to the trappings of Great War commemoration denoted 'West-Britishness' the prac-

tice of celebrating Remembrance Day ceased. The Memorial Park to commemorate the Irish dead of the Great War, designed in the 1920s by Edward
Lutyens, was allowed to decay. The subject of service in the British forces
during the Great War became almost taboo. Only in Northern Ireland was the
sacrifice of the men of 1914–18 acknowledged, and then, often, in a manner
which further exacerbated the racial and religious tensions which scarred the
Six Counties for decades.

Let us leave the last word on the conflict, as the dust of war settled over
Flanders, Picardy, Gallipoli, Salonika and Palestine, to Cpl. David Starret, the
Belfast loyalist who spent three years dodging bullets intended for Percy
Crozier. The valedictory phrases in his memoir sum up the disillusionment of
a working-class man who now realises for whom he's been risking his life.
Certainly not family and friends.

> So the curtain fell, over that tortured country of unmarked graves and
> unburied fragments of men: murder and massacre: the innocent slaugh-
> tered for the guilty: the poor man for the sake of the greed of the
> already rich: the man of no authority made the victim of the man who
> had gathered importance and wished to keep it. Greed and lust of
> power, that was the secret. We were said to be fighting to stop future
> war, but none believed it.[76]

# Notes

### 1 The Old Contemptibles

1 Breen, John, interview with Kieran Sheedy, 1973, RTE Sound Archive.
2 Gilbert, Martin, *The First World War* (London, 1994), p. 36.
3 Lucy, John, *There's a Devil in the Drum* (London, 1938), p. 74.
4 Johnstone, Tom, *Orange, Green and Khaki* (Dublin, 1992).
5 Gilbert, op. cit., pp. 47–8.
6 Lucy, op. cit., pp. 13–14.
7 Ibid., p. 84.
8 Wylly, Col. H.C., *Crown and Company—The Historical Records of the 2nd Battalion, Royal Dublin Fusiliers, Volume 2, 1911–1922*, p. 15.
9 Lucy, op. cit., p. 97.
10 Campbell, Jack, interview with the author, 1990.
11 Ibid.
12 Lucy, op. cit., pp. 118–19.
13 Ibid., p. 122.
14 King, John, interview with Kieran Sheedy, 1973, RTE Sound Archive.
15 McDonagh, Michael, *The Irish at the Front* (London, 1916). The reason for the caveat 'supposed' is that McDonagh's book is a propagandist exercise aimed at maximising recruiting in Ireland at a particularly sensitive time and is a highly suspect publication.
16 Campbell, interview with author.
17 Kipling, Rudyard, *The Irish Guards in the Great War* (London, 1923), p. 9.
18 Lucy, op. cit., pp. 145–6.
19 Campbell, interview with author.
20 McDonagh, op. cit., pp. 27–8.
21 Information from Greacen, Lavinia, *Chink: A Biography* (London, 1989).
22 McDonagh, Michael, *The Irish at the Front* (London, 1916), p. 23.
23 Jervis, Lt. Col. H.S., *The 2nd Munsters in France* (Aldershot, 1922), p. 2.
24 Rickard, Mrs Victor, *The Story of the Munsters at Etreux, Festubert, Rue du Bois and Hulloch* (London, 1918), pp. 9–10.
25 Jervis, op. cit., p. 5.
26 Rickard, op. cit., unidentified soldier, p. 65.
27 Rickard, op. cit., pp. 68–9.
28 Ibid., p. 78.
29 Ibid., p. 79.
30 Johnstone, op. cit., p. 32.
31 Ibid., p. 33.
32 Hyland, Frank, interview with Kieran Sheedy, 1973, RTE Sound Archive.
33 Kipling, p. 11.
34 Ibid.
35 McDonagh, op. cit., p. 27.
36 Kipling, p. 12.
37 Brown, Malcolm, *The Imperial War Museum Book of the Western Front* (London, 1993), p. 34.
38 Ibid., undated letter.
39 Breen, John, interview with Kieran Sheedy.
40 Lucy, John, op. cit., p. 164.
41 Brown, p. 35.
42 Ibid.
43 Lucy, op. cit., pp. 163–4.
44 Whitton, Col. F.E., *The History of the Prince of Wales Leinster Regiment, Vol. 2* (Aldershot, 1926), p. 229.
45 Doyle, Phillip, interview with Kieran Sheedy, 1973, RTE Sound Archive.
46 Brown, op. cit., p. 35.
47 Hitchcock, Capt. Frank, *Stand To: A Diary of the Trenches, 1915–1918* (Norwich 1988), p. 37.
48 Ibid., p. 261.
49 Kipling, op. cit., p. 54.

### 2 Gallipoli: The V Beach Landings

1 Lt.-Col. Tizard, memoir, p. 5, papers of Lt.-Col. G.B. Stoney, IWM.
2 Ibid., p. 5.

3  Kerr, J. Parnell, *What the Irish Regiments Have Done* (London, 1916), pp. 138–9.
4  Wylly, Col. H.C., *Neill's Blue Caps—Vol. 3 1914–1922* (1923), p. 29.
5  Tizard pp. 6–7.
6  Wylly, op. cit., p. 30.
7  McDonagh, Michael, *The Irish at the Front* (London, 1916), p. 62.
8  Wylly, op. cit., p. 32.
9  Tizard, p. 8.
10  Geddes, Capt. G.W. Papers lodged in IWM—a memoir, p. 3.
11  Capt. Lane, included in Tizard account, lodged in Stoney Papers, IWM, p. 9.
12  McDonagh, op. cit., p. 64.
13  Leavy, Thomas, inteview with Kieran Sheedy, RTE Sound Archive.
14  Geddes, letter 30/4/15, IWM.
15  Tizard (Stoney Papers), p. 9.
16  Tizard, p. 8.
17  Wylly, op. cit., p. 33.
18  Geddes, memoir, p. 4, IWM.
19  Tizard, p. 10.
20  Nightingale, collected letters, p. 17, IWM.
21  Nightingale, Lt. Guy, Letter to his mother, 1/5/15, IWM.
22  Nightingale, letter to his sister, 4/5/15, IWM.
23  Lane, quoted in Tizard account, p. 9.
24  Geddes, letter 30/4/15, IWM.
25  Tizard, p. 16, Stoney Papers, IWM.
26  Nightingale, letter to his sister, 4/5/95, IWM.
27  Tizard, p. 18.
28  McDonagh, op. cit., p. 147.
29  Wylly, op. cit., p. 39.
30  Nightingale, letter to his sister, 4/5/15, IWM.
31  Wylly, op. cit., p. 38.
32  Nightingale diaries, 27 April, British Public Record Office, PRO 30/71/3.
33  Ibid., 28 April.
34  Ibid., 1–2 May.
35  Wylly, op. cit., p. 39.
36  Nightingale, letter to sister, 4/5/15, IWM.
37  Fox, Sir Frank, *The Royal Inniskillings in the Great War* (London, 1928), p. 183.
38  Nightingale Letters, IWM, p. 10.
39  Ibid., 14 May.
40  Ibid., 4 June.
41  Ibid., 13 June.
42  Nightingale diary, British PRO, 29/7/15.
43  Ibid., 9 June.
44  McCance, op. cit., p. 55.
45  Nightingale, diary 29/7/15.

*3  Suvla Bay*

1  Cooper, Bryan, *The Tenth (Irish) Division in Gallipoli* (Dublin, 1993), p. 21.
2  Hargrave, John, *The Suvla Bay Landing* (London, 1964), p. 128.
3  Lee, J.J., *Ireland 1912–1985, Politics and Society* (Cambridge, 1989), p. 172.
4  Laird, Frank, *Personal Experiences of the Great War* (Dublin, 1925), p. 25.
5  Hargrave, op. cit., pp. 59–60.
6  Cooper, op. cit., pp. 38–9.
7  Whitton, Col. F.E., *The Prince of Wales Leinster Regiment—Vol. 2*, p. 187.
8  Ibid., p. 188.
9  Hanna, Henry, *The Pals at Suvla Bay* (Dublin, 1916), p. 59.
10  Memoir of Sir Ivone Kirkpatrick, IWM, p. 15.
11  Laird, op. cit., p. 33.
12  Papers of N.E. Drury, National Army Museum, London, Vol. 1, p. 81.
13  Hanna, op. cit., p. 65.
14  Kirkpatrick, op. cit., pp. 15–16.
15  Hanna, op. cit., pp. 95–6.
16  Hargrave, op. cit., p. 78.
17  Ibid., p. 80.
18  Laird, op. cit., p. 34.
19  Edgar Poulter, interview with Kieran Sheedy, RTE Sound Archives.
20  James Cahill, interview with the author, December 1990.
21  Hargrave, op. cit., p. 95.
22  Cunliffe, Marcus, *The Royal Irish Fusiliers 1793–1968* (London, 1970), p. 294.
23  Hargrave, op. cit., p. 198.
24  Ibid., p. 101.
25  Gilbert, Martin, *First World War* (London, 1994), p. 181.
26  Drury Papers Vol. 1, p. 85.
27  Hargrave, op. cit., p. 147.
28  Laird, op. cit., p. 36.
29  Letter of Capt. Paddy Tobin to his father, 13 August, 1915 (copy in author's possession through Kevin Myers).
30  Laird, op. cit., p. 34.
31  Cooper, op. cit., pp. 79–80.
32  Johnstone, Tom, *Orange, Green and Khaki* (Dublin, 1992).
33  Hanna, op. cit., p. 74.
34  Laird, op. cit., pp. 36–7.
35  Tobin letter, op. cit.
36  Hanna p. 82 (unidentified soldier).
37  Tobin letter, op. cit.
38  Col. Downing, letter to his wife, 12/8/15

(copy in author's possession through Kevin Myers).

39  Edgar Poulter, interview with Kieran Sheedy, RTE Sound Archives.
40  McDonagh, Michael, *The Irish at the Front* (London, 1916), p. 9.
41  Poulter, Sheedy interview.
42  Johnstone, op. cit., p. 128.
43  Poulter, Sheedy interview.
44  Laird, op. cit., p. 43.
45  Whitton, op. cit., p. 191.
46  Ibid., p. 193.
47  Kirkpatrick memoir, p. 17.
48  Johnstone, op. cit., p. 130.
49  Hargrave, op. cit., p. 130.
50  Ibid., p. 129.
51  Tobin letter, op. cit.
52  Letter from Billy Richards (copy in the possession of the author).
53  Kirkpatrick memoir p. 19.
54  Cooper, op. cit., p. 87.
55  Hargrave, op. cit., p. 177.
56  Cooper, op. cit., pp. 92–3.
57  Kirkpatrick, p. 21.
58  Curtayne, Alice, *Francis Ledwidge, A Life of the Poet* (London, 1972), p. 125.
59  Cooper, op. cit., p. 49.
60  Hanna, op. cit., p. 124.
61  Kirkpatrick memoir, p. 21.
62  Cooper, p. 88 .
63  Kirkpatrick memoir, p. 22.
64  Hanna, p. 128 (unidentified soldier).
65  Poulter, Sheedy interview.
66  McDonagh, op. cit., p. 87.
67  Hargrave, op. cit., p. 208.
68  Cooper, op. cit., p. 102.
69  Hargrave, op. cit., pp. 216–17.
70  Kirkpatrick, p. 25.
71  Ibid., p. 27.
72  Gilbert, op. cit., pp. 188–9.
73  Curtayne, p. 126.
74  Poulter, Sheedy interview.
75  Cooper, op. cit., pp. 100–1.
76  Hanna, op. cit., pp. 109–10 (unidentified soldier).
77  Hamilton, Ernest, letter to Dr Tobin, (copy in possession of the author through Kevin Myers).
78  Information from Kevin Myers.
79  Hargrave, op. cit., p. 230.
80  Hanna, op. cit., p. 111.
81  Hargrave op. cit., p. 231.
82  Johnstone, op. cit., p. 138.
83  Hamilton, Gen. Sir Ian, *Gallipoli Diary* (London, 1920).

84  Hargrave op. cit., p. 227.
85  Nightingale letters, IWM, 25/8/15.
86  Cooper op. cit., pp. 128–9.
87  Poulter, Sheedy interview.
88  Cooper, op. cit., p. 131.
89  Nightingale diary, 12 Sept.
90  Ibid., 4 October.
91  Gilbert, op. cit., p. 226.
92  Bredin, Brigadier A.E.C., *A History of the Irish Soldier* (Belfast, 1987), p. 434.
93  Drury papers, Vol. 2, p. 102.
94  McDonagh, op. cit., p. 101.
95  Johnstone, op. cit., p. 133.
96  Kerr, J. Parnell, *What the Irish Regiments Have Done* (London, 1916), p. 155.
97  Kilbracken, Lord Arthur & Godley, Gen. Sir Alexander, *Letters* (Private pub., 1949), p. 49, 23/8/15.
98  Quoted in Dixon, Norman, *On the Psychology of Military Incompetence* (London, 1994), p. 221.
99  Kirkpatrick, p. 46.
100 Ibid., p. 47.
101 Ibid., pp. 49–50.
102 Ibid., p. 50.

## 4  The Drury Diaries

1   Papers of Capt. N.E. Drury (Drury Papers), Vol. 2, p. 103, National Army Museum.
2   Ibid., Vol. 1 p. 28.
3   Ibid., p. 99.
4   Ibid., p. 102.
5   Ibid., p. 104.
6   Ibid., pp. 104–5.
7   King, John, interview with Kieran Sheedy, RTE Sound Archives.
8   Drury Papers, Vol. 2, p. 10.
9   Ibid., p. 11.
10  Ibid., p. 18.
11  Ibid., p. 20.
12  Ibid., p. 150.
13  Ibid., p. 21.
14  King, John, interview with Kieran Sheedy.
15  Gilbert, Martin, *First World War* (London, 1994), p. 208.
16  Drury Papers, Vol. 2, p. 31, 2 Nov. 1915.
17  Ibid., p. 49.
18  Poulter, Edgar, interview with Kieran Sheedy.
19  Drury, Vol. 2, p. 40.
20  Ibid., p. 59.

21 Johnstone, Tom, *Orange, Green and Khaki* (Dublin, 1992), p. 129.
22 Drury Papers, Vol. 2., p. 75.
23 Ibid., p. 78.
24 Ibid., p. 81.
25 Ibid., p. 86.
26 Ibid., p. 87.
27 Drury Papers, Vol. 2, p. 90.
28 Poulter, Edgar, interview with Kieran Sheedy.
29 Gilbert, op. cit., p. 246.
30 Drury Papers, Vol. 2, p. 163.
31 Ibid., p. 167.
32 Ibid.
33 Ibid., p. 28.
34 Johnstone, op. cit., p. 318.
35 Drury Papers, Vol. 3, p. 42.
36 Ibid., pp. 31–2.
37 Ibid., p. 40.
38 Ibid., pp. 71–2.
39 Ibid., p. 76.
40 Ibid., pp. 87–8.
41 King, John, interview with Kieran Sheedy.
42 Lt.-Col. F.E. Whitton, *The Prince of Wales Leinster Regiment*, Vol. 2, p. 480.
43 Drury Papers, Vol. 3, p. 112.
44 Ibid., p. 106.
45 Ibid., p. 108.
46 Ibid., p. 120.
47 Ibid., p. 139.
48 Ibid., p. 151.
49 Ibid., p. 159.
50 Ibid., p. 169.
51 Ibid., p. 170.
52 Ibid., Vol. 4, p. 82.

5 *The Battle of the Somme*

1 McDonagh, Michael, *The Irish on the Somme* (London, 1917), p. 27.
2 Falls, Cyril, *The History of the 36th Ulster Division* (London, 1922), p. 43.
3 Crozier, Percy, *The Men I Killed* (London, 1937), p. 80.
4 Grange, Bob; Christie, Jack; Jordan, Tommy: interviews deposited in Somme Association Archive.
5 Falls, op. cit., p. 47.
6 Brennan, p. 8.
7 Orr, Phillip, *The Road to the Somme* (Belfast, 1987), p. 156.
8 Crozier, Percy, *A Brass Hat in No Man's Land* (London, 1930), p. 98.
9 Lynas, William J., letter to his wife, IWM.
10 Falls, op. cit., p. 51.
11 McDonagh, op. cit., pp. 36–7.
12 Orr, op. cit., pp. 165–6.
13 Falls, op. cit., p. 52.
14 Tommy Ervine, interview with Joe Little, 'Survivors of the Somme' RTE Sound Archive.
15 Orr, op. cit., p. 161.
16 Starret, David, memoir, IWM p. 63.
17 Crozier, op. cit., p. 100.
18 Starret, pp. 63–4.
19 Orr, op. cit., p. 178.
20 Grange, Bob, Somme Association Archive.
21 Falls, op. cit., p. 53.
22 Fox, Sir Frank, *The Royal Inniskilling Rifles in the World War* (London, 1928), p. 69.
23 Christie, Jack, Somme Association Archive.
24 Miller, Charles Cecil, memoirs, IWM, pp. 22–3.
25 Bredin, A.E.C., *A History of the Irish Soldier* (Belfast, 1987), p. 442.
26 Orr, p. 169.
27 Bell, Leslie, interview with Richard Doherty.
28 Orr, op. cit., p. 170.
29 Gallaugher, Henry, letter to his father (copy in the possession of the author).
30 Crozier, op. cit., p. 105.
31 Ibid., p. 102.
32 Ervine, Joe Little interview, RTE Sound Archive.
33 Starret, IWM, p. 64.
34 Starret, ibid., pp. 64–5.
35 Falls, op. cit., p. 56.
36 Ervine, Tommy, interview with Joe Little.
37 Falls, op. cit., p. 56.
38 McDonagh, op. cit., p. 43.
39 Orr, op. cit., p. 170.
40 Christie, Somme Association.
41 Starret, IWM, p. 67.
42 Ibid.
43 Christie, Jack interview, Somme Association.
44 McDonagh, op. cit., pp. 44–5.
45 Crozier, op. cit., p. 109.
46 Orr, op. cit., p. 172.
47 Crozier, op. cit., p. 108.
48 McDonagh, op. cit., p. 53.
49 Crozier, op. cit., p. 110.
50 Johnstone, Tom, *Orange, Green and Khaki* (Dublin, 1992), p. 233.
51 McDonagh, op. cit., p. 42.
52 Falls, op. cit., p. 57.
53 Starret, IWM, p. 68.

54  Harry Bennett, quoted in Doherty, Richard, *The Sons of Ulster* (Belfast, 1992,  p. 23.
55  Orr, op. cit., p. 191.
56  Lynas, William John, letter to his wife 15/7/16, IWM.
57  James Conaghan quoted in Doherty, op. cit., p. 18.
58  Orr, op. cit., p. 195.
59  Gilbert, op. cit., p. 264.
60  Dixon, Norman, *On the Psychology of Military Incompetence* (London, 1994), p. 82.
61  Grange, Bob, interview with Richard Doherty (tape in possession of author).
62  Gilbert, Martin, *First World War* (London, 1994), p. 263.
63  Brennan, Anthony, memoir, IWM, p. 9.
64  Orr, op. cit., p. 201.
65  Jordan, Tommy, Somme Association Archive.
66  Grange, Bob, Somme Association Archive.
67  Seeger, Alan, *Rendezvous*


6  *The 16th (Irish) Division at the Somme*

1  Whitton, Col. F.E., *The Prince of Wales Leinster Regiment*, Vol. 2 (undated), p. 232.
2  Hitchcock, Capt. F.C., *Stand To: A Diary of the Trenches 1915–1918* (Norwich, 1988), p. 142.
3  Ibid., pp. 306–7.
4  Memoirs of William Adelbert Lyon, IWM, p. 63.
5  J.F.B. O'Sullivan, letter to his mother 10–13/9/16, IWM, pp. 4–5.
6  Ibid., p. 5.
7  Ibid., p. 6.
8  Ibid., p. 25.
9  Denman, Terence, *Ireland's Unknown Soldiers* (Dublin, 1992), p. 81.
10  Whitton op. cit., p. 309.
11  Hitchcock, Frank, *Stand To* (Norwich, 1988), p. 129.
12  Johnstone, Tom, *Orange, Green and Khaki* (Dublin, 1992), p. 241.
13  Ibid., p. 241.
14  Lyon, p. 65.
15  Ibid., pp. 63–4.
16  Ibid.
17  O'Sullivan, p. 30.
18  Ibid., p. 31.
19  Ervine, Billy, 'Battle Lines', *Journal of the Somme Association*, No. 5, 1991, p. 12.
20  Johnstone, op. cit., fn p. 448.

21  O'Sullivan, p. 32.
22  Whitton, op. cit., p. 310.
23  O'Sullivan, p. 34.
24  Ibid., p. 35.
25  Lyon, pp. 64–5.
26  Denman, op. cit., p. 86.
27  Breen, John, interview with Kieran Sheedy, RTE Sound Archives.
28  d'Alton, Emmet, interview with Padraigh O'Raghallaigh, RTE Sound Archive.
29  de Margry Papers, IWM, 'In Memoriam' p. 2.
30  Ibid., p. 4.
31  Feilding, Rowland, *War Letters to a Wife* (London, 1929) 7 Sept., p. 111.
32  Ibid., 10 Sept., p. 112.
33  O'Rahilly, Alfred, *Father William Doyle, S.J.* (London, 1932), p. 439.
34  Ibid., p. 449.
35  Feilding, 10 Sept., p. 116.
36  Whitton, op. cit., p. 316.
37  Ibid.
38  McDonagh, Michael, *The Irish on the Somme* (London, 1917), p. 148.
39  Denman, op. cit., p. 98.
40  O'Rahilly, op. cit., p. 349.
41  McDonagh, op. cit., p. 149.
42  Ibid., p. 150.
43  Ibid., p. 154.
44  Laird, Frank, *Personal Experiences of the Great War* (Dublin, 1925), p. 108.
45  Interview by author with Kevin Myers.
46  McDonagh, op. cit., p. 151.
47  Redmond, Major William, *Trench Pictures from France* (London, 1917), pp. 74–5.
48  Denman, op. cit., p. 99.
49  Redmond, op. cit., p. 82.
50  Feilding, op. cit., 10 Sept., p. 117.
51  Staniforth letters, IWM, 12/9/16.
52  O'Brien, Jimmy, interview with Kieran Sheedy, RTE Sound Archive.
53  Miller, Charles Cecil, memoirs, IWM, p. 23.
54  O'Brien, Kieran Sheedy interview.
55  Miller, IWM pp. 23–4.
56  Brennan, Anthony, memoirs, IWM, p. 17.


7  *1917*

1  Falls, Cyril, *History of the 36th Ulster Division*, p. 82.
2  Feilding, Rowland, *War Letters to a Wife*, pp. 189–90.
3  W.A. Lyon Papers, IWM, p. 68.

4   Laird, Frank, *Personal Experiences of the Great War* (Dublin, 1925), p. 143.
5   Lyon, IWM, p. 69.
6   Laird, op. cit., p. 145.
7   Ibid., p. 86.
8   Feilding op. cit., p. 183.
9   Laird, op. cit., p. 144.
10  Godley, Alexander and Kilbracken, Arthur, *Letters* (London, 1949). p. 91.
11  O'Rahilly, Alfred, *Father William Doyle S.J.* (London, 1932), pp. 506–7.
12  Papers of W.A. Lyon, IWM, p. 69.
13  Lt.-Col. F.E. Whitton, *The Prince of Wales Leinster Regiment*, Vol. 2, p. 362.
14  Fox, Sir Frank, *The Battles of the Ridges— Arras-Messines, March-June 1917* (London, 1918), p. 103.
15  O'Rahilly, op. cit., pp. 511–12.
16  Falls, op. cit., p. 92.
17  McElwaine papers, IWM.
18  Gibson, Thomas, interview with Richard Doherty.
19  Doherty, Richard, *The Sons of Ulster* (Belfast, 1992), p. 24.
20  Laird, op. cit., p. 152.
21  O'Rahilly, op. cit., p. 514.
22  Ibid.
23  Brennan, Anthony, memoir, IWM, p. 21.
24  Ibid.
25  Lyon, IWM, p. 69.
26  Ibid., p. 70.
27  Ibid., p. 71.
28  Feilding op. cit., p. 189.
29  Gallaugher, Henry, letter to his parents, 19/5/17 (copy in possession of author).
30  Quoted in 'The Distinguished Service Order' p. 249.
31  Feilding, op. cit., p. 219.
32  Redmond, Willie, *Trench Pictures from France* (London, 1917) quote from Fr Edmond Kelly in Introduction, p. 28.
33  Ibid., p. 30.
34  Breen, John, interview with Kieran Sheedy, RTE Sound Archive.
35  McElwaine papers, IWM.
36  Feilding, Rowland, *War Letters to a Wife*, pp. 191–2.
37  Godley, op. cit., p. 91.
38  Denman, *Ireland's Unknown Soldiers*, p. 115.
39  Feilding, op. cit., p. 191.
40  Bredin, *A History of the Irish Soldier*, p. 455.
41  Falls, op. cit., p. 100.
42  O'Rahilly, op. cit.

43  McElwaine papers, IWM, p. 76.
44  Christie, Jack, Somme Association Archive.
45  Ibid.
46  Brennan, Anthony, memoirs, IWM, p. 22.
47  Breen, John, interview with Kieran Sheedy, RTE Archive.
48  Byrne, Ned, Kieran Sheedy interview, RTE Sound Archive.
49  Lt.-Col. F.E. Whitton, *The Prince of Wales Leinster Regiment*, Vol. 2, p. 367.
50  Christie, Jack, Somme Association Archive.
51  Hitchcock, Frank, *Stand To*, p. 290.
52  Gibson, Thomas, Richard Doherty interview.
53  Christie, Jack, Somme Association Archive.
54  Bennet, Harry, Richard Doherty interview.
55  O'Rahilly, Alfred. op. cit., p. 527.
56  Grange, Bob, Richard Doherty interview.
57  O'Rahilly, op. cit., p. 533.
58  Walker, G.A.C., *The Book of the 7th Service Battalion—The Royal Inniskilling Fusiliers— from Tipperary to Ypres* (Dublin, 1920), p. 111.
59  Johnstone, Tom, *Orange, Green and Khaki*, p. 285.
60  Falls, op. cit., pp. 112–13.
61  Denman, p. 118.
62  Staniforth letters, IWM.
63  McCance, Capt. S., *History of the Royal Munster Fusiliers—Vol. II—from 1861–1922* (Aldershot, 1927), p. 72.
64  Falls, op. cit., p. 113.
65  Brennan, Anthony, memoir, IWM, p. 23.
66  Gibson, Thomas, interview with Richard Doherty.
67  Gibbs, Phillip, *The Realities of War* (London, 1920), p. 388.
68  Breen, John, interview with Kieran Sheedy, RTE Sound Archives.
69  Johnstone, Tom, op. cit., p. 295.
70  Ibid., p. 296.
71  O'Rahilly, op. cit., pp. 535–6.
72  Ibid., p. 542.
73  O'Brien, Jimmy, interview with Kieran Sheedy, RTE Sound Archives.
74  O'Rahilly, op. cit., p. 556.
75  Denman, op. cit., p. 124.
76  O'Rahilly, op. cit., p. 517.
77  Denman op. cit., p. 124.
78  Curtayne, Alice, *Francis Ledwidge: A Life of the Poet* (London, 1992), p. 187.
79  Orr, *The Road to the Somme*, p. 205.
80  Miller, Charles C., memoir, IWM, p. 28.
81  Feilding, Rowland, *War Letters to a Wife*, p. 202.

82 Gibbs, op. cit., p. 388.
83 Falls. op. cit., p. 122.
84 Knightley, Phillip, *The First Casualty* (London, 1982), p. 78.
85 Gibbs, op. cit., p. 389.
86 Johnstone, op. cit., p. 298.


8 *1918: From Calamity to Triumph*

1 Falls, *The History of the 36th Ulster Division*, p. 184.
2 Ibid., p. 185.
3 Capt. F.C. Hitchcock, *Stand To: A Diary of the Trenches 1915–1918*, pp. 266, 17/8/18.
4 Kipling, Rudyard, *The Irish Guards in the Great War*, p. 191.
5 Denman, Terence, *Ireland's Unknown Soldiers*, p. 156.
6 Miller, Charles Cecil, memoir, IWM, pp. 29–30.
7 Miller, p. 29.
8 McElwaine, p. 89.
9 Miller, p. 30.
10 Johnstone, Tom, *Orange, Green and Khaki*, p. 340.
11 Hitchcock, Frank, *Stand To*, pp. 257–8.
12 Nightingale papers, British Public Record Office, PRO 30/71/3, 18/2/18.
13 Miller, pp. 30–1.
14 Ibid.
15 Lt.-Col. F.E. Whitton, *The Prince of Wales Leinster Regiment'*, Vol. 2, p. 445.
16 Nightingale, 16/3/18.
17 Falls, p. 190.
18 Hitchcock, op. cit., p. 262.
19 Whitton, p. 447.
20 Unidentified soldier, quoted in Kipling, op. cit., p. 193.
21 Falls, p. 195.
22 Gough, Sir Hubert, *The Fifth Army* (London, 1931), p. 271.
23 Johnstone, p. 344.
24 Whitton, p. 455.
25 Miller, p. 31.
26 Ibid., p. 33.
27 Ibid., p. 34.
28 Johnstone, p. 356.
29 Nightingale papers, PRO 22/3/18.
30 MacWeeney, Desmond, memoir, National Army Museum, pp. 1–3.
31 Ibid.
32 Feilding, op. cit., p. 270.

33 Ibid., p. 274.
34 McMahon, Bill, interview with Kieran Sheedy, 1973 RTE Sound Archives.
35 McBride, Peter, Kieran Sheedy, interview, 1973, RTE Sound Archive.
36 Falls, op. cit., p. 216.
37 Falls, p. 203.
38 Staniforth, IWM, 2/5/18.
39 Laird, Frank, *Personal Experiences of the Great War*, p. 155.
40 Ibid., p. 157.
41 Ibid., pp. 163–4.
42 Brown, Malcolm, *The IWM book of the Western Front*, p. 210.
43 Johnstone, p. 388.
44 Denman, p. 166.
45 Nightingale, 24/4/18.
46 Ibid.
47 Ibid.
48 Gilbert, Martin, *World War One*, p. 410.
49 Johnstone, p. 390.
50 Feilding, op. cit., p. 286.
51 Drury Papers, Vol. 4, p. 11.
52 Ibid., p. 22.
53 Nightingale, 7/9/18.
54 Ibid., 13/9/18.
55 Hitchcock, F., *Stand To*, pp. 282–3.
56 Ibid., p. 286.
57 Nightingale 18/10/18.
58 Hitchcock p. 306.
59 Whitton, p. 477.
60 Gilbert, p. 459.
61 Nightingale, 21/10/18.
62 Falls, p. 292.
63 Whitton, p. 478.
64 Hitchcock, p. 306.
65 Whitton, p. 479.
66 Hitchcock, p. 313.
67 Starret memoir, IWM, pp. 131–2.
68 Nightingale, PRO, 18/11/18.
69 Poulter, Terence, interview with Kieran Sheedy, RTE Sound Archive.
70 Drury Diaries, National Army Museum, Vol. 4, 11/11/18, p. 57.
71 de Stacpoole, E.H.M., interview with Kieran Sheedy, RTE Sound Archive.
72 Cusack Tommy, ibid.
73 Kelly, Denis, interview with Jim Fahy, RTE Sound Archive.
74 Information from family sources supplied by Michael Colgan.
75 Denman, op. cit., p. 174.
76 Starret, IWM, p. 133.

# Bibliography

MANUSCRIPT SOURCES

*Imperial War Museum, papers of:*

| | | |
|---|---|---|
| A.R. Brennan | W.V.C. Lake | G.W. Nightingale |
| F. de Margry | W.J. Lynas | J.F.B. O'Sullivan |
| G.W. Geddes | W.A. Lyon | D. Starret |
| Sir Ivone Kirkpatrick | C.C. Miller | G.B. Stoney |

*National Army Museum, papers of:*
N.E. Drury
Desmond McWeeney

*Somme Association, interviews with:*
Jack Christie
R.T. Grange
Tommy Jordan

*Private Collections*
Letters of Henry Gallaugher
Letters of Paddy Tobin

*British Public Record Office*
Letters of G.W. Nightingale PRO 30/71/3
Diaries of G.W. Nightingale PRO 30/71/3
Letters of H. Waterman

ORAL SOURCES

*Interviews with the author:*
Joseph Cahill
Jack Campbell

*Interviews with Joe Little*
Tommy Ervine
Tommy Jordan

*Interviews with Richard Doherty:*
Harry Bennet
Thomas Gibson
R.T. Grange

*Interview with Pádraigh Ó Raghallaigh*
Emmet d'Alton

*Interview with Jim Fahy*
Denis Kelly

*Interviews with Kieran Sheedy*

| | | |
|---|---|---|
| Paddy Barry | Pat Farrelly | Bill McMahon |
| John Breen | Michael Fitzgerald | Bill Molloy |
| Edward Byrne | Frank Hyland | Jimmy O'Brien |
| Michael Byrne | Michael Keane | James Phillips |
| William Butler | John King | Edgar Poulter |
| Tommy Cusack | Thomas Leavy | Terence Poulter |
| Phillip Doyle | Peter McBride | E.H. de Stacpoole |

PUBLISHED SOURCES

Beckett, Ian F.W., *The Army and the Curragh Incident* (Army Records Society, London, 1986).
Bolger, Dermot, *Francis Ledwidge: Selected Poems* (Dublin, 1992).
Bredin, Brigadier A.E.C., *A History of the Irish Soldier* (Belfast, 1987)
Brown, Malcolm, *The Imperial War Museum Book of the Western Front* (London, 1993).
Cooper, Bryan, *The Tenth (Irish) Division in Gallipoli* (Dublin, 1993).
Crozier, Percy, *A Brass Hat in No Man's Land* (London, 1930).
— , *The Men I Killed* (London, 1937).
Cunliffe, Marcus, *The Royal Irish Fusiliers 1793–1968* (London, 1970).
Curtayne, Alice, *Francis Ledwidge, A Life of the Poet* (London, 1992).
Denman, Terence, *Ireland's Unknown Soldiers* (Dublin, 1992).
Doherty, Richard, *The Sons of Ulster* (Belfast, 1992).
Dixon, Norman, *On the Psychology of Military Incompetence* (London, 1994) p. 221.
Falls, Cyril, *The History of the 36th Ulster Division* (London, 1922).
Feilding, Rowland, *War Letters to a Wife* (London, 1929).
Fox, Sir Frank, *The Royal Inniskillings in the World War* (London, 1928).
— *The Battles of the Ridges—Arras-Messines, March–June 1917* (London, 1918).
Gibbon. Monk, *Inglorious Soldier* (London, 1968).
Gibbs, Phillip, *The Realities of War* (London, 1920).
Godley, Alexander and Kilbracken, Arthur, *Letters* (London, 1949).
Gough, Sir Hubert, *The Fifth Army* (London, 1931).
Greacen, Lavinia, *Chink: A Biography* (London, 1989).
Hamilton, General Sir Ian, *Gallipoli Diary* (London, 1920).
Hanna, Henry, *The Pals at Suvla Bay* (Dublin, 1916).
Hargrave, John, *The Suvla Bay Landing* (London, 1964).
Harris, Henry, *The Royal Irish Fusiliers* (London, 1972).
Hitchcock Frank, *Stand To: A Diary of the Trenches 1915–1918* (Norwich, 1938).
Jervis, Lt.-Col. H.S., *The 2nd Munsters in France* (Aldershot, 1922).
Johnstone, Tom, *Orange, Green and Khaki* (Dublin, 1992).
Kerr, J. Parnell, *What the Irish Regiments Have Done* (London, 1916).
Kipling, Rudyard, *The Irish Guards in the Great War'* (London, 1923).
Knightley, Phillip, *The First Casualty* (London, 1982).
Laird, Frank, *Personal Experiences of the Great War* (Dublin, 1925).
Lucy, John, *There's a Devil in the Drum* (London, 1938),
McCance, Capt. S., *History of the Royal Munster Fusiliers—Vol II—from 1861–1922* (Aldershot, 1927).
McDonagh, Michael, *The Irish at the Front* (London, 1916).
— *Irish on the Somme* (London, 1917).
O'Malley, Ernie, *On Another Man's Wound* (Dublin, 1979).
O'Rahilly, Alfred, *Father William Doyle, S.J.* (London, 1932).
Orr, Phillip, *The Road to the Somme'* (Belfast, 1987).
Redmond, Major William, *Trench Pictures from France* (London, 1917).
Rickard, Mrs Victor, *The Story of the Munsters at Etreux, Festubert, Rue du Bois and Hulloch* (London, 1918).
Walker, G.A.C., *The Book of the 7th Service Battalion— The Royal Inniskilling fusiliers —from Tipperary to Ypres* (Dublin, 1920).
Whitton, Lt.-Col. F.E., *The Prince of Wales Leinster Regiment*, Vol. 2 (undated).

# Index